BING

BING

The Authorized Biography

by

Charles Thompson

David McKay Company, Inc.
New York

First American Edition 1976

10 9 8 7 6 5 4

Library of Congress Catalog Card Number: 75-37320
ISBN: 0-679-50590-3

MANUFACTURED IN THE UNITED STATES OF AMERICA

Acknowledgements

This book is the culmination of four years' hard work for me, but it has only been possible due to the selfless help of many other people.

Patrick Doncaster deserves a special mention for applying his considerable talent and experience to the tough task of editing the manuscript and making it readable. Well done, mate! Sue 'Speedy' Crane also comes into this category—it was she who typed the final manuscript.

Apart from the two hundred or so show business personalities who gave up their valuable time to talk to me about Bing, thanks go to all the girls in the Crosby office in Beverly Hills for their help and patience. They always greeted my persistent pesterings with the utmost kindness and good humour.

The late Larry Crosby was a great source of encouragement and information and it saddens me that he should have died during final preparations for publication and never saw the finished product. I, like Bing, owe him much for his tireless devotion.

British Caledonian Airways deserve acknowledgement too for safely transporting me to many parts of the globe in search of people and material. And my heartfelt thanks to Russ and Clare Miller, who played their part in putting me up and feeding me up during a number of extended stays in Holly-wood.

Finally, my eternal thanks to Bing; not only for supplying

all the photographs used in the book, but for being himself and achieving so much. Without him, it can truly be said for once, none of this would have been possible . . .

Charles Thompson

'They feel I'm more like one of them, rather than a professional. My singing is sort of natural and I don't suppose its stylistic. It doesn't sound like a trained voice and most of them think: "Well he sings about like I do, you know, when I'm in the bathroom, or in the shower, and feel good and woke-up with a gay feeling." Why they think I'm one of the fellas.'

Bing Crosby
Wednesday, 2 August 1972

Chapter One

On a hot and humid autumn afternoon in the year of 1925, a battered black Ford Model-T clattered and coughed to a halt in a shallow ditch on the crest of a ridge high above the Promised Land of the 'twenties—the city of Los Angeles, with its boom suburb of Hollywood.

As its dishevelled occupants, two young men, clambered stiffly from the stricken machine, the boiling and ravaged radiator gave one last dying shudder and blew a fountain of steam into the hot sun-filled Californian sky like a whale in full spate. The pair slumped exhausted beside the sign that said 'Wheeler's Ridge' and gazed sadly at the dirty, but faithful, tin lizzie that had carried them for more than a thousand miles, along the three-week-long pioneer trail from Spokane to the City of the Angels.

There had been over a hundred punctures and blow-outs; dozens of parts replaced and much vocal coaxing from the owners. But the steep, fifteen-mile climb to the top of the ridge had been too much. It was like losing a relative, even though it had only set them back eight dollars.

The elder of the pair took the tattered hat from his head, pushed his other hand through his already thinning light brown locks and remarked that the sign chalked on one side of the Ford 'wasn't funny any more'. *Eight million miles and still enthusiastic*, it proclaimed proudly. But this was the end of the line. Eighty miles from the city of their dreams, they were stranded and broke.

As the pair wearily pulled their suitcases and a drum kit from the dusty back seat, and prepared to abandon ship for the long walk ahead, an equally battered old vegetable truck croaked and groaned its way over the brow of Wheeler's Ridge.

The driver was unable to ignore the forlorn faces and proffered thumbs. As they piled the cases and drums high on the cabbages at the back and jumped gratefully into the cab, the boys learned they were to be taken as far as the Padre Hotel on the main highway leading into Hollywood. From there, burdened with their kit, they walked and staggered the last mile and a half to their destination.

Thus was the ignominious entry into Hollywood, the very heart of show business, of Harry Lillis Crosby, struggling drummer-vocalist, and his pianist pal Alton Rinker.

It was an inauspicious start to an unparalleled career that was to encompass fifty golden years and establish the name, face and voice of Bing Crosby as the world's best loved entertainer. And Hollywood, which offered no hand of welcome that hot and dusty September day, would later rank him as its leading citizen and hail him as the Super Song Salesman of the twentieth century.

But it wasn't to be an easy road . . .

Chapter Two

Bing was the fourth of seven children—five boys and two girls—born to Harry Lowe Crosby and his wife Katherine, née Harrigan, in the small country town of Tacoma, in the State of Washington.

He was baptised Harry Lillis Crosby in St Patrick's Church, across the street from his birthplace, a pleasant, detached white-painted wooden house at 1112 North Jay Street.

Pa Crosby came from seafaring stock. His grandfather Nathaniel was a celebrated clipper-ship captain who sailed the raging seas around the Horn to China and all points East. He died in Hong Kong and is buried there. During World War II a Liberty ship was named after him and launched by Bing's father.

According to brother Larry, Bing's forebears were among the Vikings, the eighth–tenth century Scandinavian pirates who settled in Ireland, Scotland and the North of England after amusing themselves raiding and plundering the coast-lines of Britain. The name Crosby is of Danish origin and means 'Town of the Cross'.

The early Crosbys settled in Ireland and records show that there was an ancient Irish House of Crosby at Ardfert in County Kerry, where they acquired the noble but now extinct title of Earl of Glandore.

Further lustre was added to the family tree in 1601 when a Crosby was appointed Bishop of Ardfert, and there was also a

3

dashing knight called Sir Pierce Crosby who had his castle somewhere in County Tyrone, now part of Ulster.

A fair Crosby maiden crossed to England and married Thomas Brewster, one of the Pilgrim Fathers who set sail for the brave new world in the *Mayflower*.

Larry also traced a Crosby coat of arms which he said Bing was allowed to wear on a blazer. It shows a large lion rampant, with two red hands prominent above it. Legend has it that the hands signify a rash deed of one of Bing's sea-going ancestors. He had sighted land, but was unable to get ashore because of rough weather. Ancient custom decreed that the first person to actually touch a new land could claim it as his own. The brave Captain Crosby is supposed to have cut off one of his hands and hurled it ashore, thus staking his claim.

Captain Nathaniel Crosby made his home in Massachusetts, but as the family evolved it moved gradually westwards to Portland, Oregon—of which he was a founding father—then up to Washington State where he helped found the town of Olympia, and on to nearby Tacoma.

It was there that Bing's father, a bookkeeper, met and married Miss Harrigan, affectionately known as Kate, the daughter of a builder from County Mayo in Eire. It was a marriage not without problems—Crosby senior was a Puritan. But before the big day he became a Catholic.

The exact date of birth of their fourth child is the subject of some controversy. When asked, Bing says: 'May 2, 1904.' But there are those who disagree and say it was 'May 2, 1901', including brother Larry—who became Bing's publicity director. When he talked to the author for the BBC's Radio 2 fourteen-week radio biography on Crosby, he said: 'During his early days at Paramount, people thought that everybody had to be young and I let them think that Bing was born in 1904.'

A number of seemingly reputable publications have also pegged Bing's year of birth as 1901, but there is still an element of doubt. It appears there is no birth certificate as such; in those days Catholics were issued with baptismal certificates giving only the surname and sex of the child. So there are *five* male Crosby certificates, with a variety of ages, to choose from.

Younger brother Bob Crosby finds the controversy highly amusing and reveals that 'age-vagueness' was a family trait: 'Mother tore the page out of the family Bible that gave her

4

birthdate,' he said. 'We never knew how old she was. It got to be a kind of kidding thing to try and guess how old mother was. She used to say, "actually, I'm much younger than most girls of my age . . ." '

Little Harry—he had yet to acquire the name the world would know him by—spent the first years of his life in the house on North Jay Street.

Then the family moved on to Spokane, centre of a logging and mining area also in Washington State, where Dad had a job keeping books for the local brewery. It was a smallish, yellow house on Sinto Avenue and there lived next door a boy named Valentine Hobart, a few years older than Harry, and a lad with some perception. He was the first person in the world to call Harry, 'Bing'.

Harry was seven at the time and it happened like this: both boys were fans of a Sunday newspaper comic strip entitled 'The Bingsville Bugle', which featured a character called Bingo, who had large, protruding floppy ears. Harry's ears weren't floppy, but they did stick out (Hollywood had to pin them back years later) and Master Hobart wasn't slow to notice this. So Harry became Bingo. 'They called me that for a while,' says Bing, 'then they dropped the O.' And thus was born a name for life . . .

Life, however, was not one of plenty for the good Catholic family Crosby, which came to a halt at seven with the birth of Bob in 1913.

Brother Larry had been born in 1895, Everett in 1896, Ted in 1900 and sisters Catherine in 1905 and Mary Rose 1907.

The home was well furnished and there was always enough food, but the family only managed to scrape by on Dad's meagre brewery pay. Space was also a big problem and the children had to double up two to a bed at night.

There were none of the luxuries that many of today's children expect. Bing feels this was for the best. It made the Crosbys tough and self-sufficient: 'My mother always told us, after we got into high school, that they would provide us with a place to live and good meals. But if we wanted anything special—such as clothes, spending money, theatre tickets, play-things, tennis rackets, or whatever—we'd have to buy them ourselves. So that's what we all did. We all worked and did anything to pick up a little money.'

5

In his time, and mostly whilst still at school, Bing did a variety of part-time jobs: he had an early morning paper round; he mowed lawns; picked apples; washed cucumbers in a pickle factory; became a lumberjack and even worked for a time as a janitor in a workingman's club: 'I'd go down there every morning before school and mop it up and clean it out. I never liked to work and I hated that kind of work, but I wanted the money to buy theatre tickets, ice-cream and candy. It was the only way I could get it.'

He could rough it with the best. He was only nine years old when he first started to get up each morning at 4 a.m. to deliver *The Spokane Spokesman Review* to the sleeping citizens of the neighbourhood, and in winter trudging through the snows that fall heavily in those parts. But he still found time and energy to take a keen interest in all sports at Webster Grade School. He was in the football team, the basketball team and the baseball team. At the age of eight he merited a parental spanking for swimming in the river. Four years later he won seven medals for swimming, most of them firsts.

According to Leo Lynn, one of his class-mates of those early days and who was later to become his right-hand-man and confidant, Bing was a bright pupil too: 'He was ready to have fun at any time, but he seemed to get his homework and studies done with the minimum of effort and time.

'He could rattle off Latin, was terrible at mathematics, good at Greek and history. I don't think I ever saw him take a book home. He was just a fast study. Some people have to plod and try hard to get it, but he managed with the minimum amount of effort.'

And Bing still maintains he was never a mathematician.

His musical education began at the Crosby home in Spokane. His father played the guitar and mandolin and often sang with his wife in local Gilbert and Sullivan productions.

So bitten by the music bug was the elder Crosby, that he risked Kate's displeasure and spent some of his first month's pay from the brewery on a phonograph. It caused quite a stir with the family and Bing still remembers it with pride: 'It was the kind of machine you wind up. It had a daffodil-type horn and instead of discs there were cylinders. He had the Peerless Quartet on there and some of the old-timers like Henry Burr, Harry Lauder and John McCormack. We must have been the first in the neighbourhood to have such an instrument.'

The next piece of musical apparatus to enter the Crosby household, also bought by Dad, was a piano. Bing never learnt to play it, but his two younger sisters did. Meanwhile, brother Ted was showing promise as an electrical engineer and managed to build one of the first crystal radio sets ever seen, or heard, in Spokane. This gave the boys access to music from Seattle and an idea of the popular tunes of the time.

It was therefore only to be expected that the young Bing should spend much of his time, at work and play, humming, whistling and singing to himself. Also of help was his uncle George Harrigan, one of his boyhood idols; a big, tall, good-looking Irishman who was a court reporter. Bing remembers well his strong tenor voice and there is little doubt that Uncle George greatly inspired Bing: 'He was so popular and famous. His big song was "H A R R I G A N spells Harrigan", which became a sort of identification for him. He always had to sing that, no matter where he went.' He was a legend in Tacoma and Seattle and Bing says had he gone into show business he would have been a big star.

When the Crosbys weren't listening to the crystal set, or the phonograph, they gathered round the fireside and sang, making their own entertainment.

It was while at grade school that Bing began to sing seriously. He was in a number of choral groups and, by the time he was twelve, his mother felt he ought to study music properly. Something no one else in the family had ever done!

He was despatched to a music professor, who irked the young Crosby somewhat by giving him scales to practise. Bing wearied of these rapidly and, when the professor told him to stop singing popular songs and concentrate on the old standards, he gave up altogether.

There are those, of course, who argue that it was a good thing Bing had no real formal training. A freedom from conventional singing technique helped to produce the relaxed crooning style that made him unique. The Groaner himself, however, disagrees and now regrets his hastiness those many years ago: 'I never did learn how to breathe the way you're supposed to breathe. There's no question about it—even today—running scales helps the singer's voice. The vocal chords are really a muscle and they have to be exercised.'

He was twelve when he gave his first public singing performance—at a concert in the parish hall. He opened with a ballad about 'Sweet Alice Benbolt', a girl with hair so brown. Then there was a sadder one that mentioned joy and pain and bemoaned the loss of 'One Fleeting Hour'. After exiting to 'rather desultory applause' he returned to the stage dragging an empty dog leash for his encore song, which went like this . . .

> 'I've got a dog named Rover,
> Here Rover, come Rover,
> He roams around all over,
> He's only home three times a day,
> (*Whistles*) I'm looking for my dog called Rover,
> (*Whistles*) I'm looking for him now all over,
> He's a hunter's dog all right,
> He keeps me huntin' day and night,
> This is what I worry over,
> Who put the rove in Rover,
> (*Whistles*) Sometimes I wish I were a tree,
> Then Rover'd have to look for me,
> Oh where's that doggone, doggone, doggone dog of mine.'

The Crosby larynx was developing in other directions as well. He moved on to the Jesuit-conducted Gonzaga High School, where public speaking was a priority subject and elocution competitions were held regularly.

Bing made the finals a couple of times and collected a winner's medal on one occasion. His speciality was the dramatic poem. Robert Service was his favourite and Bing was at his best reciting such works as 'Whispering Jim', 'Spartacus at the Bridge' and 'The Cremation of Sam Magee'.

The young Crosby was also a keen and regular member of the Gonzaga debating society. This, combined with elocution, gave him—he considers—a good vocabulary and taught him to 'talk and think on his feet'. It also gave him a great love of the English language and he feels that much of his later success as an actor was due to this early training.

The brothers and sisters Crosby say that Bing was clearly their mother's favourite and that she went out of her way to pay special attention to the fourth eldest child.

Like most Irish mothers of large families she nursed the hope that one of her sons might enter the priesthood—and Bing was the most fancied one. But the nearest he came to her ambition was to serve at the altar in St Aloysius' Church, where all the family attended Mass every Sunday.

Certainly he was no 'mother's boy', despite this favouritism. Street gangs flourished in Spokane, a tough town with one of America's biggest railroads—the Great Northern—based there, and Bing earned himself a reputation with the Boone Avenue Gang.

He fought in the ring as well as the streets. One of his classmates, Jimmy Cottrell, who later became America's North-West middleweight champ, coached him to victory in the Gonzaga contests. 'Bing was a good amateur boxer,' he said. 'He had a good right hand and could hit like hell. The only thing I used to kid him about was that he could never hit with the left hand like I could—and you've got to be a two-handed puncher to get along.'

Bing acknowledges the value of Cottrell's coaching: 'Yeah, he gave me some pointers. I had to fight a left-hander and he said the only way to beat a left-hander is . . . every time he throws his left, you throw the right. You've got a shorter distance to go. I tried that and hit him every time—pop! It was kind of automatic.'

He was also the victor of his first-ever schoolboy scrap way back in 1914. His sister Mary Rose, who had a weight problem, came home crying because some rude boy had called her 'Fatty!' Retribution was left to brother Bing.

'All the gang showed up,' he recalls, 'back of somebody's house in an empty lot and we held a formally staged contest. This was with seconds and was like a duel. My representatives met his and we agreed to have a confrontation. We did and I finally cut him up fairly good and they stopped it.'

He could be hasty as well with his retaliation. While he was still in kneepants, he began to date a girl named Gladys Lemmon, 'a real doll with fluttery eyelashes'. When he one day returned home for dinner after tobogganing with Gladys, big brother Larry teased him: 'Where have you been? Out squeezing that Lemmon again?'

Bing picked up the leg of lamb waiting to be carved on the table and hurled it at him.

9

He collected his fair share of punishment both at home—mother used to hand it out with hairbrush or strap—and at school.

At grade school the head even took trouble to write to Bing's parents. 'If Harry doesn't behave better,' the letter said, 'the Principal will have to deal with him.'

Bing duly reported to mother: 'He dealt with me, bent over a chair.'

At Gonzaga he logged up a considerable total of hours locked in the punishment room, where he was made to learn passages from Virgil and had to recite them to gain release. And he was not averse to playing truant or the occasional petty theft.

He and a boyhood friend one day filched a haul of pies and pastries from a baker's wagon. When they were unable to cram any more into their mouths they decided to throw the rest at passing cars—one of which, unfortunately, turned out to be a police car. Off they went to the lock-up. When the police called Bing's mother, she told them to 'keep him there overnight, it'll do him good'. He remembers spending a cold night in the juvenile detention ward.

Bing was still in his early teens when he got his first real taste of show business. He landed a part-time job in the props department at Spokane's Auditorium Theatre, a greasepaint Mecca on the great American vaudeville circuit which brought to town such giants of the day as Gallagher and Shean, Eddie Cantor and Al Jolson, as well as travelling shows from Broadway such as George White's Scandals.

'I worked whenever I could,' says Bing, 'for a chance to be backstage and rub elbows with those guys and watch them work. Jolson came through twice and I worked both his shows.'

'I'd heard his records, of course, and I knew about his vocal abilities, but his chief attribute was the sort of electricity he generated when he sang.

'Nobody in those days did that. When he came out and started to sing, he just elevated the audience immediately. Within the first eight bars he had them in the palm of his hand.'

Jolson worked almost entirely in black-face and Bing remembers him as a sort of one-man entertainment business: 'He had great drive and inexhaustible energy. He was all over the theatre; checking the box-office and receipts; singing the lead and ordering everybody about. He took full charge and it didn't effect his performance because he only had one speed and that was full-bore, no matter what he was doing.'

He made a great impact on the young Crosby and was probably the only singer ever to really influence him. Decades later it would be Bing who would be instrumental in bringing Jolson out of retirement and back into show business . . .

It was at the Auditorium that Bing trod the boards as an actor for the first time—in college productions of Shakespeare! A gravedigger in *Hamlet*, a soldier who falls in the line of battle in *Julius Caesar*. But playing a corpse had its dangerous moments.

'I was supposed to be lying there stone dead when I saw the curtain starting to come down on top of me. So I just got up and walked out of the way! Self-preservation, but it got quite a laugh!'

Self-preservation brought Bing's first serious brush with the law during a school holiday. With a friend—Paul Teters—he decided to hop a goods train to Portland, Oregon, where brother Everett was working in a hotel.

They spent four days and nights dodging railway security guards and eventually arrived broke, dishevelled and starving. They hot-footed it to a Chinese restaurant and went right through the menu. When faced with the bill, Bing hurriedly pushed over a pile of boxes and the pair ran off. A few minutes later the cops caught up with them in Everett's hotel room.

After several hours in the hoosegow, they were brought before a magistrate who lectured them on the follies of stealing from Chinese restaurant owners and told them to 'get out of town and never return'.

It was on their way back to Spokane that Bing worked as a lumberjack—until he put an axe into his leg. He was laid up for three weeks . . .

Back at high school Bing caught another show business bug—drumming.

Enthused by a scratch band of youngsters calling themselves 'The Juicy Seven', with whom he played around, he bought himself a kit on the never-never—'a little set of drums with a Japanese sunset painted on the front of the bass', he says.

'I used to have an awful time with them, because they'd move as I used the bass pedal and I had to move with them! I was never much of a drummer . . .'

Show business, however, was not yet to be his chosen calling, despite his great affection for it. Late in 1920 he entered Gonzaga University to study law under the Jesuit Fathers who played a great part in shaping his character.

'There were some very great men there. One of the best was Father Sharp, who was a marvellous guy, just like one of the boys—slangy, out-going, big-hearted, but tough when he had to be. Another was Father Kennelly—a massive man, very strong, who used to dispense real harsh discipline.

'Father Shepsey was probably the most important influence on me, though. He was an English Lit. specialist and encouraged me to read and write a lot. He was a marvellous man.'

Then there was Father Gilmore, who messed around with chemicals and invented, among other things, a concoction calculated to encourage the growth of hair. Even then Bing's was beginning to thin and Father Gilmore went to great lengths to persuade him to use it. 'But it didn't do any good,' says Bing.

In the early months at university the study of law was all-consuming. His main aim was criminal law and he longed for the day when he would get up in court to make dramatic appeals to judge and jury.

To gain experience he worked for some months in the law offices of the Great Northern Railway—where he learned to handle Writs of Garnishment—and bent the rules to help out friends.

These writs were issued when an employee of the railway owed money to tradesmen and the only way of getting it was to have it seized from his salary. Bing received the writs first—and, if the employee scheduled for this treatment happened to be a pal, Bing would advise him to draw on his salary before service of the writ . . .

By the end of that first varsity year, his early enthusiasm for the law had waned and he feels there were two reasons for this. He was 'too lazy' and would never pass the Bar examinations; there was more money to be made from something new he had got into . . . singing with a band.

Chapter Three

The 'twenties got off to their roarin' start with the sound of music. The jazz age, they called it, an era fostered by the introduction of Prohibition—the total ban on intoxicating liquors across the nation from 17 January 1920. New bands blossomed throughout the United States and the mood, with World War I now becoming a memory, was one of gaiety. In Spokane it tugged at the sleeve of Alton Rinker, a fellow-collegian of Bing's, who formed and led from the piano a five-piece outfit called 'The Musicaladers'.

Al's brother Miles was on clarinet; the brothers Bob and Clare Pritchard were on saxophone and banjo and Jimmy Heaton was blowing cornet. They lacked a drummer and they were determined to find one. Somebody told them about this guy Bing Crosby, who had been giving impromptu drumming sessions in various parts of town.

'So we had him come over to my house,' says Al, 'and he brought his drums and sat down and played. Then he sang a couple of things and we said, "Oh, boy! This is great!" '

Bing was in, taking his first steps along the long hard road to fame. Faltering steps. For singing in Al's parlour was very different to singing in public. Thus the crooning Crosby was mighty nervous when he stepped from his drums to sing his first solo with the Musicaladers at a high school dance. The song: 'For Me and My Gal', which he never did put on disc.

Bing the vocalist, as band singers were then described, had arrived.

Not one of the Musicaladers could read a note of music. Everything was learned by ear. Bing and Al would take themselves off to the Bailey Music Shop in Spokane and listen to the band discs of the day. Records by Paul Whiteman, Fred Waring, McKinney's Cotton Pickers, The Memphis Five, The Mound City Blue Blowers.

They couldn't afford to buy them, but they would listen to as many as they could and memorise the tunes—then rush home to rehearse with the rest of the group.

'Al had a great ear for music,' says Bing. 'He could play practically anything after he heard it a time or two. He would play the right harmony too.

'He'd pick out a part for each guy and then voice the harmonies just to show what line to follow. We were really a novelty in Spokane! We would have an arrangement taken from a hit record and could play it. That really made us unique!'

It wasn't only the record shop that Bing and Al haunted. The vaudeville theatres had them as non-paying guests as well.

'We would sneak in,' says Bing. 'We found out where the fire exits were and would wait for an opening and slip in. We'd stay through three or four shows until they threw us out. We followed vaudeville any chance we got.'

The experience began to pay off. Now the Musicaladers brimmed with confidence and people were talking about those hit arrangements. It led to their first steady job—at a dance pavilion some ten miles outside town. They were paid three dollars each a night. Then other venues started beckoning them and the money went up to five dollars a head.

Now Bing was singing more and more, crooning—in this pre-microphone era—through a little megaphone.

As their reputation grew so did the variety of work they were offered. 'We'd take anything,' says Bing. 'We were non-union and had no scale—no minimum, no maximum. It wasn't much, but in those days you didn't need much.

'We wore grey slacks and some sort of a blue coat. I suppose if we netted seven-and-a-half dollars for the night it had been a pretty good night.'

Some of the tough guys around Spokane held little regard for fellows who sang for a living. It was considered a sort of sissy occupation and they weren't backward about showing their disapproval. As Bing found out during a date at the Lareida roadhouse on the outskirts of town. He used to croon with his eyes closed—'to concentrate on the meaning of the lyrics'—and this particular evening he was drumming and singing 'Peggy O'Neil'. As one he-man of a dancer neared the stand he shouted out 'Pansy!'

Bing's eyes were open quickly enough. He stopped drumming and singing and dashed out on to the floor and asked the guy to repeat the insult. Then Crosby flattened him with one punch, returned to his astonished colleagues, whose music was flagging without him, and picked up the beat and the words where he left off . . .

But it was a short-lived career for the Musicaladers. The band began to split. The two Pritchards went off to college. Al's brother decided to quit show business for other things. Jimmy Heaton joined a travelling band and eventually wound up in the Goldwyn studio orchestra. It was a sad blow for both Al and Bing. Nevertheless, they weren't going to give up that easily. They could still sing together with Al at the keyboard. So along they went to auditions being held for The Clemmer Theatre, a little movie house that had live entertainment before the main picture show. They landed a job at their first try.

The Clemmer already featured a resident quartet—but it wasn't resident much longer, after the twosome was hired. The manager fired the quartet and said to Bing: 'Why don't you do a solo and let Al play in the pit for you?' There was no need to say it twice.

Al tells it this way: 'Bing would sing things like "They Call Me Red Hot Henry Brown", then he'd do a little dance and then I'd start kind of singing with him, harmonising. We got thirty dollars a week apiece, which was big money in those days.' Says Bing: 'Our songs were mostly chosen to fit the movie of the week. A sea picture—something about the sea. For a Western picture a Western song and so on.'

It was a good showcase, but the glamour wore as night followed night, month after month. They both began to get restless, Bing more so than Al. Like his ancestor he felt the call of the sea—but as an entertainer, not a mariner! The theory being that whatever you made you couldn't spend on board during a long trip. Like the renowned Nathaniel Crosby he set his sights on China. He applied for a berth on sailings from Seattle, Portland and San Francisco but without success.

After much heart-searching, Bing and Al came to the conclusion that their future—if there was to be one—lay in Los Angeles. Al already had a sister there making a name as a blues singer: Mildred Bailey, one of the first ladies of jazz, who now has her place in musical history. Bing's elder brother Everett was also there, working as a truck salesman.

The momentous decision was made. Los Angeles it would be. They had their own transport—the old Ford Model-T that had originally been bought by the Musicaladers for thirty-five dollars. When the split came, the pair bought it back for eight bucks.

They packed their bags and pooled the little money they had—about one hundred dollars.

Al Rinker remembers the autumn morning vividly: 'I went over to his house and said, "Bing, get out of bed, we're going." So he did, and we said goodbye to his family, then saw my folks and then we just took off and headed West towards Seattle.'

The journey had all the ingredients of a script for the 'Road to . . .' series with the Model-T the main character. Over the three weeks they had to coax and cajole it on to its final resting place at Wheelers Ridge by day and work by night. The Butler Hotel gave them a booking at the end of the first leg to Seattle. In other places they played small theatres, speakeasies and private parties—frequently illegal drinking ones in this era of Prohibition. They slept in the faithful Ford some nights, but if there was a chill on the air they would work their hotel trick.

Bing would go in first and register and Al would sneak in later. And sneak out again next day. The bill was always for one person!

After their mile-and-a-half walk into Hollywood, the last lap to Al's sister Mildred's home in downtown Los Angeles was made by street-car. They were tired, dusty and hungry. Mildred gave them a warm welcome and a meal and the world began to look a brighter place. Bing's drums were stashed away in the basement and the talk was of show business and ambition.

Mildred was singing the blues nightly in the city's most popular speakeasy, The Silver Grill, and took the boys along to watch. It was an amazing sight. Like a nightclub of today, with people sitting at tables and booze being sold and drunk openly as if Prohibition had never happened—let alone having been in force for six years.

Bing had sampled moonshine liquor on street corners back in Spokane, but neither he nor Al had ever seen anything like The Silver Grill. 'It was great,' says Bing.

They were exciting times. There was much to see and to do. Hollywood was growing day by day and they hung around the movie studios soaking up the mysteries of film-making. Mildred, meantime, was asking around for a job for them, but it wasn't going to happen all that quickly.

Money began to get short, very short. Bing took one last lingering look at the fading Japanese sunset on his bass drum and sold it. He had to lean on big brother Everett for help too.

Eventually Mildred came up with a gleam of hope—an audition with Mike Lyman, who ran the Tent Café in downtown Los Angeles and was the brother of bandleader Abe Lyman. But even the audition wasn't without its problems. Bing didn't have a tuxedo—and they were currently advertising themselves as *Crosby and Rinker, two boys with a piano . . . own tuxedos . . . go anywhere*!

Again there was Everett on hand with tux and accessories. 'Oh! how I robbed that poor man!' says Bing.

The audition was a success and the double act of Crosby and Rinker started singing and playing for their supper at the Tent Café. 'We only had about five or six numbers,' remembers Rinker, 'but people seemed to like us.' They also worked the Lafayette Cafe where Harry Owens, who later wrote Bing's smash hit 'Sweet Leilani', was the bandleader.

It wasn't long before they were noticed by the Fanchon and Marco organisation which ran vaudeville shows in some forty West Coast theatres from Los Angeles to San Francisco.

Fanchon and Marco put the boys into a touring show called 'The Syncopated Idea' which began its tour in Los Angeles at the Boulevard Theatre on Washington Boulevard. 'This was the first time we'd ever played in a big place and we were frightened,' says Rinker. 'But we got out there and started cutting-up with our songs and, lo-and-behold, they liked us!'

There were other compensations. Also in the show were eighteen lovely precision-drilled Tiller Girls from England and there were those among them who succumbed to the charms of the blue-eyed Bing. The money was good as well—seventy-five dollars a week each now—even if the work was tedious; two weeks here, two weeks there.

The act was neat and polished. Instead of drumming, Bing now beat out the rhythm on a cymbal attached to Al's piano. And they both played kazoo—a comb-and-tissue-paper instrument that responded to the resonance of the voice.

'Terrible sounding things,' Bing laments, 'but we used them for jazz numbers. They were a thing we picked up from the Mound City Blue Blowers, an outfit from St Louis, who used two kazoos and a banjo. They had a couple of records that sold very big.'

Crosby and Rinker tired of the vaudeville circuit and living out of suitcases after eighteen months and went to see Arthur Freed, a songwriter and impressario who later found fame as a top Hollywood producer. With colleague Will Morrissey he was running a successful revue called 'Morrissey's Music Hall Revue' at the Orange Grove in Los Angeles.

'I was a kid myself,' he recalled, 'and the show had been going for about two months when two kids walked in looking for a job. One was Al Rinker and the other Bing Crosby. We loved Bing, but didn't know what to do with him because the show was already running. So we put him in the pit to sing between acts and he went over so big that we had trouble raising the curtain for the second act!'

They stayed with the show for nearly three months and moved on with it to San Francisco, where Bing was able to renew his friendship, formed during the vaudeville tours, with Bill Hearst, son of William Randolph Hearst, the newspaper tycoon.

'We got along very well,' says Bill, who was then a student at Berkeley University near San Francisco, 'because he's very easy to know. If he likes you and you like him, it's like old friends right off the bat.'

It was a friendship that led to what Bing describes now as 'a kind of infamous episode'.

As Hearst tells it: 'I asked Bing over to a sort of "beer-bust" on the campus. It was Prohibition, of course, so we couldn't officially have liquor, but we could have beer which we would "spike" with alcohol. This thing developed into quite a noise. It started in the afternoon and ran into the evening before the campus cop, as they used to call him, came and broke it up.'

Bing, who was beginning to acquire a real taste for the high life, transported the whole Morrissey show to the university campus—including chorus girls—and was very much in the fore-front of the revelry.

As Bing tells it: 'There was a wash-tub, with a block of ice in it, a couple of oranges and the rest was gin—solid gin!

'It was served like a punch and these little girls were dipping into it. They'd never had any experience with it before and everybody got pretty well boxed-up.

'I think we marched down to a big monument in front of the administration building of the university and put on a performance which was pretty disorganised. The students almost lost their fraternity charter and two or three of the boys were suspended . . .'

Shortly after the Berkeley incident, the curtain came down on the Morrissey show as well. So, broke once again, Crosby and Rinker signed a contract with impresario Jack Partington and Paramount Publix and spent about six months alternating between the Metropolitan Theatre in Los Angeles and the Granada and Warfield in San Francisco.

The year was 1926 and it was going to be a most fateful one for Crosby . . .

Chapter Four

No one took any particular note of the two faces among the crowd of fans who went along to the railroad station in Los Angeles to watch the Paul Whiteman Band steam into town. But Crosby and Rinker were there, excited like the rest, trying to catch a glimpse of their hero and his musicians.

Whiteman, a former taxi driver from Denver, Colorado, was the biggest name in post-war music and his discs were selling in millions even in those days. His record of 'Whispering', made soon after the end of World War I, had sold a phenomenal 1,800,000 copies.

Rinker, younger than Bing, was really impressed as he stood there in silence staring at the huge bulky figure of Whiteman with his moustache and receding hair. 'We just went down to the train to watch these guys get off,' says Al, 'We never met any of them, but wanted to see them because we'd been playing their records for years.'

Whiteman had never heard of Crosby and Rinker, now being billed at the Metropolitan as *Two boys and a piano—singing songs in their own way.*

But he would . . . and pretty soon.

It was his manager who caught their act.

'He came to me one morning,' Whiteman recalled, 'and said, "I heard a couple of great boys last night who you ought to have in the band" and I said "why?" He said, "Well they sing real cute." I said, "I need them like I probably need two holes in my head and double pneumonia! I'm a little heavy with singers," and he said "I think you'll find them kind of interesting." '

Whiteman sent two of his band—pianist Ray Turner and viola player Matty Malneck—to check out the talents of Bing and Al. They were both impressed. Turner reported that it was a 'very cute act'. Malneck found that the pair 'had a style that was infectious . . . like hearing a great jazz player for the first time'.

So Crosby and Rinker were summoned to the court of jazz king Whiteman—known as Pops to friends and the band—in his quarters at the Million Dollar Theatre in Los Angeles.

It was a meeting Bing has never forgotten: 'Whiteman was seated on a massive bed, looking like a giant Buddha, and he had a pound of caviare in his lap and a bottle of champagne on his breakfast table. I thought that was really the ultimate in attainment, to have reached the stage where you can have caviare and champagne for breakfast!

'He talked to us for a while and asked us about our background. Then he said he thought the act was fine and wanted to know if we wanted to join him and we said yes.'

Yet Whiteman had never seen them, although he led them to believe that he had. The moment of decision came, he revealed many years later, when he asked them what sort of things they sang. Said Bing—who had already told Whiteman that he thought his singers pretty corny: 'We don't sing any of that vo-de-odo stuff. We do a brand new thing called the hotcha-cha.'

They were in . . . Whiteman offered them more money than they had ever seen. Because he was under twenty-one, Al had to get his father down from Spokane to sign the contract. Bing turned to brother Everett and asked him to give up selling trucks and manage the Crosby future instead. Everett shook hands on that and it was the humble founding of a great new showbusiness empire.

The agreement was that the two boys should join the band some weeks later in Chicago, the Windy City, which at that time was getting the best in music and the worst in gang warfare. But the boys had two other things in mind first. They had already been invited to make a record by orchestra leader Don

Clark, who wielded his baton at the Biltmore Hotel in Los Angeles. And they also planned to go home to Spokane to give the folks a farewell concert before hitting the trail with Whiteman.

The record was cut on 10 October 1926, in a converted warehouse in Los Angeles. The song: a vocal duet called 'I've Got the Girl'. It was the first disc Bing ever made . . .

The studio was primitive. Against one wall stood an ancient, battered upright piano. Opposite, a megaphone-type contraption—which Bing had to sing into—protruded from a pine-planked recording booth.

The recording machine was a great hulk of a thing and a steel needle carved the sound of Crosby and Rinker into the thick wax that was used in those days. But there was no stopping and starting, as there is with the tape of today, when various 'takes' can be edited and joined. Once you began to record you kept right on to the end. After a couple of takes, Crosby and Rinker had a master disc and recording history had been made. For Bing it was the first of thousands . . .

But 'I've Got the Girl', issued on the Columbia label, didn't set the world alight. It didn't sell a million. Nor did it bring anyone running with a recording contract. It was a start and that was the nicest thing that could be said about it.

The return to Spokane that winter of 1926 was much more stirring. Both families turned out to welcome home their boys who, with Whiteman contracts in their pockets, were already local celebrities.

They took the stage to waves of applause from a packed house at the Liberty Theatre. There were reunions with lots of old friends, then lots of goodbyes as they boarded the train to Chicago. 'Everybody saw us off,' says Rinker.

They arrived in Chicago, the former Indian trading post once known as the Mud-hole of the Prairies, to find the massive urban sprawl in the grip of vice, lawlessness and corruption. It was known as 'the only completely corrupt city in America' and they read in the *Chicago Tribune*: 'A reign of terror is upon the city. No city in time of peace ever held so high a place in the category of crime-ridden, terrorized, murder-breeding cities as is now held by Chicago.'

The cause of the crime-wave was Prohibition, which was to last until 5 December 1932, giving birth to a whole new era of graft—the sale of black market alcohol. In complete control of the crime-wave was a slum-bred Italian delinquent called Alphonse 'Bottles' Capone.

Al Capone, also known as 'Scarface', managed what no other single gangster had, or has, ever achieved: he took over a modern American city, made it his own and then bled it dry with the air of an ancient Roman Emperor. During Prohibition, more than 700 people died in Capone's drink-traffic war—many of them brutally gunned down on the streets in open gangland fighting.

This was the backcloth as Crosby and Rinker faced the biggest challenge of their young lives so far—opening night with the best band in the land at the Tivoli Theatre.

As they waited off-stage in the wings they were both in a state of extreme nervousness. In fact they were petrified. The walk to Al's white upright, already waiting on stage, looked like a mile. Would Chicago like them and their particular brand of rhythm? It could be a tough old town.

Then the cue came and the waiting was over, but not the nerves. Whiteman, with his legendary sense of humour, was introducing them to the packed audience: 'I found these kids in an ice-cream parlour in Walla-Walla . . . I want you to meet Crosby and Rinker . . .'

The moment of truth. They trotted on and went into their first number. There was an explosion of applause as they finished the final bar. They were going to be a hit all right. And Pops Whiteman beamed a chubby smile. By the close of their fast moving 'hotcha-cha' act, the audience was in raptures and the clapping thunderous.

All Bing and Al had to do now was push the piano off stage—but, yes, it wouldn't budge! They grinned at the audience and heaved once more. Still the darn thing stuck. Now Whiteman grinned at the crowd, then walked over and put his twenty-one stone behind the upright. Over it went—and the three of them! It was a bonus laugh for the customers.

The tremendous reception was no real surprise to Bing; in discovering the criminal reputation of the city, he had also found that Chicago was the stomping ground of jazz. Musicians and singers, with such immortals as Louis Armstrong, Billie Holiday and Jelly Roll Morton (who was also a highly success-ful pimp until Capone threw him out), abounded. 'Chicago,'

23

says Bing, 'was orientated in the direction of new musical styles; always has been.'

The stature of Crosby and Rinker grew apace at the Tivoli as they captured audiences night after night. Whiteman was much impressed and decided that it was time for them to record with the band.

Matty Malneck, the viola-playing Whiteman 'spy' in Los Angeles, had been working on a vocal arrangement of a song called 'Wistful and Blue' and persuaded Pops to let the two boys loose on it. It was a smash hit.

Everything was coming up roses, like the song says.

With money in his pocket, Bing set out to explore the city. He'd seen Capone's illicit beer trucks, often with police escorts, delivering openly in the streets and it didn't take him long to discover where the booze was going.

Chicago had twenty thousand speakeasies, producing more than six million dollars a week in revenue for Capone and the other gangs that ran the city. In addition to beer, hard liquor and wine, the speakeasy provided entertainment—usually a Dixieland band of clarinettist, banjo-player, pianist and drummer.

Although most speakeasies, also known as 'blind pigs', were hidden behind respectable fronts such as soft drink parlours, coffee shops, restaurants and drug stores, Bing and most of Chicago's population of three million found no difficulty in getting in. After seven years of Prohibition, deaths from alcoholism in Chicago had risen by a staggering six hundred per cent and the number of drunk drivers had increased by almost five hundred per cent.

Entry to a speakeasy was often through a fake telephone booth. You knocked three times and, after being carefully eyed through a peephole, were admitted to a sleazy, smoke-filled room. Tables were covered in red-checked cloths, on which stood bowls of popcorn. The booze—nicknamed 'coffin varnish', 'rot gut', 'tarantula juice' or 'sheep dip'—was served in china tea-cups.

Bing's first speakeasy venture almost ended in disaster. He went out alone, but befriended a couple of strangers in the first bar he was able to get into. They introduced him to brandy for the first time and the last thing he remembered was setting out on a tour of other speakeasies. A few days later he awoke on a sofa in a strange room.

24

Across from where he lay, at a table and in deep conversation, sat a huddle of men 'with', says Bing, 'padded-shoulders, snap-brim hats and sallow faces'.

He quickly checked that his wallet and money were intact, and then, thanking the men, said he would leave. But not so fast, buddy ... For, as the men explained, while Bing was drunk there had been a shooting and someone had been hurt, and they were holed-up in the hotel room. Bing sought out the bathroom, 'feeling terrible with a case of the whips and jingles'. Suddenly there was the staccato sound of gunfire from the next room.

The door of the bathroom burst from its hinges and a burly policeman thundered through with revolver drawn—to find Bing calmly drinking a glass of water. He told the astonished lawman that he was a singer with Whiteman's Band and had just popped-in after hearing shooting to 'check that nobody was hurt'.

At first they didn't believe him, but after—as he later admitted—'the finest acting performance of my career', Bing convinced them and was allowed to leave. On the way out, he noticed that the hotel room had been peppered with machine-gun bullets and that a couple of his 'companions' had been slightly wounded.

A few days later, he found out that he had been holed-up with no less a mobster than Machine Gun Jack McGurn—Al Capone's chief bodyguard and torpedo—who was arrested on suspicion of murdering five gangsters during June and July 1927.

McGurn, who like many Sicilians, had adopted an Irish alias in preference to his real name of de Mora, was freed due to lack of evidence and Bing was to meet up with him again a few years later after leaving Whiteman's band.

Meantime, there was more to come. Bing, like most of Whiteman's musicians, found that the illegal clubs and speakeasies cried out for people to drop in and perform. According to jazz pianist Earl Hines: 'Scarface got along well with musicians. He liked to come into a club with his henchmen and have the band play his requests. He was free with hundred dollar tips.'

Bing, the one-armed trumpeter Wingy Manone and Bix Beiderbecke were three Whiteman stars who took most

25

advantage of the opportunity to give extra performances, but they soon discovered that flying bullets and beatings-up were occupational hazards.

The late Kenneth Allsop, in his book *The Bootleggers* (the gangsters who enabled a theoretically dry America to be 'wetter than it had ever been'), described what happened when Wingy Manone was in the middle of his solo of 'Clarinet Marmalade' one night at the Manley Club: 'A man at a table pulled a tommy-gun from under his overcoat and raked the front of the bandstand in an attempt to stop an acquaintance who was hurriedly leaving.'

Allsop also describes what happened when Beiderbecke joined Bing to perform at a private party at The Greyhound in Cicero —a Chicago suburb completely occupied by the Capone mob. The party proved to be 'made up mostly of blue-jawed young men in dark double-breasted suits with blondes to match'. One of them took to yelling 'at the band and Beiderbecke offered to get off the stand and punch him on the nose if he did not shut up. The heckler glowered but shut up.'

The heckler was Capone himself. When guitarist Eddie Condon pointed this out, a very white-faced Beiderbecke and Crosby remarked in unison that they were 'very glad' that the mob had not taken up the challenge.

It was something of a relief when the Whiteman Band had to pack its bags for a tour that took in some of the less bullet-swept cities of the Mid-West. It was a happy tour for Crosby and Rinker. First Cleveland took them to its heart. Then Detroit, Pittsburgh, St Louis and Indianapolis followed suit. Now they were all set to storm New York.

This was the big date, the famous Paramount Theatre, one of the nations' greatest showcases. They arrived with the confidence of conquering heroes, but it was a mood that was not to last very long. When they took the stage at the Paramount they were a colossal flop . . .

Why? They just couldn't understand it. Loved everywhere else, but not in New York. Bing took it badly. Al was even more upset. Perhaps it was just the first night audience. So they tried again, but it was the same story.

The worried Paramount manager Bob Weitman called a crisis conference. 'You've got to cancel those boys,' he told Whiteman. 'Get them off! They're not going over here.'

Pops broke the news to them and they were feeling very down—and puzzled, although the reason for the big flop was simple, in retrospect. These were the days before microphones on stage and the Paramount was much larger than any theatre they had played before. The audience just couldn't hear them . . .

But, characteristically, Bing didn't cry too hard or too long. 'I was baffled, but we were having a lot of fun. We went out to Harlem every night, to the Cotton Club and Connie's Inn and all the famous places there, hearing all the great music around New York.

'I couldn't care less, really. I knew that Whiteman had to pay us—we were contracted and I just felt something'd show up.'

Something did. Whiteman started using the boys on recording sessions. They cut a number of tracks for the Bix Beiderbecke memorial album, sang some musical comedy songs and Bing also soloed 'Ol' Man River' and 'Make Believe' on the band's recording of the musical *Show Boat*.

Other tasks that were dreamed up to keep Bing busy weren't as pleasant. Pops had him working at sound effects off stage and even pulling a transparent curtain.

The band were featuring Tchaikowsky's 1812 Overture, with its big finish of bells ringing and cannon firing. It was Bing's job to pound the chimes off stage with a mallet and witnesses recall that it was a wonder the bells survived the onslaught. 'Bing just played hell with them,' said Matty Malneck, 'because it was some job for a singer to come down to.'

Whiteman also had Crosby and Rinker busking in the Paramount lobby—to keep the second house happy while they were waiting for the first house to clear. Then Pops decided to give them a second chance at his nightclub on Broadway. But again it was a large venue and there was the added competition of the noise of eating and drinking. 'So we laid our second egg,' said Rinker. And for Bing it was back to bells and curtains. The pain was eased only when the band took to the road again. The theatres were smaller and once more the pair could be heard and the audiences were appreciative.

Back home in Spokane, the family kept in close touch with Bing's progress—up or down. He used to send younger brother Bob all his records and Bob was very impressed with what he heard.

27

'I thought Bing had something I couldn't hear any other singer do, which was a way of reading a lyric. But he didn't send me only his own records. Most of them would be jazz records of Tommy and Jimmy Dorsey, Bix Beiderbecke or Louis Armstrong—whom he had a great admiration for—and I think that whetted my appetite for jazz.' Bob, of course, would eventually lead his own Dixieland band into the jazz annals.

After a successful tour, Crosby and Rinker returned to New York with the Whiteman band and made one more try at wooing the big city audience. Once more they failed. It was the end of the road for *Two Boys and a Piano—Singing Songs in Their Own Way*, although Pops didn't lose faith in them entirely. He was always being invited to big parties and used to take the boys along to keep their hand in.

At this time there appeared on the scene an unlikely-looking saviour, a small man who slept little and suffered from a racking cough. Name of Harry Barris, who was literally bashing a piano in George Olsen's New York nightclub.

He payed hot and loud and at times he would slam the piano top down to the beat of the number. His singing style was aggressive and only the stone deaf could ever complain that they couldn't hear Harry.

With a touch of genius, Matty Malneck fathered a far-seeing brainwave to save Crosby and Rinker from impending obscurity. Why couldn't they team up with Harry Barris and make a noise as a threesome for Whiteman? Providing they all wanted to, of course. Harry was Matty's pal anyway—they were both from Denver, Colorado—and there would be no difficulty in all of them talking it over. Harry was, after all, a man of some experience as well and had been in an early local group with Glenn Miller back in Denver.

The future for Crosby and Rinker, as Malneck saw it, was decidedly black: 'You guys are either going to be shipped back to Los Angeles or something, because you're not pulling those curtains very good anyway!'

So they went along to watch the livewire Harry belting away. Not only were they impressed by Harry's flair, they thought they could get along with him as well. And everything was okay by Harry. Now the idea had to be put to Whiteman. It didn't take him long to see the light and the wisdom of it all.

And thus was born Paul Whiteman's Rhythm Boys, a revolutionary partnership that was destined to hit the road to greatness.

Harry was a real driving-force, full of ideas and how to sell them. First the Rhythm Boys worked out an act, then the non-stop Harry sat himself down in a New York apartment with Bing and wrote a song for this sparkling new trio. The title: 'Mississippi Mud', now a standard, and a big hit at the time. When they sang it at Whiteman's Broadway club, where they were doing a stint as an intermission group, the customers actually stopped chattering and listened, something that rarely happened to the intermission act.

Then came a Barris–Crosby song called 'From Monday On', another smash helped on its way with a three-trumpet chorus from Bix Beiderbecke and, surprisingly, Tommy and Jimmy Dorsey.

When the boys appeared with the orchestra, the disciplinarian Whiteman made them sit in with the rest of the band—holding fake instruments.

'They tried me on different things,' says Bing, 'like the French horn—but I got it to produce some sort of noise. I couldn't resist it. Finally they got me a violin with rubber strings so I could just saw away and look great'.

Whiteman was very fond of the violin and at every performance played a chorus of 'My Wonderful One'—much to the annoyance of the rest of the band and particularly their top solo violin, jazz great Joe Venuti. Says Bing: 'Joe always teased Pops about his intonation and as Pops never practiced it was somewhat suspect. At one matinee, as Whiteman concluded his solo and was taking a bow, Joe stepped out from the band, shook Pops by the hand, took his violin, salted it from a huge salt shaker—and proceeded to eat it! The band fell apart, the audience roared and Pops stood aghast.'

A wide smile was back on the big man's face a few days later when a major American car manufacturer signed the band for a national radio broadcast, which Paul told Bing would feature him and the Rhythm Boys.

Back in Spokane, the news was greeted joyfully and Bing's father went out and bought a new radio set specially for the big moment. Bing's elder brother Ted described what happened at the Crosby home that day: 'Half an hour before the time for the broadcast we grouped ourselves about the radio set, hardly able to conceal our restlessness or impatience.

'None of us, I am sure, listened consciously to the numbers played by the band, but when the announcement came—"a brand new number, 'Great Day' ", followed by Bing's unmistakable voice singing the refrain, we smiled incredulously at each other.'

As the song ended, the Crosby clan shuffled even closer to the crackling set. 'Would they call him Harry or Bing?' they asked themselves. But no announcement came and the Whiteman band swung immediately into another number: 'Bing had not even been given an acknowledgement! His was just a nameless voice to the thousands of listeners,' said Ted.

The big band life, in fact, was beginning to become one big laugh. The boys were now pulling in more than a hundred and fifty dollars a week each as one success followed another. All three began to hit the bottle—or 'the Flowing Bowl', as Crosby calls it. Especially Bing. 'I think we were a little drunk with power,' said Rinker.

They chased golf balls and girls and got lazy about their music. 'We wouldn't learn any new songs,' says Al. 'We just wouldn't get together to rehearse. We had a repertoire of twelve songs and that was that.'

They didn't fool Whiteman for one minute. 'Hey! What's going on here?' he said, angrily. 'You guys, you're out playing golf, you're out chasing girls and you're not developing any new material. Really, you're not much good to me!'.

The warning went unheeded and the act continued to suffer. So Whiteman was forced to drop them from the band. It was the Fall of 1929 and there was a tour of Britain coming up. Instead, the Rhythm Boys, in disgrace, were sent on a forty-week tour of the United States in vaudeville. But they weren't getting away from Whiteman completely.

Says Bing: 'He had a massive, monumental reproduction of himself made in plywood—with a moustache, violin and everything. And then he made a soundtrack with a little music and before we went on stage his voice came over and said: 'These are my Rhythm Boys and I beg you to give them your full attention.' Then we came out to mild applause . . .'

But a plywood model simply couldn't put a rein on them. The daily round was still golf, girls and grog, though not necessarily in that order. Trains were missed, baggage lost and even shows missed, the unforgivable show business sin.

Nevertheless, they were still getting top billing and a great response from audiences.

'But we were very inconsistent,' Bing says now. 'We all wanted to be comedians and we loved to imitate some we'd seen. The public wanted to hear the records we had made performed in person—but we finally wound up doing hardly any singing at all.'

They even evolved a phoney mind-reading act, with Harry and Al out amongst the audience and Bing in turban playing the clairvoyant on stage. 'We were running all over the place,' Bing remembers with a smile.

It was the mind-reading Bing—it got that they sometimes called him Binge in these hard-drinking times—who was pretty helpless in more simple duties, like handling the baggage and tickets to the next date. Frequently the boys went one way and the trunks another. And sometimes not at all. Bing admits to gambling them away to the click of the dice on more than one occasion. The crap game, it appears, was a favourite past-time and in those days clothes were money.

Once or twice Bing missed a show, leaving the other two to ad-lib a routine. They decided to teach him a harsh lesson after one of these falls from grace.

He turned up at the hotel next morning bedraggled and a little bleary-eyed with the excuse that through no fault of his own he had missed the train.

Harry and Al called in a husky footballer friend of theirs and persuaded him to be the offended theatre manager. Bing was sitting head-in-hands on his hotel bed and being comforted by his singing colleagues when the bogus manager burst in.

'That's it!' he stormed. 'You're fired! And what's more, I'm going to make sure that the word gets around and you'll never perform on stage again. In fact, you'll never sing again if I have my way!'

Crosby cried real tears and begged the 'manager' to reconsider. At which Rinker and Barris collapsed in laughter and Bing was angry. Very, very angry indeed.

The lesson didn't last long. Bing hit the happy trail again and—to be fair—so did the other two. By this time, Whiteman was getting a barrage of complaints from genuine theatre managers up and down the States. A stern warning was sent to the tippling threesome: 'Do what you're paid to do—or else!'

This at least threw a scare into them, but the threat had come too late.

Says Bing: 'We tried to get back to the act, but we'd lost it. So gradually towards the end of the week, we went right back to what he'd forbidden us to do. At the end of the show, for a closing joke, Harry said "do you know how to cure a horse from frothing at the mouth?" I said "no" and he said "teach him to spit!" And the curtain came down with a wham!—right in front of us and that was it. We were cancelled. So we went back to New York and Whiteman was furious.'

Surprisingly, after giving the boys a fierce man-to-man talk, Whiteman forgave them. Their youth, he felt, was largely to blame for their indiscretions. And back they went into the band. An extremely fortunate decision for Bing. Hollywood, to which he had trekked with Al, was calling. They wanted Whiteman and Company in movies!

Chapter Five

Hollywood as 1930 dawned was still an infant but growing up fast. The Talkies, after a spasmodic and imperfect start, were going to be here to stay. Prohibition still had a couple of years to run and drinking was not as secret as it used to be. But there was another word around—Depression, following the Wall Street crash. Oddly it would not cripple Hollywood. In contrast it would make it busier than ever. What the nation needed was music and laughter and the Dream Factory that was Hollywood could churn that out. The 'thirties for 'Tinsel Town', as someone dubbed it, was to be an era of romance, comedy, light-comedy—and above all music.

Universal set the pace at the start of the decade by signing the Whiteman ensemble for a mammoth musical to be based almost entirely on the character of Pops himself and to be entitled *The King of Jazz*.

The proceedings got off to a real bang-the-drum start. At the same time the band was also making a name on the national radio network in a programme sponsored by Old Gold Tobacco. So to tie-in with the making of the movie, the sponsors hired a complete train to transport the orchestra from New York to California, normally a three-day trip. But this train, called—not surprisingly—The Old Gold Special was halting in various towns or cities along the route to allow the orchestra to give a local concert or broadcast.

An entirely male train, with a ban on wives or girlfriends.

Everybody had his own compartment and drawing-room. The dining car was open day and night. There had never been a train like it and it was a ball all the way.

The ballyhoo spilled over into Hollywood. The whole band was moved into a special lodge at Universal City and anyone who wanted one could have a Ford car that carried a caricature of Whiteman in the middle of the spare tire . . .

But Whiteman wasn't exactly falling about with glee. The film wasn't ready to shoot; the script was a terrible mess and the producers had decided to completely rewrite it. In fact, it was going to be a long wait before *The King of Jazz* was ready to roll. Universal hadn't yet got to grips with making pictures with sound—and certainly not musicals.

As Bing recalls: 'It was sort of the birth of talking pictures. They didn't know much about techniques. Everything took a long, long, time. Shooting a musical number was a big project; particularly if there was a band involved and a lot of dances— so we had a ball of a vacation really!'

Drink was easy to come by, and the fine weather gave the boys ample opportunity to play that great love of their lives— golf. Bing was, as usual, the first to spot the course opposite the Universal studios.

'We could see it across the way. It was called Lakeside. So we'd play golf and then check-in to get our pay every week. Sometimes Paul would say, "Well, thanks a lot for managing to get over here for your cheques—thanks a lot!" '

After weeks of this the King of Jazz—known also by many as the Fat Fiddler—blew his top and took the band back to New York aboard The Old Gold Special. Only this time they picked up a few extra passengers—including a struggling song-writer named Hoagy Carmichael.

'Paul Whiteman let me get on the train,' said Hoagy years later, 'although I didn't have a nickel in my pocket. And Bing let me use his upper berth to sleep. That was my first real contact with him'.

Hoagy, of course, also became a success and penned several Crosby hits, with 'Stardust' probably the best known.

At last Universal were ready to shoot. But this time there was no special train to the West Coast, or any special lodge when the band got there. The free-loading was over and ac-commodation had to be paid for.

Most of the band moved into rented apartments, Matty Malneck among them, who found a modest place which had twin beds that came out of the wall. His landlady surprised him one day when he returned. 'Mr Crosby has moved in with you,' she announced. When Matty asked why, she replied: 'Well, he didn't have his rent money this month.'

But there was still a free drink or two to be had at the private parties that were now so fashionable in Hollywood. Bing and Al Rinker were invited to their fair share and they remember fondly one lavish do given by Beatrice Lillie, Gertrude Lawrence and Jack Buchanan.

Each guest had to play, sing or dance for his or her supper, which was little problem for Bing and Al. But Bea Lillie was the hit of the night with her impersonations and a finale that had her poised on a settee, champagne in hand, bottom protruding exaggeratedly and shouting loudly: 'There—dignity! England with its ass out!'

The film, in which Bing was scheduled for a solo number, 'Song of the Dawn', and others with the Rhythm Boys, dawdled along at snail-pace. Which was time enough for Bing to get into trouble once more. Let him tell it himself:

'I was driving home from this party and I had a young lady with me in the front seat. We were going down Hollywood Boulevard at a moderate speed, because I was going to turn right into the Roosevelt Hotel. I had my hand out and I was sober. Then a guy in a car hit me from behind and this young lady flew out over the windshield! I picked her up, a crowd gathered and I took her into the hotel lobby and sent for a doctor. Then a policeman came round taking notes. He smelt my breath and said, "You've been drinking!" and I said I'd had a few. So he said, "Well, you can come along with me." And he took me down to jail and locked me up.'

At about 2.30 a.m. the phone rang in the apartment that Bing was now sharing with Whiteman's concert master, Kurt Dieterle. Crosby had been expected home earlier—and his dinner was dried up on the stove.

'Where the hell are you?' bawled Kurt.

'Down in the jail here! It's colder than hell. Will you come down and bring me some blankets.'

Kurt did just that—then phoned an angry Whiteman, who bailed his troublesome boy out when morning came.

Two weeks later Crosby appeared in court charged with reckless driving and suspicion of drinking. Typically, he went to court straight from the golf course: 'I was in knickers (plus fours) with Argyll socks and a loud sweater—I looked very fetching!'

The judge solemnly read the details of the case then looked sourly at Bing and said: 'Here I see H.B.D.'

'What does that mean?' asked the innocent-eyed crooner.

'Has been drinking,' the judge explained.

'Oh! Yes. I had a few.'

'Don't you know that there's a Prohibition law in the United States and liquor is forbidden?'

'Yes—but nobody pays any attention to that!'

'Well, you'll have thirty days to pay some attention to it!'

And clang! There was Crosby in clink.

At first he was kept in his cell and treated like every other inmate, but later he was moved to the front office and put to work typing. Then, due to Whiteman's influence, he was transferred from downtown Los Angeles to a smaller station in North Hollywood—and allowed out on special 'day-release', which made him available for filming.

Each day an armed guard—an affable Irishman—would escort Crosby to the Universal studios and take him back at night. But Bing lost his solo spot. 'Song of the Dawn' was given instead to actor John Boles to sing and he made quite an impression with it.

There was some compensation. Bing's day-releases from the lock-up came in time for him to put on a top hat with the Rhythm Boys and join the three lovely Brox Sisters in the number 'A Bench in the Park'.

The remarkable thing was that Bing's behaviour, or perhaps misbehaviour, never really affected the progression of his career. Most musicians drank during Prohibition and the rare abstainer was considered an oddball. Whiteman recognised this, but even so he stood more from Crosby than anyone else, probably because of his obvious talent plus that rare quality—youthful innocence. But it couldn't go on for ever.

The crunch came not many weeks after the film was finally in the can and the Whiteman band had taken to the road again. It started with a confrontation between band manager

Jimmy Gillespie and ended with the three Rhythm Boys packing their bags.

Says Bing: 'Jimmy was a nice guy, but he guarded Whiteman's interests very severely. At the time, we were in Seattle and I bought a bottle of gin from a bootlegger friend of Jimmy's and he claimed I didn't pay for it. Jimmy was going to take it out of my salary and I raised hell.

'But that wasn't really the reason—it was the culmination of a lot of things. Nothing serious, we weren't doing anything; we weren't working; we were lazy and we weren't producing and developing new material—you just had to develop new material.'

So that was it. Contracts would be terminated when the tour reached St Louis and the threesome would keep the title the Rhythm Boys but drop Whiteman's name.

If there was anger over the parting, it was forgotten over the years. Said Pops before his death in 1967: 'Nobody could love Bing more, nor could a fellow ever have been kinder than Bing has always been.'

Says Bing: 'He was a majestic figure and he had great humour. He wanted the best. I don't think he had a great musical talent, but he had a great ear. He knew what was good.'

With the parting of the ways, Pops set out to try to replace the rebel three. He made an offer to one Perry Como, a young fellow just beginning to make a name with a small band—but was turned down. He brought in Johnny Mercer, who was to become one of the world's greatest songwriters. But a tremendous success like the Rhythm Boys is not easily duplicated. Pops kept it in the family instead by hiring Al's sister Mildred Bailey.

The wheel had turned full circle . . .

Bing, Al and Harry headed West once more to the Californian sunshine. Even though the nation was now in the depths of the Depression and the Buddy-can-you-spare-a-dime days—the song was yet to come and Bing would make a hit of it—they were able to take things easy for a little while and spent most of their days on the golf course. But the business was still gnawing at them. Al worked out some new routines for the trio. Harry wrote some new songs—while Bing tried to reduce his golf handicap!

When the bright lights eventually lured them back the venue was an intimate and fashionable nightspot called the Montmartre Café on Hollywood Boulevard. They felt at home there and after a somewhat quiet start quickly became the darlings of the Hollywood set. But what was more important was that they were now working harder both at new songs and new material.

A Montmartre regular then was Rudy Vallee, who was just beginning to establish himself as a singer and was to become, along with Crosby and Russ Columbo, one of the Big Three crooners.

He recalled how the Rhythm Boys improved as the evenings went by: 'The piano was against the wall and Barris, who was playing, had to face it when he sang—so his voice went into the wall and didn't mean very much.

'The other two boys faced the audience, which was down below seated at tables, eating. But, since they didn't have any amplification in those days and didn't use megaphones, nobody paid the slightest attention to them.'

Bing was the first to notice this and he decided to do something about it. Why not leave the stage and head for the audience?

Rudy Vallee, who hardly knew Bing at the time, was impressed: 'Suddenly, the room was as quiet as a grave. Out in the middle of the floor was one of this trio, singing. The crowd was quiet, very quiet, and when he finished the place went into ecstasy.

'They applauded like mad and this young man walked right off the floor with no expression whatsoever on his face. No triumph! No elation! No conquest! It was as though he were deaf like Beethoven and couldn't hear that the audience had liked what he did.'

Vallee had witnessed an early example of a side to Bing's character that is seldom seen in public—the cool Mr Crosby—vastly different from the usual hail-fellow-well-met image for which he is world renowned.

Both the experience and the money were good at the Montmartre—some four hundred dollars apiece. The only way the boys could go now was up and soon they were signed to star at the area's best known nightclub, the celebrated Cocoanut Grove at the Ambassador Hotel on Wilshire Boulevard, where Gus Arnheim and his orchestra were in residence. It meant sitting in with a band again, but for Bing it was another momentous turning point. He became a solo singer.

The Grove was the real in-place for the stars, as Ben Lyon— one himself then—recalled: 'We all put on our white ties and looked quite English and had dinner and a lovely evening dancing. Bing sat on the stand with a ukulele—although I don't think he played a note. When the band finished its dance numbers, a little white piano was wheeled out and the Rhythm Boys came on to the floor. Everybody loved them.'

As they became more popular, they gradually superseded Gus Arnheim's sweet-music trio which included Russ Columbo, then one of his violinists but soon to become in the eyes of the public one of Bing's rivals in song.

There at the Grove the true Bing began to develop. Despite the finesse and success of the threesome, his solos began to steal the show.

Now, when he started to sing, the patrons would stop dancing and turn to face the stage. Then, as he sang, they would sway gently to the music. The warmth generated by the closeness of the audience and the intimacy of the room was matched only by the warmth of his voice.

There, beneath the Grove's plastic palm trees and artificial monkeys, he began to sing with what has since been described as 'a glowing depth'.

His solos, he later said himself, started to have a 'cry in them' and fans noticed for the first time a 'tear' or 'gravel-throating' creeping in. 'The Crosby Cry', they christened it.

His two partners were being left behind—and they weren't surprised. 'That's the way it had to be,' said Al Rinker. 'Bing emerged as a soloist, which he wasn't before.' But the boys stuck it out together and were in residence for more than a year.

At the Grove they were also able to reach out to a far wider audience than the high and mighty of Hollywood who patronised the club. A two-hour nightly broadcast went out from a special room above the club. 'A new thing in those days,' says Bing. 'We could be heard up in San Francisco and the North-West and it was a great showcase for us. We could try out new songs, new material and we built up a little bit of a name.'

The first song he sang over the air from the Grove was 'Just

One More Chance'—a plea he had frequently made to Whiteman.

The Rhythm Boys matured there, but they couldn't forsake the good times for work completely. Bing stayed out nights and his attendance record was far from perfect.

To try to curb him, Abe Frank, who ran the Grove, hired a girl singer, Loyce Whiteman (no relation to Pops).

'They heard me on radio station KFWP and were looking for somebody not actually to replace Bing,' she said, 'but to scare him a little—so he would not walk out so much and so he would get on with the job more often. He was being a little naughty.'

Loyce's début brought forth a bad attack of first-night nerves.

'I was petrified; I was backstage and Bing was sitting there, and he said, "Oh come on kid, don't get worried about it, I'll walk out there with you on your first song."

'So, he took my hand and we walked out. He sang one chorus and then he made me sing it, and then he came in in harmony on the end of it. It was precious and it gave me a lot of assurance.'

But her arrival at the Grove failed to put an end to the revelry. Bing was soon up to his old tricks. Jack Mass, who was later to go into a music publishing business with Bing, saw much of the fun-loving Crosby.

'He was a great fan of Louis Armstrong, who always played the Cotton Club,' said Jack. 'And after the Cocoanut Grove engagement, when he was through at one o'clock in the morning, he'd generally go to the Cotton Club and listen to Louis or Duke Ellington. He loved both those men.'

Bing also had a lot of time for a young clarinet player from Cleveland, Ohio, named Artie Shaw, who had just arrived in Los Angeles, at the tender age of nineteen, to seek fame and fortune.

'I was working with a little band at the Roosevelt on Hollywood Boulevard,' said Artie, 'a sort of mecca for producers, stars and agents. I remember Bing showing up quite often and asking to be allowed to sing a song. It was a place for him to get heard by some of the important people.

'Even in those days, you knew there was something special about him. He was doing something that hadn't been heard before. It was his own. Most people don't understand it, but musicians do hear a little more acutely—not better necessarily, but more acutely.'

At the Grove, Crosby met someone who was to be vitally important in his life. A girl named Dixie Lee. It was love at first sight . . .

Chapter Six

Miss Wilma Winnifred Wyatt had everything going for her when she arrived in Hollywood at the age of seventeen. She was a girl with all the attributes of a new and sparkling blonde bombshell. A wide, generous smile and not unlike Betty Grable when she posed by a pool in swimsuit. In a few years she had come a long way from her hometown of Harriman in Tennessee.

She had first caught the public eye and ear when she won a competition to find 'The girl who could sing most like Ruth Etting', a torch singer of national acclaim who later was to take the Hollywood trail herself to film with Eddie Cantor.

After her victory, Miss Wyatt understudied Miss Etting during a Chicago engagement. Then she went on to greater things—a hit Broadway musical called *Good News*. It was certainly good news for Miss Wyatt, who landed a three-year contract with 20th Century-Fox and came to the celluloid city with the new professional name of Dixie Lee. They put her first into a vehicle entitled *Movietone Follies* and again she attracted considerable attention. Stardom was getting close . . .

Attracted to her more than anyone else was the young up-and-coming crooner Bing Crosby nightly airing his larynx at the Cocoanut Grove. A fortunate Mr Crosby, for he happened to be a pal of her current escort Dick Keene, a musical comedy star from New York, also under contract to Fox. And through

Keene, Bing was able to engineer a meeting—oddly a three-some . . .

'We went out double-dating one night—that's how I met Dixie,' he admits.

There had been many girls in his life, many dates along the way—but no big romance. Now he was thoroughly enchanted by the lively Miss Lee from Tennessee.

The feeling seemed to be almost mutual. Dixie became a fan of the crooner's and a regular patron at the Cocoanut Grove. Said Connee Boswell, of the famed Boswell Sisters singing trio and a friendly observer of the romance: 'I believe it was almost love at first sight. Bing fell in love with Dixie and that was that . . .' But the path of love was anything but smooth.

Here was a starlet, still in her teens, with world fame nearly within her grasp. Here was a hell-raising singer with some way to go yet and some ten years her senior. Her future at that time, in fact, promised much more than his.

It became an on-and-off affair with a courtship that could only be described as hectic. Bing would ask Dixie to marry him only to be told that she would not wed a man who 'spent twice as much as he earned'. Once she described him as 'the bump-tious baritone'.

There was pressure from Dixie's friends as well, who urged her not to consider marriage to 'that crazy crooner with neither security nor future'. But Bing eventually persuaded her to say yes—after crooning to her over the phone a song that was to become a Crosby classic—'I Surrender Dear'. Followed by a talk over a cold chicken meal at the Grove.

They were married on 29 September 1930, at the Blessed Sacrament Church on Sunset Boulevard. She was almost nineteen.

None of that midnight, justice-of-the-peace Hollywood-style quickie wedding stuff for Bing. Despite his somewhat irre-sponsible behaviour sometimes, he had stayed faithful to the church in which he had been reared.

As Loyce Whiteman, his colleague at the Grove, recalled: 'There was one thing he'd never miss—church. No matter what happened, any time he went off, drunk or not, he sure found his way to Mass every time. He'd crawl to church. That's one thing that was beautiful about him.'

Crosby remembers the anti-brigade well: 'One of the things

they threw at Dixie was that she'd have to support me for the rest of her life. She did—but not the way they meant; the support she gave me was more important than money. We could always count on her for the truth about ourselves, which is a rare and helpful commodity in Hollywood.'

The marriage certainly never rated any blazing headlines in the local Press. One Los Angeles newspaper carried this small paragraph: 'Dixie Lee, the movie star, has been married to a Mr Bing Crosby, who is described as a singer.' Bing still laughs at a heading that went: 20*th Century Fox Star Marries Obscure Crooner*.

It was a tag that wouldn't be with him for much longer. The Victor Record Company thought it time to give him a whirl on disc and teamed him with the Gus Arnheim band for a session in Los Angeles. The date was 19 January 1931, and he had been married nearly four months. Both the sides had been written by Harry Barris—'I Surrender Dear' and 'It Must Be True'. 'I Surrender' caught the public ear and became Bing's first big solo hit.

Even with marriage, however, there had been no immediate settling down to the steady life for Crosby. Golfing and what he calls 'bibulous behaviour' interfered with his work at the Grove. Bossman Abe Frank decided to get tougher and planned to fine Bing every time he missed a show. The first time he tried it, Crosby turned on his heel and, stopping only to collect Harry and Al, walked out on Abe and the Grove.

'I don't remember all the details,' he says, 'but I went to Caliente and didn't come back. It was a spa just over the border in Mexico and we'd go down there once in a while to gamble and have fun. I didn't get back in time and missed a couple of nights. Abe docked my salary—so I walked out.'

Rinker and Barris went with him and it was virtually the end of the Rhythm Boys . . . for Abe Frank retaliated by getting the Musicians' Union to 'black' the trio and they found it impossible to work. Eventually the split-up came and they went their separate ways. A decision, thought Rinker, that was not entirely due to Abe's reaction. 'The break-up was inevitable,' said Al. 'I think we'd reached the end of what we were doing and there was no point in going on. We weren't going forward, we were just doing a job. It was fun, but it couldn't go on for ever.'

Al Rinker went on to become a highly-respected radio then television producer, and his contacts with old school-buddy Bing became fewer and rare . . . something that caused him some bitterness over the years.

Harry Barris, also finding romance at the Grove, married Loyce Whiteman. He appeared in some of Crosby's movies, continued with his songwriting and was successful as a solo act on stage and radio. Their daughter Marti Barris took to the boards as a cabaret artiste and received a certain amount of help along the way from the Crosby organisation.

Bing decided to go it alone, despite the union ban, and called on personal manager brother Everett to play a more active role in his career.

Everett had been a tough top sergeant in World War I and younger brother Bob Crosby maintains that he was the only person in the world who could have handled Bing. He tried to instil the discipline and ambition that Bing lacked. He also interested him in the business and legal side of his calling—a must in view of the union blackballing.

Dixie went to work on this pressing problem as well and came up trumps with a lawyer named John O'Melveny, a respected legal eagle for the film business whom she had met at Fox. He was a member of one of America's top law firms and he got Bing out of his trouble, but even years later would never tell how. That initial success really impressed Crosby. O'Melveny remained his lawyer for forty-five years . . .

Says Bing: 'Any trouble I got into over a contract or law suit, like guys who said I sang a song they wrote and somebody stole, why he'd sort them out.

'Generally, these lawyers were "ambulance chasers" or shysters and when you told them—"well see my lawyer John O'Melveny", that chilled their ardour a little and they thought twice before pursuing the suit any farther. In that way I avoided a lot of legal entanglements.'

While the ban was being sorted out, Everett Crosby went knocking on the door of Mack Sennett, legendary movie maker who gave Charlie Chaplin his first chance and also gave the world the illustrious Keystone cops.

Everett, who turned out to be a real go-getter, came away with a contract for Bing to appear in a series of short films—each to be based on songs with which he was associated or had recorded; each to run about twenty minutes at seven hundred and fifty dollars a time . . .

They were all shot in 1931 and there were six of them: *I Surrender Dear, Just One More Chance, Billboard Girl, Dream House, Sing Bing Sing* and *Where the Blue of the Night*—and each was produced in typical Sennett custard-pie tradition.

Bing certainly found Max Sennett's way of working unusual: 'Yeah, he had a method. He had some writers, but they put very little on paper. They'd have meetings before they started a picture to talk about what they were going to do and a secretary would take down notes. From those they developed a sort of a skeleton script—no dialogue, just locations.

'You had to fake your own dialogue, but the films always wound up in a chase. In every short a conflict would develop and the heavy would be chasing the hero. They'd have these wild chases through the Hollywood Hills, with cars going willy-nilly through the traffic, and then at the end the lovers would meet!'

Sennett retained much of the slapstick from the old Keystone Cops days. Bing was dunked in water tanks and fish would slide down his shirt. And once he was called upon to be drowned in quick-rising dough . . .

The crooner says he also made two shorts for the Christy Brothers and another for comedy king Hal Roach.

Bing describes Everett as a hustler and good mixer, who could 'holler and shout' and pound the table and stamp up and down.

To good effect . . . When the musicians' ban was finally lifted, he made national radio his next objective. All the country should hear brother Bing, he felt. So into the mail to CBS and NBC, the major networks based in the East, went recordings of Bing with the Arnheim orchestra.

William Paley, president of CBS, lent his experienced ear to the crooning tones of Crosby and was first on the ball. 'Can you get the boy to New York for an audition?' he cabled Everett—for Paley was in the middle of the Atlantic Ocean on a cruise liner bound for Europe and had only got around to playing Bing's 'I Surrender Dear' after a number of days at sea. Paley didn't have to repeat the invitation. Bing was quickly signed for his first national radio show in his own right at six hundred dollars a week. It was still 1931, still the days of Depression.

But the first broadcast from New York was a disaster and Bing shudders at its memory: 'I lost my voice completely. I rehearsed a long, long time. I had a bit of a cold and tried to sing over the cold. But it got worse and finally when it came to go on I couldn't produce a sound.'

The crisis came earlier during the afternoon, at a three-hour rehearsal. Bing found that his voice was getting shriller and shriller. Bandleader Freddie Rich called a halt. 'Maybe I just have a loose tonsil,' suggested Bing, 'let's try it again.'

But after a few songs, Bing's voice was no more than a hoarse croak and Everett came rushing from the studio control room yelling, 'Get him to a throat specialist fast.'

'There were a lot of stories about nervousness,' Bing says, 'but it was just over-use. Although, truthfully, I was night-clubbing pretty heavily, with late nights and not enough rest, so the pipes blew.'

For Bing's family, waiting by their radio set in Spokane, it was a trying time. Until Everett was able to cable them, they had no idea what had happened. The announcer simply said that the scheduled programme was cancelled 'due to circumstances beyond our control'.

The news was an even greater blow to Everett. He'd already invited more than twenty top New York journalists to witness his brother's début and it was too late to stop them turning up. When the newsmen arrived, Everett plied them with drinks, told them of Bing's loss of voice and handed each a personally-autographed Crosby recording of 'Stardust'—the great Hoagy Carmichael song soon to hit the record shops.

Three nights later, with knees visibly shaking and sweat on his forehead, Bing stood before the CBS microphone with one hand resting hopefully on guitarist Eddie Lang's shoulder. As the studio warning lights suddenly blazed out the red 'on air' sign, Bing nervously cleared his throat and began to croon.

Just before midnight, the ordeal over, Bing was relaxing in his hotel bedroom with a bottle of scotch when Everett burst in excitedly waving a huge bunch of telegrams clasped in his podgy hand. 'Look at 'em!' he shouted. 'Boy, you're a hit'.

Bing quietly took the bundle and carefully thumbed through them until he found what he was looking for—a cable from Spokane: *You were fine*, it read. *Glad you are better. Don't catch cold again. Mother.*

Overnight, a radio star was born . . .

While the dramas of new-found fame were unfolding in New York, Mrs Dixie Lee Crosby stayed in Hollywood. The wife of Bing Crosby was not allowed to live the traditional married life. She was still a rising starlet under contract to Fox and their private lives and business lives were lived separately. Although she would, in fact, play only two minor roles in films after their marriage—in *Love in Bloom* and *Redheads on Parade*.

But there was no stopping Crosby now—nor Everett. Ambition, not as Bing has since claimed 'luck', took the Crosbys in hand. As Bing admitted, when he agreed to help CBS with publicity, 'I'd do anything to further my career—even stand on my head on top of the Empire State Building.'

The broadcasts grew in stature and Everett set out to search for a sponsor, and found one in Cremo Cigars.

The money pleased Bing, but the sponsorship, he knew, would be bound to cause frowns at home in Spokane. His mother detested smoking and would undoubtedly have preferred him to have continued nationally as he had begun locally on radio a few weeks earlier—selling diamonds.

For it was at 7 p.m. on 2 September 1931 that he made his first solo radio broadcast on Station KHJ in Los Angeles on behalf of the Leroy Diamond Company. He opened with 'Just One More Chance' and the programme ran for fifteen minutes.

But now, disapproving mother or no, cigars it was to be.

Then Everett pulled off the real big one . . . stardom at the Paramount Theatre, where with Al Rinker, Bing had flopped so miserably in the Whiteman days; where the management had actually stipulated that he must not sing and had gagged a voice that was to be worth millions. Now they were going to have to really buy him back.

The contract, which began in November 1931, was for ten weeks and Bing was a sort of MC who would sing a song or two and maybe do a comedy sketch with one of the acts. His salary was two thousand five hundred dollars a week. A fact which, according to Bob Crosby, greatly surprised Bing: 'Brother Everett told me that when the first pay cheque came in Bing's eyes bugged out at the size of it and he turned to Everett and said "for goodness sake book as many of these as you can, because it can't possibly last beyond sixteen weeks." '

It did. In fact, Bing broke all house records at the Paramount and stayed for a record twenty-nine weeks. His act was lengthened and, after the initial ten-week run, his salary increased to four thousand dollars a week. Two months later it was estimated that with the Paramount show, his radio contract and record sales, he was averaging some seven thousand dollars a week . . .

Which led *Variety*, the show business bible, to comment—and to accurately prophesy—as early as 1932: 'Certified Cremo Cigar Company must have stepped high to corral Bing Crosby, the rage of the radio hour, for their WABC broadcast. But, judging by his work, he's worth it.

'This must be a tough week for him, however, for he is doing four shows a day at the Paramount Theatre which, on top of his radio work in the evening, puts a heavy strain on his voice. Monday night, when caught, he showed no effects of hard usage, however, his tones being clear and vibrant as ever.

'On the air Monday night he used "Now That You're Gone", "Then She's Mine" and "Goodnight Sweetheart". All these he threw off in the manner that has brought him forward so fast in the favour of the public. It is highly individual, belongs to him alone and he need stand no fear of competition, because, while he may have imitators, there will be only one Bing Crosby.'

The same magazine, in its 'New Acts' column, reviewed his Paramount show thus: 'Crosby isn't a novice on the stage, another advantage for him over the average radio name crashing the theatre. He saw an audience before he saw the inside of a radio studio, so he must know audiences. When with Whiteman's Rhythm Boys, he struck a battered cymbal for emphasis with a drumstick and made a noise like a goose . . .'

Bing was just what Paramount needed. Audiences had been falling off and a crisis could not be far off. But it was not enough simply to have Bing on stage casually crooning the songs of the day. He had to be integrated into the show, which always had a theme. Sometimes this would be circus, or perhaps naval, and it was the task of Paramount manager Bot Weitman—yes, the man who had once told Whiteman to get Bing and Rinker off!—to make Crosby part and parcel of all the action.

Said Weitman: 'We would change his suit; change his costume; have him enter from the right, from the left, or have him come up from the audience on to the stage; or even have him on a horse. And it didn't matter, he was as fluent and as adroit and as happy as anybody that I have ever met in my life.'

Weitman was full of ideas, but—as Bing tells it—they didn't always work: 'Oh God! He had me on a crane one time singing a song. It was over the audience and the crane would move around, with drunken sailors tugging at my pants' legs from the audience.

'It got stuck often. That thing never did work. I'd finish a song and was supposed to be whipped-off stage. But there I would be with egg on my face! The audience got a big kick out of it.'

What Weitman had done was to sling a kind of bosun's chair from the front part of the crane. In this Bing sat dressed completely in black. Everything else was black, as well; the crane, stage-hands, drapes. Even the exit lights were blacked-out.

'Bing was given a small torch which he held just under his chin,' said Weitman. 'They'd wheel him out so that, when he got across the orchestra pit, he was four rows into the audience at the completion of his opening number. As he sang other songs, he'd change the flashlight to different colours. If it was a ballad he used a nice rose colour and if it was a bright number he'd use white.

'After his last number, they were supposed to pull him back, curtseying to the left and right by dipping him over the audience. But the crane stuck.'

So there was the audience tugging at his trousers. There was only one thing to do. Sing! The grabbing hands would cease to grab and normality returned. But Bing was trapped up there for thirty-five minutes before the crane would work again. 'It was one of the damndest things that ever happened in that theatre,' said Weitman.

The so-called Battle of the Baritones was another of Weitman's gimmicks to pull the crowds in. He put the handsome Russ Columbo with his Valentino looks into the Brooklyn Paramount a few miles from the Manhattan one. Russ, a former colleague of Bing's in the Gus Arnheim days at the Cocoanut Grove, was now making something of a name as a crooner. And an artificial rivalry was being whipped up purely for publicity. Bing and Columbo were really the best of friends —although the public were not led to think so.

Crosby, paying tribute to him, says: 'He was a very good

violinist, a marvellous singer and a handsome guy. His lady friend was Carole Lombard, a really big star and very beautiful. Russ and I sang some things together when we were at the Grove.'

The Battle of the Baritones warmed up (Bob Crosby swears that Columbo was a tenor!) and forces were joined by Rudy Vallee. 'In fact,' says Bing, 'there was a song out—"Crosby, Columbo and Vallee". It was quite popular and said something about the battle.'

Veteran comic George Burns, of the celebrated Burns and Allen vaudeville twosome, was around at the time.

'I played the Paramount, New York, with Crosby and then the following week I played the Paramount, Brooklyn, with Russ Columbo,' he said with tongue-in-cheek humour, 'They both sang exactly alike and I couldn't understand it. Two guys, singing alike, and they're both stars! I sang entirely different and couldn't get any place!'

George couldn't resist a gag either about the way the Paramount 'presented' Crosby: 'I don't know whether he was afraid to walk out to the centre of the stage, but they used to push him out on a little cart with flowers around it. There was a microphone there into which he'd sing and and the cart would roll about the centre of the stage. But he never walked . . .'

Tragedy was to prevent Columbo from ever proving if he was really a serious rival to Bing. He died in a shooting accident, ironically in a Beverly Hills house that was later bought by one of Crosby's most successful singing partners—Rosemary Clooney.

Next-door neighbour Ira Gershwin—brother of the brilliant George—told Miss Clooney about it years later. Until then she was unaware that Columbo had died in the 'den' of her home on 2 September 1934.

'Evidently,' said Miss Clooney, 'there was an old Civil War revolver which was rusted and used for a paper weight. No one thought there was a charge inside, but apparently a charge went off and a ball ricochetted off three places in the room and killed Russ immediately. It was such an extraordinary story that it was under investigation for a long, long time. Now my children, when they are a little afraid and it's all dark downstairs, say "Hello, Russ, are you around?" It's kind of funny . . .'

Some people thought that life for Crosby might have been

more difficult had Columbo lived. Rudy Vallee, third of the triumvirate, was among them. 'Bing was hitting the bottle quite heavily,' he said, 'and it's possible he would have lost much of his popularity and might never have achieved the success that he did.'

Ace lyricist Johnny Mercer firmly disagreed: 'Colombo would have done very well, but I don't think he had what Bing had. He didn't have Bing's original talent. He copied Bing. He didn't have Bing's line of talk and he didn't have Bing's personality. He was a different kind of man.'

Bing himself has always been phlegmatic about the controversy: 'I don't think there was any competition. There was room for everybody really. There were so few of us . . .'

During those heady days in New York, the fancy-free Bing was doing his best to cram two days into one. While Dixie kept the home fires warm in Hollywood he was notching up a formidable total of sixteen hours singing out of twenty-four—yet still finding time for a spot of golf, a whirl at the roulette table or a visit to the races, nightclubbing and tots of tequila. Something had to give. And did. His voice gave out and it was one of the biggest shocks of his life.

'During the week,' he says, 'I was singing five times a day. On Saturdays and Sundays we'd do six shows a day. They were long shows—about an hour and forty to fifty minutes—and then I was staying up every night.

'We'd finish at 11.30 and then go right to Harlem and to Club Olsen (run by dance and Broadway bandleader George Olsen), or the Chateau Madrid and then the Richmond Club, or some place, to hear the latest singer and the latest comedian. We'd get to bed at two or three o'clock in the morning and then up again at seven or eight for recording dates.'

So it was exit voice . . . 'I couldn't produce a sound, so I went to see a throat specialist, Dr Simon L. Ruskin. He sent me to a guy named Chevalier Jackson, who was a real specialist in this kind of thing. He said that the chords, through constant and over-use, had developed little warts and callouses.

'He said, "I can operate on them—take them off—but it might change the timbre of your voice. You might become a boy soprano!" I didn't relish that. So, he said, "if you rest and don't even answer the phone—don't talk, don't do anything— they'll recede".'

A very worried Bing took this advice and the warts, or nodes, to be more precise, disappeared. When his 'new' voice returned, it was a tone or two lower than before. And there are many who said it was even better and warmer.

And it was ready for its first full-length Hollywood movie. . . .

Chapter Seven

The only other fellow to make the Hollywood big time with jug ears was Clark Gable, and even he was turned down because of them by Warner Brothers. When, in 1931, he started to hit instead with rival M-G-M this sign went up in the Warner studios: *'Do not forget to make up men's ears!—Jack Warner'*. Sound advice that no doubt echoed through the rest of town.

Thus a certain amount of attention was paid to the jutting Crosby appendages when he returned West from New York to be featured in *The Big Broadcast of 1932*—to be reunited with Dixie and a belated first wedding anniversary.

He had been beset with this particular form of ear trouble before, during those early days in Los Angeles with Al Rinker, when perseverance and near poverty won him a test and interview at the Fox studios. Bing sang a few songs and read a few lines for a casting director.

'Pretty good,' said the casting director, 'but I don't think there'll be a chance for you in films—the ears are too wingy . . .'

Crosby thought he had said 'the years are winging' and protested that he was still only 'twenty whatever-it-was'.

'No,' the casting director persisted, 'your ears stick out too far and we'll never be able to photograph you—be tough to do . . .'

It was an unrewarding introduction to the Dream Factory. Ears, of course, would not really concern the slapstick purveyor Mack Sennett. The more wingy, possibly, the better for comedy.

They didn't matter either when the three Rhythm Boys made a brief appearance in an RKO-Pathe short filmed during July and August 1929 and released a year later. It was a campus comedy with the trio as college boys and it was the first time Bing had been seen on the screen. He was paid twenty-five dollars for it.

He made another RKO short—said to have been called *Ripstitch the Tailor*—which was considered unsatisfactory and was scrapped and so never shown in public.

His appearance in—for him—the disastrous *King of Jazz* was short as well and the producers had bigger troubles than Bing's ears.

That same year, 1930, Crosby was heard in a film entitled *Check and Double Check*—but not seen. The great jazzman Duke Ellington was master-minding the music and he revealed the full story shortly before his death in 1974: 'Two guys had written a song called "Three Little Words" and the director had got a little chick in at the last minute to sing it, but the first thing that came into our minds was to go and get Bing and the Rhythm Boys from the Cocoanut Grove.'

This the Duke did, but when the film was shown Ellington's trumpeters were filmed as if they were singing the song instead.

There was one more fleeting appearance to come that busy year—in *Reaching for the Moon*, starring Douglas Fairbanks Senior and the late Bebe Daniels, wife of Ben Lyon. The scene set aboard ship, had the Gus Arnheim Orchestra in residence, with Bing as vocalist. He sang a song from the Irving Berlin score called 'When the Folks High Up Do the Mean Low Down', and Bebe afterwards joined him in a duet. He also spoke his first screen line: 'Hello gang!'

When the film came out, there was no screen credit for Crosby. But when it was revived in 1946 at the height of his fame the billing said *Featuring Bing Crosby* and made no mention of Fairbanks or Bebe Daniels.

There was one more short filmic glimpse to come before *Big Broadcast*. The Rhythm Boys were cast as entertainers at a high school dance in a Paramount production called *Confessions of a Co-ed*—a nostalgic scene for Bing and Rinker, who had started out on the long haul to fame doing just that . . .

Now worrying glances were being cast at Bing's ears at Paramount. He had been cast in a leading role as a radio crooner in *Big Broadcast* and the public were going to see him a lot more closely.

Starring with him were other stalwarts of the airwaves such as Kate Smith, Burns and Allen, The Mills Brothers, the Boswell Sisters and Arthur Tracy, who traded as The Street Singer. And it was decreed that the Crosby lugs should be stuck back.

Says Bing: 'They did it for a couple of movies, with glue and adhesive tape; it felt terrible! If you got in the hot lights for five or ten minutes, the glue would weaken and the ears would pop out. Then everybody would have to go and sit down while they pinned my ears back. Jack Oakie said I looked like a whippet in full flight.'

By this time, Bing was now regularly wearing a thatch, as the business fondly calls a toupee—but the millions who would see him on the screen would wait years before they shared the secret. There was nothing, however, that Hollywood could or wished to do to enhance the dulcet Crosby tones. The voice was and always would be pure gold . . .

Bing took his film-making very seriously, which rather surprised George Burns, who found him a little cold. 'Nobody could get very close to Crosby,' he said. 'You'd do your scene and then run to the dressing-room where, as we were all radio acts, everybody had writers stashed away. I had my writers and Crosby had his.'

Arthur Tracy disclosed another reason for this apparent lack of communication between artists: 'Most people think that, because you are appearing in the same film, everybody knows each other well, but it wasn't always the case.'

Astonishingly, Bing and Tracy, who were seen together singing 'Here Lies Love' in the film, worked three thousand miles apart . . .

'I was tied up with theatre work in New York,' said Tracy, 'so I shot my portion out on Long Island at the Paramount studio and then the things were pieced together in California.'

Bing had trouble trying to stick to his new serious image during the making of *Big Broadcast*—an image which didn't last long incidently—because all his old drinking and gambling pals kept turning up on the set. Elder brother Larry, who was making his first trip to Hollywood, was given the task of dealing with them: 'I tried to keep some of his pals off his back, because he was taking it seriously at that time. In fact, Bing gave me a thousand dollars—which was more money than I'd ever seen in my whole life—and told me to take the gang away and keep them away as long as possible, so he could get on with the picture.'

Because, possibly, he was taking things too seriously, Bing accidently mixed up the lyric of his hit number, 'Where The Blue Of The Night'. He sang '. . . . and the blue of her eyes crowns the gold of her hair . . .', instead of '. . . . and the gold of her hair crowns the blue of her eyes . . .' It was one of many Crosby indiscretions that have remained for all to see or hear—and one of the strangest.

It was then the only song to credit Bing as the lyric writer and it had by then become nationally known as his signature tune.

He had to find a regular opening number for his national début over CBS. 'I Surrender Dear' had been his biggest hit up to then and was an obvious front-runner. He also considered 'Love Came Into My Heart', but something told him that a newly-written piece provisionally titled 'When the Gold of the Day Meets the Blue of the Night' was the one.

'It was written for me,' he says, 'for the first sustaining programme by Roy Turk and Fred E. Ahlert. They wrote the music and I set the words to the verse.'

By the time Bing had finished with the lyrics the title had been switched to 'Where the Blue of the Night Meets the Gold of the Day'. With the studio orchestra of Victor Young behind it, it was to become the best-known theme song in the world.

But Paramount were extremely pleased with their new boy—muffed lines or not. Before *Big Broadcast* was half through, Crosby was signed to a long-term contract—to make five films over a period of three years with a fee of three hundred thousand dollars. It was a flying start to an association that was to last for twenty-three years of unbroken success.

The man responsible for signing Crosby was studio boss Adolph Zukor, one of the fathers of Hollywood and motion pictures. Shortly after his hundredth birthday, in 1973, Zukor—still remarkably razor sharp—explained how he got Bing: 'I talked to him first in New York and told him he could be doing very well in Motion pictures. "Well," he says, "I can't, because I'm not an actor, I'm a singer." I told him. "Whatever you do, you do well and the fact you do it the Crosby way is different from what everybody else is doing, and that's what I want." He asked me if I believed that he could make good and I said, "I wouldn't suggest for you to do it unless I felt that you are going to be a star." '

How right Zukor was. Over the years, Bing would make fifty-eight pictures for Paramount—including some of the biggest box-office successes of all time. Adolph Zukor says he did well in every single one of them: 'Very well—because he acts natural. He doesn't have to act; he can just be himself and that's enough. That's what he was and that's why he was different to anybody else, and yet he reached stardom and popularity not only in this country but all over the world.

'He is a very odd individual, is Bing, when you talk to him, he'd rather you tell him what his faults are than praise him. He doesn't like to listen to praise. He likes to listen to criticism.'

Bing's devotion to this new calling, however, was not all-absorbing. He still felt the call of the road and after *Big Broadcast* was safely wrapped up he decided to tour and to take with him guitarist Eddie Lang, a former Whiteman buddy, and one of the all-time greats of jazz, and pianist-conductor Lennie Hayton.

Eddie had been with Crosby on his radio shows and recording sessions, and he had accompanied him in the film as well. He was much admired by the crooner.

'He had a tremendous ear,' says Bing, 'and had a stroke on the guitar that nobody had employed up until that time. It was a marvellous accompaniment to sing a rhythm song to. It just made you feel like you wanted to ride and go.

'If he heard a thing once, he could play it—he never read music very well. His style was unique and other guitar players really looked up to him. They couldn't understand how he did it, without being more of a technician.'

Eddie had also earned himself another big reputation—at pool. And, according to Bing, it was pool that played a large part in Eddie's decision to tour: 'He was making, in New York on radio and recording dates, probably five or six hundred dollars a week and I couldn't afford to pay him much more than that.

'When I broached the prospect, he was very keen about it and I discovered why a little later. We opened in Cleveland and after the first matinee he disappeared. He didn't come back till show time, about six in the evening, played the show, then disappeared again.

'I found he was going over to the local pool hall—in those days they used to have big gambling in pool—and playing some of the local guys who figured they were pretty good. He'd allow himself to get licked a little—lose small sums of money, ten, fifteen dollars—and then during the last three days he'd pull out his "A" game and pick up four or five hundred dollars.'

Thus Bing discovered that Eddie, the quiet unassuming guitar genius from Philadelphia, was a hustler: 'He was delighted to come out on the road, because everybody knew him around the pool halls in New York and he couldn't make any money there. He always dressed very nice and looked like a librarian or something—the last guy in the world you'd think would play brilliant pool.'

It was during this tour that Bing met up again with Al Capone's right-hand-hoodlum Machine-gun Jack McGurn.

Bing had been booked into the Oriental Theatre in bullet-happy Chicago and after his first rehearsal was told there was a case of champagne waiting for him at the stage door. He didn't drink champagne and told the manager to send it back.

'The fellow who sent it wouldn't like that,' warned the manager. 'He's Jack McGurn . . .'

Bing had to agree. 'I'd better keep it then,' he said.

The next day McGurn sent a note to the theatre saying he would like to play golf with Crosby, an invitation that caused Bing considerable concern.

'I thought about it for a long time,' he recalls, 'because I didn't want to get involved. But in those days you couldn't get into a country club as an actor unless you knew somebody and as he was big in Chicago I thought he'd probably have access to a pretty good golf course.'

So Bing phoned McGurn and they arranged to play. 'He arrived,' says Bing, 'in a big limousine with two or three guys in black hats and black overcoats. He looked like a university football player and was a good-looking man. We went for miles in this limousine—I guess he had to get to a safe place. We played golf and he got me back in time for the first matinee show.'

But Bing realised he was getting in deep, for McGurn was

facing seven charges of first-degree murder for his alleged part in the St Valentine's Day Massacre—when seven members of the rival Bugs Moran gang were machine-gunned to death in a Chicago garage.

Although Bing tried to ignore constant phone calls from McGurn, he eventually had to speak to him: 'He wanted me to go to dinner with him,' says Bing, 'and I went once. He had a girlfriend with him—a blonde—who swore that he was in Miami at the time of the massacre. She became known as "the blonde alibi" and I had dinner just this one night. I thought I'd get caught in the crossfire and didn't call McGurn any more. I got worried about it,' Bing admits.

McGurn, who Bing thought 'a very nice guy,' was credited with more than twenty-five murders during his time with Capone and eventually died in a hail of machine-gun bullets in a Milwalkee bowling alley in February 1936.

Bing remembers him not as a murdering gangster but as a golfer: 'In fact he could play very good golf. He filed an entry in the United States Open Championship and played under an assumed name. He managed about eight holes before they found out who he was and asked him to withdraw.'

On that 1932 tour, Crosby was to meet another fellow who was to play a vital role in his life and career—a young comic named Bop Hope. They were on the same bill together at the Capitol Theatre in New York. 'He used to do an act with a girl —a very bad act!' Bing says with a smile. 'He was a good billiards player as well and was always looking for clients. I think he could have become a pool hustler if he hadn't gone into show business . . .'

The pair didn't actually work together then—it was to be another seven years before the classic partnership would be formally born. In the meantime, they found a common interest across the road from the Capitol—O'Reilly's Bar, one of the first to enjoy the liquid legality that had come with the ending of Prohibition a few days earlier.

It was there, between shows, that Hope and Crosby displayed their natural but competitive good humour. Many of the patrons thought they were indulging in plain old bar talk, but as Bob was to reveal more than forty years later, they knew it was the start of something big: 'The chemistry was so good and it was a great piece of electricity, because things were happening all the time—new, fresh things and that's always great for anything.'

New York, unfortunately, was one of the last dates Eddie Lang was to play with Bing. He died at his peak in 1934 following routine surgery for the removal of his tonsils. Eddie simply bled to death . . . It was a great blow for Bing, both personally and musically. He had come to rely on the brilliant guitarist as principal music consultant and friend.

Life, meantime, hurtled on for the busy Bing at a relentless pace. There were records to cut, radio shows to air and those films to make. 'A normal home life was an impossibility', says Bing.

The first movie under his three-year contract was called *College Humour*, co-starred Jack Oakie, Richard Arlen and Mary Carlisle and began shooting in 1933—a typical, razzamataz campus epic with the chaps in long racoon coats and trilbys with tipped-up brims. The first day's shooting called for Bing only to nod his head a few times which earned him the immediate nickname of Old Hinge-neck. He was also still being ribbed about his jutting ears, which prompted him to observe one day: 'I don't know—there's a fellow by the name of Gable doing pretty well and we haven't got a high enough wind for me to take-off!'

But Crosby was taking his film career seriously. 'He worked very hard at it,' said Richard Arlen. 'He wanted to be good and he was. He looked like a million dollars.

'You'd do one rehearsal and we'd shoot it. He was very quick on dialogue.

'I never knew him to blow a line, or forget and if he started a song he went right through it—whether it was good, bad, or indifferent. He'd wait until the director yelled "cut" and if the director said "do you want to try another one, Bing?", he'd say. "Yes, I think I could do better." '

Mary Carlisle was making her first appearance as a leading lady in the picture. She was very young and inexperienced, and Bing befriended her after the director—the talented Wesley Ruggles—reduced her to tears during one of the early scenes. 'I was supposed to cry,' recalls Mary, 'and I didn't know how to cry. I had nothing that made me unhappy so I just stopped in the middle of the scene. In those days there were no play-back tapes, you did it "live" with the beautiful orchestra—and the director just looked at me and said, "Why did you stop?"

'I said, "Well I wasn't crying," and he said, "Just who do you think you are? I'm the director and I'll tell you when to stop." Well, of course, I started to cry my heart out and he shot the scene. I was still crying afterwards and Bing put his arms around me.'

From that point on, Bing and Mary became firm friends and, to while away the waiting hours on the set, she introduced him to backgammon.

'She was pretty good too,' remarks Bing. 'She came from the East, where they played a lot of backgammon. I thought I knew some pretty good games, but I'd never played backgammon. She took a lot of money off me too; she used to really clip me!'

Bing, always a competitive gamesman, got really hooked on the game—but couldn't beat Miss Carlisle. 'When we finished the picture, he owed me three hundred dollars,' she said.

Each time he lost, Crosby refused to pay up and demanded the right of a re-match. 'When you get hooked on a game,' he explains, 'whether its backgammon, poker, or golf, and you lose a substantial amount, the only way you can get out is by double-or-quits. So, she'd get me in pretty deep and I'd suggest this. She'd say no, but I'd finally convince her that she ought to give me a chance and she'd win again. That's how I lost so much money to her.'

Mary had to wait four years before she got the chance to see the colour of Bing's money, when they were teamed once more for a film called—ironically enough—*Double or Nothing*. Even then, as she laughingly recalls, Crosby wasn't going to pay up without a fight: 'I kidded him, saying "I think the only reason you are having me in this picture, is that you don't want to pay me the three hundred dollars." So, we kept playing all through the picture and just before we finished it we had a very big game—it was twelve hundred dollars he owed me—and he doubled it up and won. We didn't play again and I told him it would probably be the last picture I'd ever make with him—and it was.'

Towards the end of filming *College Humour*, Bing's new-found seriousness slipped a little, and with Richard Arlen as a willing companion, took to the town for a spot of merry-making. Their antics didn't go entirely unnoticed.

'We were doing a big production number and we must have waited two hours for Mr Crosby to arrive,' says Mary Carlisle. 'I was just leaving the set when he drove up, his eyes all bloodshot. We looked at each other and smiled and he said, "I'm not going to make it today." He was so nice about it, and so apologetic. Nobody could get mad at him, because he did it so beautifully.'

There was an excuse for some of the Arlen–Crosby outings. Both were expectant fathers at around the same time. And when the stork delivered there were babies' heads to wet.

Gary Evans Crosby, first of Bing and Dixie Lee's four sons, arrived lustily into this world on 25 June 1933. He had blue eyes like Pop and was baptised Gary after Crosby's great friend and fellow-actor Gary Cooper.

Said Bing to Arlen, not without some pride, of the safe delivery of their two bonny children: 'Not bad for a couple of old birds who are seldom on the nest . . .'

Life, in fact, was being lived at a fevered pace. But Bing now knew where he was going—in three directions at once. Records, radio and films. *The Big Broadcast* was now proving itself a success and it was to be the final shot in the celebrated if fabricated Battle of the Baritones.

According to Rudy Vallee it had been something of a toss-up whether he or Bing got the crooning part in the film: 'I was working at the Brooklyn Paramount, Bing in the New York one, when they took a vote of all Paramount employees as to whether Bing or I should do *The Big Broadcast*. He won by two votes . . .'

But a little earlier Vallee had already seen the writing on the wall—after hearing Bing singing 'Beside a Shady Nook'. Vallee sang the same song on his radio show and told eighteen million of his listeners: 'This man Bing Crosby, who has recorded this number for Gus Arnheim, is going to push me right off my throne.'

Said Vallee years later: 'I knew it was only a question of time before he would completely eclipse me and eclipse me he did.'

Thus in 1933 the pattern was evolving. Crosby had truly arrived on all three fronts and was much in demand on each of them. Watching his startling progress with a very professional eye was Miss Marion Davies, long-time girlfriend and mistress of newspaper magnate William Randolph Hearst. She was one of Hollywood's biggest—but already fading—musical stars. Yet not so faded in Mr Hearst's book. He lavished untold dollars on her and was now backing a film to be called *Going Hollywood* in which she would star. And for which she wanted the lively, going-places Bing.

There was one snag. Hearst didn't much care for the way Crosby sang and impresario-songwriter Arthur Freed, who had written six of the film's seven songs, had to be called in to mediate.

He managed to talk Hearst round, promising him that Bing and Marion would make the typical American boy and girl—a stage of life the pair had already left far behind. But Hearst liked the idea and Paramount loaned Bing to rivals M-G-M, who were scheduled to make the movie.

It was an all-revealing exercise for the crooner, who was to find what 'Going Hollywood' meant in real life.

'Marion Davies,' he discovered, 'lived in great style on the M-G-M lot. She had a vast bungalow with six or eight rooms—kitchen, dining-room, music-room—and we'd have long Continental lunches. She'd come in at nine-thirty to work, maybe get one take done by noon and then we'd break for lunch until three-thirty or four o'clock. Those long lunches would be laced with Rhine wines, maybe a brandy or two, and a few highballs before lunch, and everybody would go back half-boxed—including the leading lady.

'She always had an orchestra on the set, a six-piece outfit playing hits of the day. And, of course, you couldn't get a great deal of work done because the orchestra would start playing something we knew and everyone would have to sing and dance to it.'

Mr Hearst, of course, was footing the bill. Not that he appeared to worry about it very much. 'He never bothered anybody,' says Bing. 'He'd come on the set and he'd be amused by what was going on and laugh and talk with everybody.'

He would also invite the cast for long weekends, usually from Thursday night to Sunday, at his sprawling, treasure-filled home at San Simeon, looking out over the Pacific between Los Angeles and San Francisco. A bewitching, wondrous ranch covering more than 240,000 acres, with its centrepiece the magnificent Casa Grande dominating a complex of Moorish palaces set in ornamental gardens amid palms and cypress trees.

The Casa Grande, a great twin-towered Spanish mission cathedral, stands atop the Enchanted Hill. In its dining hall a hundred and fifty guests could sit down to eat at sixteenth-century refectory tables. It was stocked with priceless tapestries and works of art; ancient English silver. Only the Vatican, possibly could compete with its many collections from round the world. In a guesthouse, one could sleep in Cardinal Richlieu's bed. There were palatial pools to swim in and Arabian horses to ride; animals from around the globe gathered in a splendid zoo. Bing says: 'I think Mr Hearst liked me a little because I always evinced a genuine interest in his massive collection of furniture and objets d'art. Few others did.'

Little wonder that brother Everett Crosby was able to drive a hard bargain for the services of Bing in *Going Hollywood*. His fee was a surprising—for those days—two thousand dollars a week. As the movie took almost five months to complete between parties on the set and safaris to San Simeon, Bing was almost forty thousand dollars richer in the end.

Nevertheless, *Going Hollywood* was a success at the box office and put him among the top ten film draws (he was seventh) for the first time. And Mr Hearst was able to laugh a little more on his way to the bank.

Crosby himself was grateful not only for the money and the growing acclaim, but for the fact that the film gave him for the first time a chance to attempt a dramatic song: the now ever-green 'Temptation'.

It also reunited him with an old school pal from Gonzaga, Leo Lynn. Leo had worked as a stand-in for the British star Clive Brook but was then without a job. It was Leo's lucky night when he bumped into Bing at the prizefights after the day's shooting had ended. The studio were looking for a stand-in for Crosby. Bing hired him; the studio also hired him and he drew two salaries.

He still draws one. He has stayed with Bing during his entire career and can be found today in the small Crosby office in Beverly Hills.

With so much going for him in those frantic early 'thirties how could there be any time left for the crooner's favourite sport? He found a way. On his journey to Paramount in the morning he would stop off at the Lakeside Club at 5.30 a.m. and play nine holes. When the day's filming was through he'd stop off and play another nine before going home to join Dixie.

At Lakeside the caddies had a tag for anyone who swung a club. Western star Randolph Scott was, for instance, 'The Cowhand'. Bing became 'The Groaner', even in those early times.

It was an affectionate nickname and he would eventually become The Old Groaner. It was Tommy Dorsey who added the age reference after discovering that his friend wasn't as young as his publicity hand-outs claimed. Not that Bing would ever mind; not with the way life was to turn out . . .

Chapter Eight

One of the most depressing decades in modern history could only be described as the Thriving 'Thirties for the developing family Crosby.

Its rapidly-growing empire now encompassed all the clan with the exception of brother Bob, but even his progress would be enchanced by elder brother's fame. Mother and father packed up home in Spokane and headed west to be installed in a sumptuous home in Hollywood. Dad would eventually become a familiar figure around the town as Bing's book-keeper. His pockets bulged with Press cuttings eulogising his celebrated son; and he would be dubbed Hollywood Harry by the locals.

Brothers Larry and Ted (only briefly in Ted's case) joined Everett in the fostering and handling of the varied Crosby enterprises. But their mother Kate would be the dominant influence in the fountainhead's life.

It was because of her strong aversion to cigarettes that Bing gave them up and took to the pipe that was to be something of a trademark well into the 'seventies. It also led to the break-up of a lucrative radio contract.

One of his early sponsors was Chesterfield Cigarettes. 'I had quite a crisis there,' Bing admits. 'They always wanted me to do some of the commercial advertising on the programme, which I was loathe to do. My mother was death on cigarettes. Even when her daughters were grandmothers themselves, she wouldn't let them smoke around her. They always had to go into the bathroom to smoke.

'Anyhow, Chesterfield had a commercial they wanted me to do for Mother's Day—something about "Don't forget to buy your mother a carton of Chesterfield's for Mother's Day" —and they really got adamant about that. I said I was not going to say it and that ended the contract.'

An added influence arrived in 1934. Just over a year after the arrival of baby Gary, Mrs Dixie Lee Crosby gave birth to twins on 13 July . . . Dennis Michael and Philip Lang. Dennis was named after his grandfather Harrigan and the Lang in Philip's name was a tribute to the late guitarist Eddie Lang.

Poor Dixie! As she endured the pangs of childbirth, there was more concern for the health of her husband.

Wrote one sobbing journalist at the time: 'Bing suffered so while the stork was being delayed for one reason and another that he nearly died . . .'

Another jubilantly reported: 'It's twins at the Crosbys and Bing is doing splendidly.'

But it was virtually the end of Dixie's professional life. She retired to devote herself to bringing up the family, although she did record two duets with Bing later—Jerome Kern's 'Fine Romance' and 'The Way You Look Tonight'. It was their only professional appearance together. She was not even teamed with him on radio, which launched him as a major public personality in those early 'thirties; a career that was to span some twenty-five years. For eighteen of them he would be the nation's Number One star of the airwaves with a weekly audience in excess of twenty millions.

But it was his records that were to enshrine him in the hearts of millions more in every nation across the world that had gramophones or record players. He was to sing through the years some four thousand different songs on disc and rack up astronomical sales of four hundred million. The figure is only an estimate. No one could ever put a finger on the exact number. It grows day by day and still they come. Even films were a fleeting thing in comparison. They still turn up on television, but like diamonds the record is for ever. And in the 'thirties he was producing them with almost assembly-line swiftness.

By 1934 Crosby was getting ten thousand fan letters a month

and there were eighty-five fan clubs spread throughout the world. It was a significant year in that Bing was to meet Jack Kapp, a recording genius who was to guide his disc destiny.

When the young Crosby first began his career on wax there were only two major record companies in the United States—Victor and Columbia. Most of Bing's early work was on the Victor label and probably he would have continued with the company but for Jack Kapp—who had a wild ambition to start his own outfit to challenge the two giants.

Records were almost in his blood. His father used to sell them from the back of a horse and cart, before he was successful enough to open a record store. Now, filled with confidence, Jack enlisted the aid of a rising young British recording pioneer named Ted Lewis (later to become Sir Edward). They got together and, with great enthusiasm, founded Decca Records. Their aim: to make and to sell records cheaper than anybody else, at a mere thirty-five cents each.

The brave new company's first signing was Bing Crosby. On 8 August 1934 he went into a studio and cut his—and the company's first record on the new label. The titles: 'I Love You Truly' and 'Just a Wearyin' for You'. The serial number: DE-100. Before long its successors would swell the coding to five figures . . .

Jack Kapp, now long dead, went on to mastermind the Crosby recording career. Says Bing of him: 'He was tremendously competent. I was impressed with what he'd done and had great faith in him. He developed a recording programme for me that involved every kind of music. I sang with every kind of band and every kind of vocal group—religious songs, patriotic songs and even light opera songs. I thought he was crazy, but I had confidence and went along with his suggestions!

'He gave me a very expanded repertoire which most other singers at that time hadn't bothered to get into. I just did exactly what he told me to do and it worked. It's a good thing I bumped into him: he was certainly influential in getting me going.'

Jack's brother Dave Kapp agrees completely with Bing about the relationship of the two men: 'They never argued at all. He'd say he didn't want to sing this or that kind of song, but usually did. His answer was always "Look, I'm the one who sings, you're the one who tells me what to sing." Many times we'd bring a demo record to Bing and he'd listen to it and say, "I don't know if I should sing this. It's pretty rotten, but if Jack wants it—I'll sing it." '

The increasing demands on Bing's time—he was now averaging three movies a year apart from the weekly radio show—made difficult the task of getting him into the recording studio, where a heavy schedule meant at least half a dozen Crosby projects on the books at any one given time.

There was only one solution. They would have to take the studio to him. Decca finally rented one as close as possible to the Paramount lot. It was there that the bulk of the early waxings were produced.

'Bing was always prompt,' said Perry Botkin, his guitarist who succeeded Eddie Lang. 'One thing about Crosby—if he told you he'd be there, he'd be there. But he didn't often tell you that. He would try to manœuvre you out of being there and find some excuse—but he'd never stand you up.'

Perry also noticed that Bing tended to make light work of those initial sessions: 'He took recording not too seriously when he was young. It was very easy for him, because he was the best in both style and quality at what he did.'

From this casual, almost knockabout but highly successful start, Jack Kapp would lead the Groaner to further pinnacles and eventually team him in golden partnership with other star names of the turntable. But meanwhile, Miss Carole Lombard awaited his attention on the Paramount set for the 1934 movie *We're Not Dressing*, a musical version of *The Admirable Chrichton* which also had a small part for a promising new actor from Britain named Ray Milland.

Bing's role called for a little more acting than usual and the dramatic highlight was a scene in which he had to slap the lovely Miss Lombard—but hard. Says Bing: 'She was always worrying about that scene and I couldn't figure out why. She kept saying, "Do you think you should slap me in this scene? It doesn't look good for a woman to get slapped; kind of makes a heavy out of you." She used all kinds of excuses.'

Aware of Lombard's concern, Bing talked to director Norman Taurog. But he was adamant that the scene stayed; arguing that he had to build up an animosity between his two stars and that what she had done to Bing in the previous scene definitely provoked a slap.

So Bing returned to the studio floor and on they went with the scene. 'But,' he recalls, 'when I slapped her she went wild and knocked me down! I didn't want to hit her back, but she kicked me in the belly, knocked off my toupée, wrecked my make-up and tore up my clothes.

'They finally pulled her off me and she was hysterical and was crying and all broke-up. Then she told us that, ever since she was a child, she couldn't stand anybody slapping her face; it just drove her mad. A phobia.'

Obviously, the director couldn't repeat the scene. So the slap which cinema audiences saw and the ensuing Lombard attack were very much for real.

Apart from that one incident, Bing and Carole—then dating the wing-eared Clark Gable—got along famously together. Bing's fondest memory of her happened during location shooting on Catalina Island.

All the cast was billeted in a small, sleepy residential hotel patronised mainly by elderly people, many of them dignified old ladies who eavesdropped all the time and hung on to the slightest Hollywood gossip.

Lombard, whose fondness for salty language was no secret throughout the movie colony, decided to shock them.

'She'd sweep into the dining room and utter some expletive,' Bing smiles. 'She really could be profane, but coming from her nobody seemed to mind. There was something about her delivery. When most women swear, it affronts you; when she swore, you just figured it as one of the fellows.

'So, when she came into the dining room at breakfast time, all the old ladies would have their ears cocked and their ear-trumpets tuned up waiting to see what she'd say. And she swept in this morning, and called all the way across the room, "Bing? Did I leave my lingerie in you room last night?" and that really broke it up.'

The last two films of Bing's original Paramount contract, *She Loves Me Not* and *Here Is My Heart*, produced the first of his really big hit film songs—'Love In Bloom' and 'June In January', both Leo Robin and Ralph Rainger compositions.

Kitty Carlisle was his co-star in these two vehicles, each of which had a happy-ever-after ending. Yet, looking back, Miss Carlisle didn't remember them as being particularly happy days.

'Bing,' she said, 'was extremely businesslike and did his work very seriously. I can't say he was unfriendly, he just wasn't terribly friendly; he was very nice and very correct. I do remember asking him one day, what song in the picture he thought would be a hit. And he said, "My dear, if I knew that, I wouldn't be putting on this toupée and this make-up every day—I'd be a millionaire!"'

Again, the cooler side of Bing . . .

If ever *She Loves Me Not* comes within your scope, watch out for his ears, apart from anything else. Some of the film was shot with them glued back; part with them sticking out. 'They kept coming unstuck under the heat of the lighting,' explains Bing. 'One day they popped out and I said, "To hell with it— that's the way they're going to stay." And so they never bothered with the glue again.'

There was one more personal triumph to come that neatly rounded off the saga of the ears. When Bing began to attend the Church of the Good Shepherd in Beverly Hills he discovered that a fellow-parishioner was the Fox casting director who had years earlier turned him down because of them.

Says Bing: 'He always sat down in the second or third row, so when I'd come back from Communion, I'd just look at him and tap my ears a couple of times and continue on back to my pew. He thought it was a great gag.'

For posterity: the casting director was one Jim Ryan.

Now, if Paramount wanted to hang on to their singing sensation, he was going to cost them more. Brother Everett, who was now relishing his task of guiding Bing's fortunes, went to work with John O'Melveny, the lawyer who solved the crooner's earlier union trouble.

Everett was aggressive and, according to brother Larry, a master of psychology. 'He was tough,' he said. 'He was tough on contracts to the point where, when the studio would come up with the first contract, he wouldn't even read the thing. He'd just scratch around it and say "now come on, it doesn't make sense". The studios naturally didn't like that, but I think it was a good idea. He didn't take the trouble to go through the fine print. He darned well knew there were a few bugs in there.'

The small print could be left to O'Melveny, who at first thought Bing 'was just another moving picture actor. Then I began to find out that this man was going to be a character—an international character—and very much liked.'

So Mr O'Melveny moved quickly and decisively.

'I went to Paramount,' he said, 'and got them to tear his contract up and give him a new one on a much bigger basis. I think I did that altogether five times and they were not unhappy about it. They were sold on the fact that he was becoming a very popular man in the amusement world. They began to see the light, as I had seen it. I was trying to get him all the money I could.'

O'Melveny had an added advantage in these negotiations: he was also one of the lawyers under contract to Paramount handling company business and therefore knew their methods and executives well.

Unlike many Californian law firms specialising in show-business work, O'Melveny's was never an aggressive outfit and Bing says he found that particularly pleasing: 'The O'Melveny office never believed in going to trial. They had a very good trial lawyer, but they always believed in negotiation and settlement and arriving at equitable terms for both parties. It was a wonderful connection; plus the fact that he was a personal friend. He was always in our home, I was always in his and we're still dear friends.'

Between filming, recording and trying to raise a family at this time Bing somehow managed to sandwich in his weekly radio show on behalf of Woodbury Soap—obviously a much cleaner way to earn a considerable crust than pushing the nicotine habit.

The Woodbury contract signed in 1934 was for thirty-nine weeks—but they fired him before the time was up! An amazing decision. For they got rid of him because they didn't like the way he talked . . . when millions were falling for the happy-go-lucky Crosby manner of speaking. In fact, an astonished Everett showed the Woodbury release document around among friends and it plainly stated that the sponsors didn't even think he could talk.

Crosby, however, would not remain in the radio wilderness for very long. But first he had to don sideburns, moustache and a girdle . . . to co-star with the comic genius W. C. Fields and Joan Bennett in *Mississippi*, his initial movie under the new contract and his first in costume.

That girdle? Bing explains: 'I was heavy then, a little adipose, and I had quite a bay window. I think I weighed around a hundred and eighty to eighty-five pounds, whereas I'm now a hundred and fifty. So I had to strap myself in to keep the paunch in, because I had to wear really tight Southern clothes; the film was set around the time of the Civil War and I had to wear tight collars. I was in agony.'

The making of *Mississippi* brought about a friendship between Bing and Bill 'My Little Chickadee' Fields. They remained pals until Fields died from an alcoholic liver on Christmas Day 1946—the day of the year he always said he detested most.

'He was very amusing to be with,' recalls Bing. 'He wasn't irascible and short-tempered at all. I played lots of golf with Bill and he was very good for an old man; a great putter and chipper and, being an ex-juggler he was very quick with his hands. He loved golf and when you played with him there were lots of laughs.'

There were two more movies to shoot during that *Mississippi* year of 1935—and there would be exciting feelers from the Kraft Music Hall, radio's best-known network programme.

Bing was invited to share an experimental Kraft show with its current host, ironically his former boss Paul Whiteman. The idea was that the Whiteman orchestra played in New York and Crosby, backed by the Jimmy Dorsey orchestra, sang from Hollywood. It went out on 5 December 1935, and was an immense success. Before the year was out Bing was signed to replace Whiteman. Another wheel had turned full circle . . .

So the Kraft show shut up shop in New York and moved to Hollywood, where the new host would soon become the nation's number one listening attraction, gathering in an enormous fifty million devotees a week.

In the move West with the Kraft wagon train was the man who dreamed the show up week by week, writer Carroll Carroll. And he, too, was to find the Groaner in that cool, efficient mood: 'When I arrived in the studio, somebody said, "Bing, this is Carroll Carroll the writer of the show." He said, "Hi, Carroll" and then walked away.

'I figured the best thing I could do would be to write, so I wrote a script and it was sent to Bing. It came back with a couple of minor word changes—but he never talked to me. I think I wrote the show for maybe three or four months before he even really knew what my name was.'

Crosby's indifference belied a great respect for Carroll's ability. 'He had a marvellous talent,' says Bing. 'We used to use a lot of opera people and concert musicians—such as Heifetz, and Menuhin and Rachmaninoff. We even had Chaliapin, which was the proudest moment of my life—to stand alongside a man like that.

'These people would sing one song of their own genre, then we'd do some kind of little light duet together. Then we'd have some comedy dialogue, which would fit the personality of the star or his work. And Carroll would write—he really put together some marvellous little spots for those folk.

'They loved to be on the show; they loved to let their hair down a little and be themselves. We used to have Ogden Nash on with his topical poetry. That was in addition, of course, to the popular singers and soloists.'

Yet at the outset Bing, possibly still smarting from the harsh criticism from the Woodbury sponsorship, objected to having to say too much. 'I'm a singer,' he had protested, 'let somebody else do the talking.' But the Kraft people wanted him to talk. 'He's become more of a person than just somebody gargling a few tunes,' Carroll Carroll argued.

Crosby also wanted to do the show without an audience. He objected strongly to phoney applause and organised applause, which every other radio show had. The deal with Kraft—at a fee of three thousand dollars a week—almost didn't go through because of Bing's insistence.

Brother Larry, who was now acting as public relations man for Bing, sorted the problem out. He judged, quite rightly, that the crooner wouldn't mind having some Servicemen around during the show and—provided they applauded in the right places—he would see that it worked. Which is what happened and why there was an audience from that day on.

Writer Carroll found Crosby anything but Mr Easy-Going. 'He was about as casual as Westminster Abbey . . .

'And he perplexed me sometimes with the changes he would make to the script. He'd change a word arbitrarily. Say it was 'beautifully', he'd change it to 'magnificently'. I'd think, well, he doesn't like 'beautifully' for some reason. So the next time

I'd want to use the word I'd use 'magnificently' instead and he'd change it back to "beautifully".'

The radio programme ascended rapidly in popularity and the public particularly liked the policy of having off-beat celebrities as Bing's guests—but not always for the same reason. Like the shoe-shine boy in New York who, when questioned, said he liked most the part where Bing had opera stars and the like with him, because 'when they come on I can go to the toilet!'

Crosby's first guest on Kraft was the late comedian Jack Benny. As the weeks and the years rolled by, the cast list would be littered with the great.

Wielding the orchestral baton was Jimmy Dorsey. He was to stay almost two years and leave because he thought he was losing his identity as a big band leader with only one limited radio exposure a week. Bing understood how he felt and let him go with his blessing.

For some time, since the inception of the Kraft show, there had been something else nagging at Crosby. Some new venture that would call for his time and energy.

Nags . . .

Chapter Nine

Even though he is colour blind and could never pick out which horse was which, Crosby has for long had a fascination for the turf. Therefore it was with some joy that he greeted the suggestion that he could be boss of a racetrack of his own.

The idea was first mooted in the 'thirties and the plan was to build a spacious entertainment complex mid-way between Los Angeles and San Diego at Del Mar, including a racecourse running down towards the Pacific to be known as the Del Mar Turf Club.

But, with the Depression still lingering, money was short and the planners would have to look around for a benefactor. There were few of them about, but there was Bing. And he would be a good bet. A big name with a clean reputation and free from the stranglehold of any mobster organisation such as the Mafia.

Crosby was all for the idea but—as brother Larry revealed—it wasn't all plain sailing. A lot of money was required and the cash wasn't in the bank. 'So we sold stock,' said Larry. 'Bing had to come up with a hundred thousand dollars in advance for a five-year lease on the track; we never owned it. A couple of months before it was due to open the builders said they needed another hundred thousand to complete the track. So Bing said to give it to them. Then, a month before the track is to be opened, they come back and there's another mistake and they need another hundred thousand. I went to Bing and told him he hadn't got the money. "Well," he says, "we can borrow it on my insurance, we've got to open the track." '

Bing never did ask anyone else for cash backing for the project, but he did need help to run Del Mar. He called first on actor Pat O'Brien, who was as enthusiastic as Crosby. 'I was an eager beaver,' he agreed, 'so we wound up with a race-track. I became Vice-President and Bing was President. We were still painting the place the day we opened it. Bing and I were taking tickets and I helped raise the flag and it was all pretty exciting.'

Even if the paint wasn't dry, the guest list on that opening day was certainly on the glossy side. They ranged from J. Edgar Hoover, head of the FBI, to such filmic greats as Spencer Tracy, Jimmy Cagney and Gable. But it was a slow start. Says Bing: 'Hardly anybody showed up for the first two weeks. It looked like we were really in for a terrible financial slogger.'

Producer and writer Herb Polesie, a member of Crosby's kitchen cabinet responsible for getting Del Mar going, remembered how he and Bing used to hopefully count the carriages of the train that brought the punters in from Los Angeles—just to see if there was one more than usual.

Del Mar even started out with its own signature tune, recorded by the Groaner: 'Where the Turf Meets the Surf', referring to the closeness of the ocean, and broadcast before every race meeting.

Polesie's wife Midge is credited as being the writer. 'We were sitting around the house,' said Herb, 'and Bing said he'd like a slogan for Del Mar. Something like "Del Mar the Best in Racing". Then Midge pipes up and says why not "Where the Turf Meets the Surf?" '

'Say no more,' said Bing, taking a pencil from behind his ear. So a song was born—and is still played at the track today.

Business did start to pick up. Along came the high society from Tinsel Town and in their wake the celebrity seekers.

Pat O'Brien was eloquent about it. 'Every Saturday night,' he said, 'there would be the greatest parties in the history of Hollywood, New York, or London. There would be Bing Crosby, Bob Hope, Jimmy Durante, Johnny Mercer, Johnny Burke, the Tracys, the Gables, the Charlie Laughtons and that great actor from 'Treasure Island'—a pretty good student of the sauce—Robert Newton; and quite a horse-player.

'The real queen of the parties was Mary Martin and everybody would get up to do something—it was like the old days when you were kids in the parlour—only this was the pros having fun. It would last until about three in the morning and Bing was the leader of the pack. These were the fun days of Hollywood and I'm afraid they have gone with the wind and I don't think they'll ever return.'

There occasionally was fun on the track itself. Like many other stars of that era, Crosby took a financial interest in a number of horses, one of which was name Ligaroti. His first time out at Del Mar happened to coincide with a day when Bing was indulging in one of his little-known hobbies: guest race commentator. Which, for a man with colour blindness was no mean task.

Unable to pick out the colours of the racing silks—even the blue and gold of the Crosby stable—he simply described Ligaroti as being in the lead all the way round.

It came last . . . The horse did atone, however. It went on to win the Sunset Handicap and the American Handicap at the Hollywood Park races and netted its owner sixty-five thousand dollars in prize money.

He bought his first horse in 1935, a nag with the unlikely name of Zombie. 'A steed of peerless lineage, but dubious ability,' says Bing, who always referred to his horses as a 'bunch of slow-coaches'. He ended up with a string of twenty-one and also became a partner with Lindsay Howard in a breeding farm called Bing-Lin that produced some fifteen foals a year.

One of the characters of Del Mar was veteran vaudeville comic Joe Frisco, a man with an endearing stutter that added to his natural humour. A lovable, compulsive gambler and usually broke. Everything he had went on horses and frequently he would lean on Bing, who by this time had something of a reputation as a soft touch.

Joe, pockets bare, would wait at the entrance for Bing to arrive, then put the hard-luck pressure on. Usually he had 'got a lot of g-g-good information' but needed 'a f-f-few bucks'. And Bing would give him twenty.

But there was at least one lucky day for Joe Frisco. With a twenty bill from Crosby to set him off, he backed five winners in a row. The big news buzzed around Del Mar and Bing went to look for him.

'He was down in the bar in the clubhouse,' says the Groaner. 'He'd got a stack of bills a foot-and-a-half high and was buying wine for everybody. He was holding forth and singing. Very festive, so I walked up behind him and just coughed—rather suggestively—and he turned round and looked up at me and peeled-off a twenty-dollar bill and handed it to me. And then he said, "Here kid, give me a c-c-couple of c-c-choruses of 'M-m-melancholy B-b-baby'." '

The crooner himself was never able to place bets with the freedom that Joe Frisco did—because of his fame. Every time he attempted to get near a window, fans would swamp him.

'I'd be trying to think and to figure the horses,' he says, 'then somebody grabs you for an autograph.' So he gave it up, or asked a friend to put on a bet for him.

It was much easier for him to make bets while working on a film up at Paramount than during his leisure at Del Mar.

'He couldn't finish a shot fast enough to get off to a telephone,' said actor Anthony Quinn, a life-long fan from Bing's early broadcast days at the Cocoanut Grove.

'At that time,' he said, 'I owned the only radio in the neighbourhood and we used to gather together to hear Bing Crosby. He was the first big hero of mine and of the whole neighbourhood. We used to follow all the stories about him that he occasionally "nipped" a bit and we were amazed that he was still able to sing—and sing so magnificently.'

Years later fate was to bring them together in *The Road to Singapore*, first of the 'Road' series of films.

It was the Del Mar Turf Club that gave Crosby the chance to involve another of his brothers in his commercial activities— brother Ted who up till then has been engaged in the real estate business. But it wasn't to turn out the happiest of associations, as Larry Crosby admitted.

'Ted got the Hollywood urge,' said Larry, 'and during Del Mar we brought him down to do publicity. But he didn't get along with the then manager, who put him in a back office and wounded his pride. He didn't want him meddling around with things—so Ted quit. He went with Electrical Industries in Washington D.C., for a time, but he wanted back home. He's a farmer-type and a hobby man, so he then left the job in Washington and went back to real estate.'

The Del Mar involvement was to come to an end in the

'forties when an American Supreme Court judge ruled—as part of the anti-Mafia and mobster campaign—that no one could own a racetrack and baseball team simultaneously.

Bing had bought a slice of the Pittsburgh Pirates and had to choose between the ball game or the racing game. Baseball won.

But no financial regrets. Del Mar had prospered over the years since that shaky start in the mid-'thirties and when he sold his interest in it in 1945 the going price was four hundred and eighty-one thousand dollars.

The Turf Club, an added and important responsibility, was never allowed to hinder or intrude on Crosby's other vital activities.

All of them, like Gary and the twins, were growing apace with each day in the 'thirties.

The Kraft show boomed, as did the records, which he was able to plug regularly over the air in those pre-disc jockey days. Everything was moving on—including the movies, where the quality of both vision and sound were improving.

But Bing was far from casual about all the changes and improvements going on around him. When Jimmy Dorsey left the Kraft show in 1937, the Groaner knew exactly where to look for his successor.

'Who's this fella who does the arrangements for Skinnay Ennis?' he asked Johnny Burke, the lyric writer and his close confidant.

Musicman Burke knew only too well who was behind the growing reputation that singer Skinnay was building with the Hal Kemp band. 'John Scott Trotter,' said Johnny.

'Get him,' was all Bing said.

Larry Crosby traced Trotter to New York and cabled him an offer to take over the orchestra.

When Trotter arrived in Hollywood, the Kraft people, pointing out that the show was a very informal one and that Harry Lillis Crosby was simply known as Bing, suggested that he should be billed as Johnny Trotter and His Orchestra.

'Look', said Trotter, 'I was a twelve-pound baby. I have never been diminuitive and I would feel more comfortable if I could be called John Scott Trotter.' And that's the way it was to be.

Bing immediately liked the big, rambling good-humoured

Trotter and allowed him to change the style of the orchestra. Basically, he took the melody away from the band and gave it to Bing and made sure that the saxophones didn't interfere with the crooner's voice. 'If you listen to some of his early records, they've got saxophones practically in exactly the same range as Bing—and that is lethal,' said Trotter.

Although he never said so, it was apparent that Crosby was happy with his new musical director. 'Bing is very undemonstrative in this way,' said Trotter. 'If he's pleased, you remain. If he isn't—it's good-bye.'

Trotter remained all right. He was to stay for more than three-hundred shows spanning several years and during that time neither he nor Bing thought it necessary to draw up a contract. John Scott Trotter's word was his bond.

What's more, not long after his arrival in 1937, the crooner brought him in to handle the music on his records. Their first disc together: 'It's the Natural Thing to Do', from Bing's *Double or Nothing* movie.

For Trotter it was the first record under his own name.

Years later, Bing summed up his feelings about John Scott Trotter: 'I'm not musically educated enough to really describe what he was in music terms. I just knew he was very good and he had marvellous taste. He was a follower of opera and classical music and had studied for both those things and knew that field very well.'

One of Trotter's early duties was to back an early Jack Kapp pairing of Bing with another star—Connee Boswell, who had gone solo after her sisters Martha and Vet married and quit the act a year before in 1936.

Connee, born in New Orleans, the spawning ground of jazz, was billed as *The Girl Who Sings with the South in Her Mouth*. Thus it was fitting that she and Bing produced one of the finest versions of the New Orleans classic 'Basin Street Blues' with the aid of Trotter and ace jazz trombonist Jack Teagarden.

By this time Bing was already such a legend that even famous girl singers teamed with him under Kapp's policy were so overawed that they had attacks of studio fright.

Patty Andrews, of the hit-making sister trio, confessed: 'I was so nervous I didn't think I'd be able to sing. He was on one side of the mike and we were on the other, facing him. But I knew that if I looked at him I wouldn't be able to open my mouth.'

She conquered her terror by looking at his feet instead. 'He never did snap his fingers when he sang. He had a thing with his foot. He would move it right-to-left, right-to-left and so on—just like a metronome.'

The foot-watching disc: 'Ciribiribin', was a whacking great hit.

With the Andrews Sisters Bing would go on to win six golden records signifying sales of more than one million each.

The delectable blonde Miss Peggy Lee was another songstress who sought solace in the Crosby hooves. She took an attack of the jitters before she was about to sing a solo on the crooner's radio show and felt that she couldn't go on. For a solo, he would normally introduce the artist, then leave the stage. But Peggy needed him. 'If you can stand where I can see your feet while I'm singing, then I'll be all right,' she told him. He did . . .

The Mills Brothers, with whom he had a long recording association, needed no such help and felt really at home with the Groaner—possibly because of a musical affinity.

The Brothers—in fact Dad and three sons—had found international stardom with their own particular brand of harmony and the recreation vocally of musical instruments. Although they are credited with being the first to put these sounds on record, they were only doing something that Bing had been doing—of necessity—back in the 'twenties with the Musicaladers.

There weren't enough instruments in the group to reproduce a faithful copy of the big band discs Crosby and Rinker used to listen to in the record shop. So Bing would thrash his drums and make a noise like a trumpet at the same time . . .

But singing stars, whether solo, pairs, trios or groups, could only be as good as their material, as Bing has frequently said.

The credit he gives the songwriters, even by his self-effacing standards, is extremely high. 'I think,' he says, 'the song was ninety per cent of whatever success those records achieved.

'I always asked for songwriters for my films—rather than them come to me and we had a great coup in getting Richard Rodgers and Lorenz Hart to write the songs for *Mississippi*.'

This was the shrewdness and perception of the casual Groaner as far back as 1935 . . . Rodgers, of course, went on to form the now historic partnership with Hammerstein that was to give the world some of its finest musical shows and movies.

Crosby was one of the first to notice the talents of Hoagy Carmichael, the struggling songsmith he first met when Hoagy bummed a lift on the *King of Jazz* publicity train returning to New York.

Back in Hollywood in the mid-'Thirties, Bing asked Hoagy to get him an invitation to a very exclusive filmland party. So stiffly exclusive, Hoagy remembered, that not a soul would venture towards the piano when he sat down to accompany the crooner.

The evening wasn't completely wasted, however. 'That same night,' said Hoagy, 'I showed Bing a tune I'd written called "Moonburn". He liked the song and a month later told me he was putting it into a picture.'

He sang it in his 1935 movie version of Cole Porter's *Anything Goes*. Later Hoagy joined forces with Johnny Mercer, one of the young hopefuls who had tried to help Paul Whiteman fill the gap when the original Rhythm Boys quit. Now he was trying to make his name writing songs in Hollywood. Together, Mercer and Hoagy churned out a piece called 'Lazy Bones'. It was one of the few numbers Bing himself decided to record in those days of Jack Kapp's astute guidance. Of course it was a hit and within a matter of months Mercer and the crooner had their first professional meeting.

Johnny still glows about that day: 'Bud Livingstone, who was a clarinet player, told Bing about a song I'd written called 'I'm An Old Cowhand'. Bing said he was interested and we met and he put it in a picture called *Rhythm On The Range* in 1936.

'I'm very grateful to him, because that truly opened the door. I'd written a little class-C picture for RKO, which didn't mean very much, but when Bing put that song in his picture—and it got to be a hit—that really established me in Hollywood.'

Bing rates Mercer as one of the greatest songwriters of all time: 'There are many marvellous things he's written,' croons the Groaner, 'unique subjects like "On The Atchison, Topeka and Santa Fe". The kind of things that really take a fertile sort of mind and imagination.'

But the thing that impressed Bing most about Johnny Mercer was his great integrity. Many years later, Mercer and two friends founded Capitol Records. 'Johnny was a pretty big stockholder,' says Bing, 'and after some years of success with the company they sold it and Johnny's share was around half a million dollars. His father had been in the furniture business in Charleston, South Carolina, and had gone bankrupt, leaving four hundred-and-some thousand dollars of debts.

'Johnny went back and paid off all of them—something he wasn't obligated to do at all. It was probably the first big hunk of money he had got hold of, but I suppose the people holding those debts were friends of his fathers—who had gone into business with him hoping to do well and had lost their money—and he just couldn't rest until they were repaid.'

Apart from writing songs for Bing, Johnny Mercer was also one of the few back-room boys to actually sing on disc with him. 'We made a few records together,' laughed Mercer. 'One was "Mister Gallagher and Mister Shean", which was rewritten as "Mister Crosby and Mister Mercer", and then we did "Mister Meadowlark", "On Behalf of the Visiting Fireman" and a few others.'

Johnny too, admits to being scared and very much in awe of Bing during those recording sessions: 'He's a little bit older and much more experienced, and a first class rhythm singer besides being a great ballad singer. But his rapport, his slang and his knowledge of the idiom made you feel at home. His ad-libs were great and he filled in for you if you were a little shy or nervous.'

The Groaner also had great respect and admiration for his lyric-writing friend Johnny Burke, who with Arthur Johnston wrote 'Annie Doesn't Live Here Any More' for him—which led to Bing giving the pair the score to do for another 1936 film, *Pennies from Heaven.*

'Johnny Burke was a great man,' says Bing. 'Everybody used to call him The Poet, because the lyrics he wrote really were quite poetic—for popular songs. He was quite a workman and a great practical joker, always perpetrating ribs on everybody. He had such a straight face he could get away with it.'

From that point on, until his death, Johnny Burke worked almost exclusively for Crosby. After Arthur Johnston, he teamed up with James Monaco for a while, before getting together with his last—and many say most successful—partner Jimmy Van Heusen.

It was a partnership that would last fifteen years, fourteen

Crosby pictures and nearly fifty hit songs, many of which would never die . . .

With Bing and his songwriters spreading their musical happiness round a world racked by depression and the gathering clouds of war, Gonzaga University thought it was high time they came up with some recognition of their illustrious old boy.

So, during 1937, the Jesuit Fathers let it be known that they would like to confer on him the honorary degree of Doctor of Philosophy in Music. But Bing, in his modesty, wasn't exactly happy about accepting the honour.

Brother Larry, as he frequently did, found a way. Why not take the entire Kraft Music Hall team up to Spokane and put on a radio show to raise funds for the university at the same time? Bing liked the idea and the double event took place that October.

Father Leo Robinson, an ex-classmate of Bing and now President of Gonzaga, read the citation before the distinguished turn-out for the great day.

'The voice and personality of Harry Lillis Crosby', it said, 'have brought pleasure and many happy moments to millions of his fellow men. In token of the high regard in which he is held by his school and his fellow citizens, Gonzaga University confers upon Harry Lillis Crosby the degree of Doctor of Music.'

Bing was nervous at having to appear before his former classmates and teachers and took along 'a flagon of spirits' to fortify him. After drinking half of it in a school locker room he had then adjourned to his old classroom to complete the task when Father Sharp, his tough but big-hearted ex-teacher suddenly appeared. With the reflexes of schooldays, Bing quickly hid the bottle in a desk.

They talked about old times, then, as they were about to leave, Father Sharp opened the desk top, took out the now three-quarter empty bottle and downed the rest in one go.

'It wouldn't be right to let a soldier die without a priest,' he chuckled, ushering an astonished Bing from the room.

Within a few weeks Doctor Crosby was back in Hollywood hard at work on a new picture aptly entitled *Doctor Rhythm*.

On the domestic front, the 'thirties saw the arrival of the final member of what was to be Bing's first family. Another boy, born on 5 January 1938 and baptised Lindsay Harry Crosby, the Lindsay being after Lindsay Howard, the crooner's racing stable partner.

A noisy quartet now that could disturb the peace of Bing's relaxation with his pipe in a rocking chair on the porch at the family home; something he liked to do in the evening if there was time.

All four would turn out to be rumbunctious children, getting into their fair share of trouble in the early years, for which Bing always blames himself. He doesn't consider that he played the part of father very well.

'No, I was away too much; more than I would have liked to have been. I could have spent some more time with them.'

Nevertheless, he was strict with them and used a leather belt on them more than once. Trying to explain why he felt he had failed with his first family he once said: 'Maybe I haven't laid into them with a belt as often as I should.'

Once the boys got into Dixie's room, took her favourite canary out of its cage and gave it what they called a 'summer suit' by plucking all its feathers . . . Bing summer-suited them by taking their pants down and 'spanking a bit of hard common-sense into the place it hurts most'.

But Dixie was a critic of his disciplinary technique. 'You punish them,' she used to say, 'then ten minutes later you're taking them to a movie.'

If Bing was strict and over-watchful, there was good reason.

All America had been shocked by the kidnapping in 1932 of the lone aviator Charles Lindbergh's baby. Even gangster king Al Capone was moved. From a jail cell he offered to muster all his underworld resources to try to recover the child if the authorities would give him only temporary freedom (they didn't).

The Lindbergh snatch was followed by others and there was also a deluge of kidnapping threats. The danger was very real for the movie-star parents of Hollywood, the Crosbys among them.

Son Gary, looking back today, says: 'I'm sure father had received threats against us that we didn't even know about and probably will never know about. Not knowing about it made it tough for us. We couldn't figure out why we couldn't do what the other guys did. So to us it was like he was chaining us up. He was over-strict, but at least it was because he really cared and was something he really felt deeply about . . .'

Gary's younger brother Dennis still remembers the guards at the gates of the family home. 'But,' he says, 'I think if kidnappers had grabbed the four of us, they'd have sure let go of us quick!'

All four today disagree with Bing's views about his being a bad father. What he did, they now realise, was for their own benefit . . .

From the earliest of ages all four went to St John's Military Academy, where they played in the band—but couldn't quite understand why they didn't have the freedom other children had.

The Jesuits would have a hand in their upbringing, as they had with father. All went to a Jesuit preparatory school.

All four would later break away from discipline and go through the tear-away phase that Dad had also gone through.

But as the 'thirties began to fade, there was to be a lighter side of life dawning for Bing. Paramount wanted him to take the road with his old drinking buddy with the ski-slope nose from O'Reilly's bar in New York City—Leslie Townes Hope, from Eltham, Eng., currently trading as Bob . . .

Chapter Ten

If the original plans for the 'Road' series of films had been faithfully followed they would have starred Jack Oakie and Fred MacMurray instead of Crosby and Hope and the first road would have led to Mandalay instead of Singapore. But that's Hollywood.

Tinsel Town was going through a period of South Sea Island films each calculated to give the world's cinema-going millions a ninety-minute or so respite from the harsh realities of life. For Paramount screen-writers Frank Butler and Don Hartman had adapted a mediocre tropical island tale called *Beach of Dreams*.

They re-titled their finished screen-play *Road to Mandalay* and Oakie and MacMurray were suggested as the leads. Both firmly said no. The next idea was to team Burns and Allen with Crosby, but the husband and wife duo said they weren't available.

Paramount went into a huddle and came up eventually with an idea that was to prove one of the best ever to come out of the Dream Factory. Why not team Bing with the fellow he was always supposedly feuding with over the air—Bob Hope?

So they were brought together in November 1939—as Britain and most of Europe became entangled in war.

It was a partnership that was to endure for twenty years and take seven roads: to Singapore, Zanzibar, Morocco, Utopia, Bali, Rio and Hong Kong.

The series would break all existing box office records and create a new style of cinema. Apart from the James Bond epics to come later, it was the most lucrative sequence of films in movie history.

Signed for the first with Bing and Bob was a former Miss New Orleans named Dorothy Lamour, a dark-haired beauty who had already become something of a resident in island and jungle pictures, and needed little wardrobe other than a sarong.

And to play the whole thing their way, Crosby and Hope hired a special gag-writer named Barney Dean, who was to spend much of his time scurrying from one star's dressing-room to another with wisecracks and ideas.

Thus prepared, the feudin' twosome went to work on the newly re-titled *Road to Singapore,* under the expert eye of director Victor Schertzinger.

'There wasn't anything real about the feud,' says Bing, 'except we'd needle one another. I'd appear on his radio programme and he on mine, and the studio people—noticing this friendly rivalry and being cognisant of the fact that it was getting some popular attention—thought we'll put these two guys in a picture and let them needle one another.'

The effervescent Hope also remembers those early days well: 'Yes, we used to kid! He used to talk about my nose and I used to say he was a nice fat little singer and would talk about his money. So, when we got together, people were just waiting for that stuff and it was a very successful kind of a friendly feud,' says Hope.

Dorothy Lamour, who was to become an instant hit as the girl both Bing and Bob tried to get, talked about it thirty-three years after her first day's filming with the pair: 'I always say that I was married to Bob and Bing longer than I've been married to my husband, which is almost thirty years now. It was fun from the very first day. We were all exuberant about the picture, never dreaming that it would end in one of the greatest series ever to hit the motion-picture industry.'

Working with the trio on that first 'Road' picture was the fervent young Bing fan Anthony Quinn: 'Interestingly enough, at that time, I was earning extra money hiring myself out to parties for two dollars a night doing imitations of Bing Crosby, Louis Armstrong and Maurice Chevalier,' he said.

'I was very happy. I was one of the few young actors to be

The young Groaner and proud parents—mother Kate
and father Harry Lowe Crosby

Bing's great grand-
father Nathaniel
Crosby II, clipper
ship captain, off
duty—and ready to
round the Horn

A rare gathering of the Crosby Clan shortly after Pa
Crosby's death. From left to right:
Seated: Sister Catherine, Mother, Mary Rose
Back: Everett, Bing (unusually without toupee), Larry, Ted,
Bob

The formal graduation from High School and the budding law student at home in Spokane

The house at 1112 North Jay St, Tacoma, where Harry Lillis Crosby was born

The Crosby home in Spokane

Top right: Bing goes racing—Chicago, late 'twenties

Top left: New Jersey, 1927—before the New York flop with Whiteman

Bottom right: Bing and Al Rinker—Los Angeles, 1925

Bottom left: Al Rinker's sister—the singer Mildred Bailey. Hollywood, Christmas Day, 1926

Top: The Rhythm Boys: Harry Barris, Bing, Al Rinker

Bottom right: Going solo with guitarist Eddie Lang

Bottom left: Paul 'Pops' Whiteman

Dixie Lee Crosby

Dixie, with Gary and twins Philip and Dennis in 1938
(*left to right*)

Top: The Boney Baritone meets the four Crosby boys in the dress uniform of the St John's Academy

Bottom: Adults all—the four boys join Dad and say, 'You're okay by us'

Before tragedy struck: Bing and
Dixie at the Elko Ranch, Nevada

'The best cure for a hangover is coffee'—a scene from Bing's first major feature film *The Big Broadcast* (1932)

The Groaner returns to the drums, with the help of (*left to right*) Jack Benny, Dick Powell, Ken Murray, Shirley Ross and Tommy Dorsey

I'm dreaming of . . .'
Bing records in Hollywood

Bing on the road to . . .
Zanzibar with (*left to right*) Una
Merkel, Dorothy Lamour, Bob
Hope

Morocco—'What, no sarong. . . ?'

Utopia—'Who's idea was
this. . . ?'

Fred Astaire with his 'favourite dancing partner' in Irving Berlin's *Blue Skies* (1945)

All eyes on Mr C, Rosemary Clooney and Danny Kaye during Irving Berlin's *White Christmas* (1954)

Grace Kelly and William Holden comfort a hungover Bing in the film *Country Girl* (1955)

'First citizen of the recording industry'
Bing's platinum records presented in 1960
(*left*); (1970) (*right*)

Bing with Irving Berlin—the man who
gave him the biggest selling record of all
time, 'White Christmas'

Father O'Malley comes to Times Square—the New York World
Première of *Going My Way* (1944)

The crooner and bandleader Glenn Miller in
London shortly before Glenn's death (1944)

(*Left*) Der Bingle—on the Western Front, France
(1944)

The baseball Bing shows his team, The Pittsburgh Pirates, how to swing . . .

And then takes the field himself (*far right*)

Preparing to take the football field at High School (*bottom left*)

...ing makes the Gonzaga Varsity Baseball
...am (*third from right, back row*) but almost
...ts squeezed out

One man and his dog
went to . . . Make a
catch . . . Bag a bird

allied with Bing and Bob in those "Road" pictures. I became like a good-luck charm around the studio, because all the pictures that I was in at the time were making such enormous money; and of course, it was all due to Bing and Bob.'

Less than four months after shooting had started, *Road to Singapore* was premièred in New York on 13 April 1940. The public flocked to it. This was something new; this was the tonic the troubled world needed. And the box office cash registers played a merry symphony. The brain-child was about to become a monster success.

Bing sang his way through two more musical movies that year—*If I Had My Way* and *Rhythm on the River*. A year that saw the war explode in Europe, the fall of France and the historic withdrawal from Dunkirk to an England now standing alone. But the long shadows of conflict were already reaching out across the Atlantic to an America where young men faced their first peace-time call-up, and the steadfast Franklin Delano Roosevelt shattered convention by being re-elected President for an unprecedented third term.

As the clouds grew darker, Paramount busied themselves planning the second 'Road' film, which would take the Crosby–Hope–Lamour trio to Zanzibar and was to prove after its release in the Spring of 1941 an even bigger box-office success than the first. By this time it had been established that one of the features of the series was to be the ad-libbing between the two principals.

And this, says Bing, caused certain problems: 'The two guys who developed them—Frank Butler and Don Hartman, who later became head of Paramount Studios—fought like hell against changing a word. The stories were nice, but they weren't really anything. We didn't pay any attention to them and the two writers would come on the set—and see us doing a scene that they had no recollection of writing. They'd make a mild objection, but we'd say "it's funny, it plays funny—what do you care?" So, they finally got inured to it and said "go ahead".'

'We ad-libbed so much on the first couple of pictures,' said Bob Hope, 'that we almost got into trouble with Hartman and Butler. We were very popular on radio—we had the two top shows in the country—and people wanted to see us, because they understood our humour. One time, Don Hartman walked on the set and I yelled, "If you hear one of your lines, yell Bingo!"; he got so mad, he went up to the front office and yelled.'

Dorothy Lamour found all the ad-libbing somewhat off-putting. 'Bob still tells this story about me,' she says. 'On the first day of shooting I had learned my script—just one line—and was standing between the two of them. The cameras started to roll and they started to ad-lib and I couldn't get my one line in. And I said, even with the cameras rolling, "Wait a minute, I can't get my line in!" Bob teases me about it to this day.'

Dorothy's fondest ad-lib memory of *Road to Zanzibar* involved the filming of what was intended to be a silent safari scene: 'There wasn't supposed to be one line of dialogue, but they set up the microphones. Now, there were something like seven takes of that particular scene, and for each take there weren't ever less than five pages of dialogue taken down by the script girl.

'That's the way it was, the whole way through; you never knew what they were going to say. You kind of had that feeling that maybe they stayed home the night before and read their scripts to see who could out-do the other.'

While *Zanzibar* was making its rounds America was plunged into sudden war with the Axis Powers by the treacherous Japanese attack on Pearl Harbour on 7 December 1941. While the nation was still reeling from this blow another of Bing's films, *Birth of the Blues*, showing the growth of jazz in the Crescent City of New Orleans, had its New York première three days later.

He only made two films in 1942—*Holiday Inn* and *Road to Morocco*—electing to devote most of his time to raising money for the Armed Forces. It was the year Americans learned to do without. There were fewer rubber tires, fewer cigarettes and shirts. There was even less Bing Crosby, for after seven years of national broadcasting with Kraft, Bing's hour-long variety show was cut to half an hour and only four songs.

On one trip in 1942 Bing and composer-friend Jimmy Van Heusen travelled more than 5,000 miles in the US performing a two-man show for servicemen and visiting hundreds of hospital wards.

On another trip, he took a large troup of dancers, a band, and comedian Phil (Sgt Bilko) Silvers as well as Van Heusen.

They averaged three shows a day at camps all over the States and these shows would continue throughout the war years.

The year 1942 produced a wealth of great keep-'em-happy films: Paramount's *The Fleet's In*, Columbia's *You Were Never Lovelier*, 20th Century Fox's *My Gal Sal*, MGM's *For Me and My Gal*, Warner Brother's tribute to vaudeville, *Yankee Doodle Dandy*, with James Cagney. But standing way and above them was one that outstripped any musical film made up until that time—the glittering *Holiday Inn*.

The magnificent Irving Berlin score included 'Easter Parade' and the hundred-million seller 'White Christmas'. And the film was another milestone for Crosby. He made his motion picture dancing début with the daddy of them all, Fred Astaire, one more Bing fan from way back.

They sang and cavorted to Berlin's 'You're Easy to Dance With'. And, according to Fred, Bing *is* easy to dance with: 'Oh sure, he's very easy! He used to joke about it and he really practised to do a few steps, but he's certainly not a dancer. I call him the kind of dancer that I am a singer.

'But he works hard and we had a few steps designed so that we could do them together. At one time, people used to ask me who was my favourite dancing partner and in order to keep myself clear—from picking one girl from another, with all the different girls that I worked with—I always said my best dancing partner was Bing Crosby.'

Astaire also threw some light on the so-called Crosby casual-ness and disagreed with the crooner's oft admitted 'I am lazy' confessions: 'I had a million laughs with him, but he was a dedicated worker. He did it in his own quiet way; you didn't realise he was working so hard. He's rather casual about a lot of things, but I think he gives it a lot more thought than that and has always given it a lot more thought than that.'

Astaire worked frantically in *Holiday Inn*. The Firecrackers sequence is said to be the fastest dance number ever recorded on film. But it took a long time to do and Bing was there to witness it.

'Fred's a perfectionist,' he says, 'and always has been. He'd rehearse, as he always rehearsed everything, for several days—maybe even weeks. He had several numbers in the picture, but spent a lot of time with that one because it was pretty intricate.

'Every step, every movement there was a firecracker let off.

Some he'd throw down like torpedoes and some he'd kick-off. He had to be in certain positions all the time to hit the right firecrackers so he'd be on camera. He'd hit this one, then get the next one, then the next one and they all had to go off in tempo. It was pretty elaborately contrived and had to be done perfectly.'

Astaire spent so much time getting the sequence perfect, that he made thirty-eight takes—a massive number—and, as Bing tells it, danced himself thin: 'I thought the first take he did was great. They all looked alike to me, but there was a little something he didn't like in each one. He about wore out the director and wore out the crew and the sequence took two or three days. Of course, Fred's a thin man to begin with. I don't know how much weight he lost, but I'd venture to say twelve or thirteen pounds and off his frame that's a considerable loss.'

In fact, Astaire started *Holiday Inn* weighing a hundred and forty pounds—which was slightly heavy for him—and ended it at a hundred and twenty-six pounds. He considered that loss perfectly natural and not at all surprising: 'I think athletes always lose weight if they're on a heavy period of work,' he said.

Nobody knew or could ever have guessed that 'White Christmas' would turn out to be one of the greatest smash hits the world has ever known. Bing, who at the last tally had accounted for some thirty million of the hundred million sales with his recording, didn't want to sing the song at all. Then there was a squabble about it with Irving Berlin himself.

Crosby, true to his religious feeling, was reluctant to be any part of a venture that would commercialise what was, after all, the most important date in the Church's calendar.

It was Jack Kapp who in the end convinced him of the song's innocence and, as always, relying on Kapp's judgement, he said: 'All right, Jack, you want me to do it, I'll do it.'

Bing blushes slightly when reminded of 'White Christmas', but remembers well the day Irving Berlin first demonstrated it to him: 'He thought it was a nice little song, or—as he said—"I have an amusing little number here". When he demonstrates a song before a picture for the cast, director and everybody—you have to hug him to hear him. He has tremendous enthusiasm, but a tiny little voice and he plays a kind of broken-down piano.

'He has a lever device on the piano, with which he can shift keys. If the key he's written a song in isn't the key he can sing it in, he just pulls the lever and changes key.'

Jack Kapp and Irving Berlin had an argument about the lyric, the opening verse of which ran: 'I'm sitting here in Beverly Hills, dreaming of a white Christmas.' Berlin, like most writers, had an affection for the line and was loathe to let it go. Kapp insisted that, divorced from the film and simply in a song on record, the offending line would mean little to the rest of the world. He was right, of course, and Berlin had finally to agree with him.

What would have happened if the Beverly Hills line had remained? Would the song have been the fantastic hit it was to become? Nobody can ever tell, obviously, but John Scott Trotter, who provided the backing for the original record, had these feelings: 'I think the song would have been a big hit, but I don't think that the original record would still be played today.'

Holiday Inn was an original idea of Berlins—'a story about a man who was lazy and only wanted to work on holidays,' explained the songwriter talking about it much later in his eighty-sixth year. 'So he opened this inn and White Christmas was one of the holidays. But America was at war and the song took on a meaning I never intended. It became a peace song.'

Bing sums it up: 'So many young people were away and they'd hear this song at that time of the year and it would really affect them. I sang it many times in Europe in the field for the soldiers. They'd holler for it; they'd demand it and I'd sing it and they'd all cry. It was really sad.'

'White Christmas' took only eighteen minutes to put on record. He wasn't known as 'One Take Crosby' for nothing—a nickname he acquired during the Whiteman days.

'He didn't care to take three or four hours making sixteen takes,' said ex-Whiteman pianist Ray Turner, one of the two people Pops sent to check on Bing's talent years back.

'Sometimes he hadn't even seen the music and he'd look at it while somebody would play it through on the piano for him. He'd sing maybe a couple of notes and then away we'd go.'

Turner was so puzzled by this habit of having the song played through that he tackled Crosby about it. And the crooner confided that it was because he couldn't read music.

'I'm working out the lyric—when the music goes up the mountain and then down again, I go up and then come down. My ear tells me whether I'm right or not,' Bing told him.

The man who had most time to assess Bing's aptitude at speedy recording was producer Sonny Burke: 'Frankly, I don't think there's anybody better in the studio than Bing,' he said. 'He and Sinatra are two of the finest people I've ever worked with from that standpoint. When Bing comes into the studio, he's there to perform and nothing else. He's a pure professional and is that much of a pro that he doesn't tolerate anyone else who isn't.'

Sonny was also impressed with Bing's ability to learn songs quickly: 'Bing is probably one of the fastest studies I've ever seen. He's got great ears. He has something approaching total recall, in that it doesn't take him long to get the feeling of a piece and learn it.'

The early 'forties were one head-long rush for Crosby; a mad dash from studio to studio (his recording output alone averaged two discs a day during his career). Apart from feature films and the 'Road' series he was still involved in the 'Rhythm' series that had begun in 1936 with *Rhythm on the Range* and would end in 1942 with *Star Spangled Rhythm*, a real morale booster.

There were forty-three stars, including Mary Martin, Dick Powell, Bob Hope, Dorothy Lamour, Betty Hutton, Veronica Lake, Fred MacMurray, Gary Cooper, Ray Milland, Susan Hayward and—making one of his rare on-screen appearances—Cecil B. de Mille.

Bing, by then Paramount's biggest and most popular star, sang as the finale the highly patriotic Johnny Mercer–Harold Arlen song 'Old Glory'. But the best Mercer–Arlen composition written for the film was the one-that-got-away: 'That Old Black Magic'.

The producers turned it down . . .

The four 'Rhythm' pictures were all relatively successful, but the 'Road' series would far outstrip them. They had their moments and their memories, however.

Bing never forgets making *Doctor Rhythm*, which starred him with Beatrice Lillie, Louis Armstrong, Andy Devine—and three hundred and fifty monkeys.

As Bing tells it: 'Andy Devine played a zookeeper and there was a scene when he goes out on the town and gets inebriated.

He comes back to the zoo determined to let the monkeys go, because he can't stand to see them imprisoned for life.

'The problem facing the production team was, of course, how to liberate all those mischievous monkeys without them really getting away. The assistant director came up with the answer: throw a net, out of camera shot, around the cage, cameras and actors.

'All very well in theory, but Devine lurched in weaving, opened the cage and the monkeys all burst out. The first one out went right up to the top of the net, took it in two hands, and pulled it apart. The monkeys disappeared all over the studio lot and all over Hollywood.

'There were monkeys all over the place. They scared people to death. People would drive home into their garages, and when they turned on the light there would be a monkey leering and chattering. Finally, the studio got about fifty back and the guy who rented the monkeys wanted to be paid for those that had been lost.'

Emanuel Cohen, who ran the Paramount studio at the time, wasn't at all keen on paying out good money for monkeys he hadn't got, so he offered a ten dollar reward for each recovered. That, Bing remembers, produced an incident which capped the whole hilarious episode: 'Manny Cohen was a little man and after he put up the reward notice a few monkeys showed up. Then gag-writer Barney Dean came in one day, and said, "There's a fellow at the front gate—he's got Manny Cohen by the hand and he wants his ten dollars!" '

Road to Morocco, third in the series, was sandwiched between *Holiday Inn* and *Star Spangled Rhythm*. And it gave a job to another old Crosby buddy—Jimmy Cottrell, the former North-west champ who had coached the crooner in his boxing days.

Life hadn't been treating him too well and he turned to Bing for help. A job was found for Jimmy in the props department at Paramount, but it didn't stop at that. He quickly assumed the role of personal manager and adviser to Crosby.

'Oh! Jimmy was so loyal', says Bing, 'that he embarassed me on a picture, because he was always rooting for my interests. If it was a comedy scene with Hope, he'd watch it closely and would give me the okay—whether or not Hope stole the scene, or whether it was even, or whether I did.'

Embarrassed or not, Bing used to listen to Cottrell's views;

he liked the little man's earthy, unsophisticated approach: 'If he told me Hope stole the scene, I'd tell the director I thought I'd better have another take. Of course, if I did something good Jimmy would pump me on the back.'

Jimmy's fervent loyalty and enthusiasm began to get too much and Bing was forced to be firmer when Cottrell started telling the rest of the cast how good Crosby was and how bad they were.

'I'd have to talk to him once a week', says the Groaner, who continued to heed him nevertheless: 'When they'd make five or six takes of a song and would start talking about which one they liked the best, he'd stand behind the director and hold up two or three fingers—for whichever one he thought was the best.'

There were, however, more important issues occupying Bing's mind in those dramatic days of war effort, notably the increasing involvement of the Crosby clan in the big hard world of business.

The Crosby office on the third and top floor of the Crosby building at 9028 Sunset Boulevard was buzzing with Crosbys and Crosby business activities. Dad was now overseeing real estate as well as finances and doubling as a liaison officer if Everett and Larry were otherwise engaged.

Bing would not hear of having a luxury office there and frequently only went near the place for a Turkish bath at a Swedish masseur's in the basement called the Finlandia Baths.

But there was much going on upstairs.

The Del Mar Turf Club had become a defence plant turning out wing-rib assemblies for aircraft. Of course they became known as Bing's Wings . . .

And to encourage frustrated inventors, the Bing Crosby Research Foundation was set up and was mainly in the hands of Larry. But he found inventors a difficult race to handle. 'An invention is their baby,' he said, 'and you just can't tell them it's no good. You've got to try to keep the peace'.

They did come up with a few things—including a better mousetrap invented by one Mr W. A. Utts. It was guaranteed to dispose of any mouse, but would never come down sharply on unwary fingers.

'Even I,' said Bing at the time, 'who knows practically nothing about anything, can handle the machine without the loss of a single digit.'

When the atomic bomb that was to blast Japan out of the war was being developed, it was reported that the Crosby Foundation was called in to research and produce a safe container for the deadly radio-active weapon. After the bomb had been used one paper headlined the news thus: *Bing Made the Container*.

Bing says this was untrue, but tells an amazing true story of how the rumour started:

'A man brought Larry an elaborate plan which he claimed would destroy Tokyo. Capture 20,000 bats from the Carlsbad Caverns, he said, where there were millions. Immobilise the bats and place them in aluminium containers after tying a tiny incendiary device around their necks. The containers would be dropped from bombers high over Tokyo and would open; the bats would revive and seek nooks, crevices and alcoves in the wooden Tokyo houses. The heat of their bodies would ignite the device and Tokyo would be in flames. The Pentagon actually considered it!' the Groaner reveals with a grin.

Crosby himself was inventive, according to his old actor friend Richard Arlen, and had long nursed an idea to concentrate orange juice with all its goodness. Eventually an inventor came along who could do it and Jock Whitney, a former US Ambassador to the Court of St James, formed a group to develop it. The product was marketed as Minute Maid and Bing went on the air five times a week to plug it, but instead of taking a fee he decided on preferential options to buy stocks and shares in the venture.

'They gave me stock at ten cents a share,' grins Bing, 'and I bought a hunk, of course, at that price—being one of the privileged stockholders. I did about a year's programmes with it, then the orange juice became successful and made money. When the shares went up to eleven dollars a share I sold.'

To come, there would be Bing's Things, Inc., marketing some twenty items ranging from toys to clothing (which made a big loss); oil drilling interests in Louisiana and Oklahoma; banking interests in California and Arizona (the Californian bank failed); 6,000 head of cattle roaming the ranges in the United States and South America; and an ice-cream distribution set-up. All of which led him to be accused one day of being a minor 'business octopus'. Although Bing says the oil was the only thing that did well.

Larry Crosby had this to say about the boss: 'I don't think anything has been a struggle for Bing. Everything comes easy, but he's not a detail man. Here at the office he thinks we can do everything in one day, when actually it takes weeks. He wants it right now! He's a pretty good boss, but I think he listens to too many people.'

Lawyer O'Melveny agreed: 'He's a very good, soft-hearted, fine fellow and almost anybody could talk him into things that I very much disapproved of.'

Strangely, another business that never did really boom was the Crosby music publishing outfit, which was formed by merging two existing companies.

There was a split publishing deal for many of the new songs Bing sang in films. 'In fact,' said Larry, 'when it got real big at Paramount we'd draw cards to see who got first pick out of the four or five songs in a picture.'

The publishing business was literally hit-and-miss and Bing himself doesn't have the fondest of memories of it: 'I was trying to get a catalogue of songs, because it's proven that, if you have a catalogue, it's an income almost in perpetuity, but we didn't do too well. Perhaps it was mismanagement, the wrong people. I don't know—never really got interested. I had too many other things. Golf, horse-racing, fishing and travel. I don't suppose I could have helped even if I had tried. Successful song publishing involves a lot of politics, coercion and even bribery,' he alleges.

But he did find time for talent during those early years of the 'forties.

During the ten years of the Crosby Kraft show a number of unknowns were given the chance to make their début on national American radio. Many of them soared to stardom and the biggest discovery by far was Danish comedian Victor Borge, who had fled Nazi-occupied Europe and was working in a petrol station in Beverly Hills for a few dollars a day.

Ironically, it was Bing's rival Rudy Vallee who first saw Borge and gave him his chance to break into American show business. The Dane, who was already quite a celebrity when he left Europe, had tried without success to get into radio in California. As a last desperate attempt he took his press cuttings scrapbook along to a little Los Angeles restaurant called The Pirates Den owned by Vallee and other Hollywood celebrities.

Vallee was having dinner that night with W. C. Fields, Gary Cooper and Fred MacMurray when a friend introduced Victor. Vallee ignored the scrapbook, but let Borge perform anyway. 'When he did his phonetic punctuation act, I fell off my chair,' said Vallee. 'I'd never heard anything like it—it was classic.'

Although greatly impressed, he didn't book Borge for his radio show. He simply gave him a hundred dollars and told him to report to the NBC studios next afternoon to do the audience warm-up. And watching this with a professional eye was Crosby writer Carroll Carroll and again the hypnotic punctuation routine paralysed the audience.

Carroll immediately snapped him up for the Kraft show and he made his American radio début with Crosby next day. The whole studio was in uproar and tears were streaming down Bing's cheeks—until he discovered that Borge had overrun his allotted seven minutes and was on his way to doing forty . . .

Drastic on-the-spot cuts were made. Out went three songs from the Groaner, out went the guest segment, three commercials and the closing announcement.

'We thought we'd get hell from the sponsor,' said Carroll, 'but as it happened they thought it was the greatest thing they'd ever had on the air.' Victor Borge stayed on for a record-breaking run of fifty-four weeks with Bing. A career was made. But for Vallee it was a cruel blow.

'His sponsor was very upset,' Borge was to find out later, 'and almost fired him because of the success I had on the Crosby show.'

Phil Silvers, Bing's armed forces tour partner, was another warm-up man to begin with the Groaner.

'When I came to Hollywood,' said Phil, 'it was very frustrating—I was the hit of everybody's party and every benefit, but I couldn't get into a picture. Then I started doing the warm-up. Time passes, I'm still not on the radio show proper, and I was a little hurt. "You think I'm so funny," I told Bing, "so why am I not on your radio show?" '

Bing never did give a reason, but he did give Phil his big chance. 'I was very nervous,' he said, 'and I don't read well from a script. We were rehearsing and I'm not reading my lines too good. I got worse and I'm waiting for my benefactor to say something, but from Mr Crosby—not a word.

'Five minutes before air-time—the show was "live"—and Bing said "can I see you for a minute?" I went to his dressing-room and he says "Do you want a shot of whisky?" I said I didn't drink. He says okay, and that was that—no encouraging words or anything.'

Phil was a great success. He showed no trace of his earlier nerves and went on to make many more appearances with Bing. Often his humour was directed at his mentor.

'I play a little clarinet, but badly,' Silvers said, 'and one day I sat in with the John Scott Trotter orchestra backing Bing with "Moonlight Becomes You".

'I was playing a nice counter-melody, but I guess I overblew it and there were some discordant notes. Bing was furious. He kept singing, but I got worse and finally he couldn't stand it any longer.'

The Groaner kicked the music stand, turned round and roared: 'Phil, you hit one more clinker and I'll bang you over the head with that pipe!'

Silvers looked up and said: 'Sing the songs, buddy, sing the songs. We'll take care of the music!'

Bing literally fell on the floor . . .

He gave opportunities on the air to the most unlikely musicians of the day. Such as Henry Fonda, who fancied himself as a trumpet player. But there was a snag, as Henry said: 'I don't read music and the only way I could do it was to draw diagrams of the trumpet's three valves on those cardboards that come back with your shirts from the laundry.'

So off he went to the Kraft Music Hall and set up his cardboards on a music stand about two-and-a-half feet from the mike. When he started to play somebody screamed from the control room: 'Back away! You're too close to the microphone.'

But when Fonda moved back, he found he couldn't see his diagrams. Undaunted, he delved into his trumpet case and produced a music holder for use in a marching band and stuck the cardboard into it. Eyes closed, cheeks bursting he began to blow. By which time Bing was collapsing and the band were helpless with laughter.

But one trumpeter from the orchestra wasn't laughing when he tackled Fonda at the stage door afterwards. Angered, he tore the movie star off a strip: 'I've studied the trumpet and made it my living for twenty years and you come along and make more money in one day, playing it badly, than I ever did playing it well.'

Fonda's fee? 'At least a thousand dollars, I would think,' he said, trying to remember many years later.

James Stewart braved the Kraft microphone with the accordion he would usually only play in the privacy of his own home.

He played quite well, but made the mistake of unstrapping his accordion when he finished his piece and putting it down, whereupon it closed itself with a long, slow groan.

'Jimmy,' observed a quick-on-the-ball Bing, 'I want to tell you that thing sure dies hard . . .'

A promising young British actor named David Niven went along to guest on the show for the nominal fee of two hundred and fifty dollars—and a gift hamper of Kraft products. He was under contract to Sam Goldwyn and part of the deal was that Goldwyn would get half of everything Niven earned outside his employ.

Not only did he send off a cheque for half of his fee to Goldwyn but also half of everything that was in the kingsize hamper. Not jar for jar—that would have been too easy. He cut all the goodies completely into two; jars, cheese trays, caramels and even the basket itself. 'Here's your half of the loot,' he said in a note to Goldwyn . . .

But the Hollywood luminaries who guested for Crosby were not always a bundle of fun. Certainly not Miss Marlene Dietrich.

She objected to the script and refused to have anything to do with the show until it was rewritten. The producers told her this wasn't possible and as a precaution asked actress Joan Bennett to stand by. Dietrich waited until the morning of the broadcast before she finally agreed to perform. Once on, she got along fine with Bing, read the script exactly as it had been written and was a big hit.

Douglas Fairbanks Junior did at least have a good excuse when he turned up two hours late for a Kraft rehearsal. He had been to collect his naval lieutenant's uniform and was due to ship out to war next day. But there was time first to laugh about a much earlier meeting with Bing on the golf course, during the crooner's days with Whiteman.

Crosby had made a screen test, which angered Whiteman, who threatened to fire him if he ever did it again. Bing sought advice from Fairbanks about his future.

'I told him he was in the best band in America,' said Douglas, 'and that the people were buying the band's records because the Rhythm Boys were on them. In films, I said, he might get a few jobs, then be out of work. He might even be a tremendous failure. He disobeyed my instructions—and look what happened!'

Mrs Dixie Lee Crosby used to go along to some of the shows, the growing family left in the safe hands of staff or relatives. One of her favourite singers was the then Great Young Lady of Jazz, Ella Fitzgerald. Seldom did Dixie miss an Ella show with Bing.

If, because of all the pressures of those early 'forties, he couldn't get in a few holes of golf as dawn broke, the Groaner would be on the tennis court at home. Dixie was keen on the game as well and partnered him regularly while the birds were greeting the new day. If not, he would call one of his colleagues from their beds. Producer Herb Polesie was a favourite stand-in on the court.

'Bing always wore a rubber sweat suit,' Herb said, 'and I guess I used to give him a pretty good work out. He was certainly an early riser. I was in the feathers sleeping good one morning when our Filipino cook knocks on the door and says there's a Mr Cross on the telephone. I don't know any Mr Cross and I tell the cook to ask him who he is and what he does. The Filipino comes back, knocks again, and says: "He say a little fat fellow, sing on radio name B-I-N-G" . . .'

The crooner was so keen on the game that he sent younger brother Bob a racket, saying, 'It's a very good game for a young man to play.' Bob became Boys' Champion of the Pacific Coast.

As a much crowded 1942 faded and the new year dawned there was a distinct smell of burning . . .

Chapter Eleven

There had been time for a round of golf with Fred Astaire after the day's work and now Bing relaxed in the Brown Derby Restaurant, a celebrated haunt of the film famous. He had studied the lengthy menu and decided what to eat for dinner before making his way home to wife and family. But, with the meal barely started, a waiter hurried to the table to tell him that there was an urgent telephone call.

At the other end of the line was a frantic Johnny Burke, the brilliant lyricist who (for once) now found himself almost at a loss for words.

He was trying in the nicest way to tell Crosby that his twenty-roomed mansion in North Hollywood had burned to the ground, that Dixie and the children had narrowly escaped with their lives but were well.

'Dixie and the boys are all right,' the faltering Burke began.

'Isn't that nice,' Bing replied drily, assuming it was another of Burke's legendary practical jokes, 'and how's your family?'

The message eventually managed to seep through and Burke implored the crooner to return home at once.

'But I just ordered my dinner,' he said, 'and Astaire's going to pay.'

Burke thought he was joking. He wasn't. He unhurriedly finished his meal before calmly driving out to view the smouldering remains of his once beautiful home.

The usual crowd that disaster attracts were there to see him arrive and to watch as he picked around in the embers with a golf club. A little later he hooked out a charred shoe and pulled from it a roll of two thousand dollars that had escaped the flames. His betting money for the races . . .

After wistfully surveying the smoking premises for several minutes, Bing drifted two houses down to the home of neighbour Bill Goodwin, where the family, with a few sympathetic friends, were gathered. As he walked in, Hollywood writer Dave Shelley looked up and casually said: 'Hiya, Bing! What's new?'

His entire record collection was destroyed, but he was able to replace much of it through the record companies. Even so, there were still some collector's items missing. Fans throughout the world—and in the United States they included Bing's idol and jazz immortal Louis Armstrong—rushed in with replacements. With duplications and records that weren't even in his original collection, Crosby ended up with more discs than he had before the blaze.

The fire had started through a short circuit in the Christmas tree lights, but the great day itself with its family present-giving had fortunately passed and 1943 had just begun. The Crosbys moved into the Beverly Hills Hotel then later into one of Marion Davies' houses.

Before the year's end flames would strike again. The forest fires which annually sweep Southern California during the dry and breezy weather that heralds the winter, destroyed the Crosby home at the Malibu Beach colony along with more than a hundred others.

The ashes had hardly cooled from what was the Black Christmas fire when Bing was back before the cameras at Paramount playing Daniel Emmett (1815–1904) who was described as the 'father of Negro minstrelsy' and the composer of the famous 'Dixie', which was taken up as a rallying song by the South during the Civil War. The film took its title from the song and was Bing's first as a star in colour. (He had been seen in silhouette in a colour segment with the Rhythm Boys in *King of Jazz* more than twenty years earlier.)

Although he could not have known it at this time, Crosby was fast approaching the peak of his career. But along the way there was to be a conflict of conscience . . .

Firstly his normally casual mood in the Kraft studio was shattered one day in May when it was suggested he should play a parish priest in a sketch. It was to be a send up of the gangster era with James Cagney, the screen's top mobster. Cagney was to parody the hoodlum roles he made famous and seek advice from the kindly Father Crosby.

Bing would have none of it. It was bad for his image, he argued, and against his religious feelings. He stressed that he didn't sing religious songs for the same reason. 'Oh, no,' he said with much determination to writer Carroll Carroll, 'you're not getting round me, never in a million years.'

The sketch went on—without Bing. Announcer Ken Carpenter took the role against Cagney.

But within a matter of weeks, Paramount were knocking on Crosby's door with the same idea. Would he not don cassock and dog collar in a movie?

The film they had in mind was called *The Padre* and was the brainchild of director Leo McCarey, a friend of Crosby. He had offered the story to RKO, for whom he had worked, and then went along to Paramount, who were more enthusiastic. He dearly wanted the crooner to play Father Chuck O'Malley and Paramount production chief Buddy DeSylva went along with that idea as well, although most of the studio bigwigs couldn't quite see their singing star and purveyor of light comedy in sober black soutane.

How would Bing react now?

'Leo was an old racetrack buddy of mine,' he says, 'and he always threatened to use me in one of his pictures. After years of joking, he finally said he wanted me to play a priest. But I told him the Church simply wouldn't stand for that kind of casting. Leo said it would. Priests in pictures were usually dramatic actors and I'd been a crooner, a sportsman, a racetrack habituary and one thing and another'.

The story impressed Crosby. And the way McCarey briefly outlined it at one meeting 'there wasn't a dry eye in the place,' says Bing. He also had immense respect for Leo's judgement and it was this that swayed the Groaner to accept the role in the end, rather than Paramount's blessing. The conflict was over, the conscience eased.

'Leo had made some brilliant successes and it had always been my axiom to get in the hands of a great director,' says Bing. 'So I just went ahead and did it.'

McCarey so believed in his project that he put his entire life savings of fifty thousand dollars into the venture. Eventually his investment would net him a return of two million dollars—but that was a long way ahead.

First, by accident, he came across a new and better title for his brain-child. Driving home one very wet evening he stopped his car to give a lift to a soaking sailor trying to thumb a lift. 'Going my way?' the sailor asked . . .

Going My Way went before the cameras in August 1943 and would take some six months to film and run into February the following year. The time spent was to be well worth it, yet the production was by no means lavish according to Hollywood standards and cost less than a million dollars to make.

McCarey cast the veteran Irish actor Barry Fitzgerald in the part of Father Fitzgibbon to support Bing's Father O'Malley, but hadn't—says the Groaner—prepared a complete script by the time shooting was to begin: 'I don't think when Leo started that he even had the full story in mind. He had his characters—Barry Fitzgerald and me—but we were never sure what we'd be doing from morning to afternoon. He made a lot of it up as we went along.'

The McCarey free-and-easy handling of Crosby and Fitzgerald created a unique partnership, as their female co-star, Risé Stevens, recalls: 'Bing loved this. He and Barry used to try out scenes together. Then they would throw in certain little idiosyncrasies of their own. And this really worked out and the results were quite fabulous.'

There was a feeling of very real affection between the two principals. Bing, in particular, had a great respect for Fitzgerald: 'He was a marvellous little man. He had a warm personality and was what we call a gaffer. A real cute, sly little man with a sly sense of humour. But you couldn't understand him half the time, because of his brogue.'

Leo McCarey found the same difficulty. In the film Fitzgerald had to deliver a sermon in his role of Father Fitzgibbon and Leo thought it might be a good idea to first get Barry to record it, then take it home and listen to it so that any imperfections in his speech could be remedied. 'We have to understand the words,' McCarey told him.

Next morning in the studio Leo asked the Irish actor if he played the record over. 'Yes,' said Fitzgerald, 'but I couldn't understand a bloody word of it!'

Bing got into his part as Father O'Malley by modelling himself on his tough, down-to-earth but lovable tutor at Gonzaga, Father Sharp, who a few years earlier had caught the crooner at the bottle. Another shrewd decision that was to pay off handsomely.

Johnny Burke and Jimmy Van Heusen were called in to write the music for the film, but found that not all the songs came easily. For one particular scene in which Father O'Malley tries to explain right from wrong to a bunch of hell-raising dead-end kids they were asked to produce a song that would embrace the teachings of the Ten Commandments.

'Yes,' said Van Heusen as if he still didn't quite believe it, 'we were told write the Commandments into a rhythm number! It was some problem and we struggled with it for days. In the end it was Bing who was the inspiration. We were at his house and one of his boys was acting up when Bing chastised him by saying "What do you want to be—a mule?" That sparked us off.'

The result was the big hit 'Swinging on a Star', which picked up an Oscar in 1944 as song of the year and had a line that ran: 'Would you like to swing on a star, or would you rather be a mule?'

When Crosby came to record the disc version of the tune the youngsters from the film weren't available and a little-known singing group called the Williams Brothers were rushed into the studio. One of them was a lad named Andy, who some twenty or so years later would become an international singing star in his own right.

Bing also sang 'Silent Night' in the film and it was to become his biggest-selling record next to 'White Christmas'.

'Silent Night' was the second time around for the Groaner. He had first recorded it in 1934 after much soul-searching and then only because the Church was directly involved.

A missionary had arrived in Hollywood from China looking for help. He had shot some film showing the mission's work and now he wanted a sound-track to go with it as part of a fund-raising scheme. So he called on the Crosbys.

Larry and Bing discussed whether or not to finance the soundtrack, then came up with the idea of the crooner singing a couple of songs for it instead and issuing them on record at the same time, all the royalties to go to the missionaries and the needy they cared for.

It was Larry who suggested 'Silent Night' as one of the sides. 'Bing,' he said, 'thought it was out of his class, but did it and took a few liberties with it—departing from the original lyrics.'

Over the years the record made thousands for the missions— and caused something of a flap in the Crosby office. Music lovers wrote in from all over the world complaining that the Groaner had tampered with their favourite song.

Larry answered them: 'I explained that it was Bing's way of interpreting the song and of putting the right feeling into it. I told them that I thought we'd get many of the younger generation to listen to "Silent Night", kids who wouldn't otherwise have heard the original. Usually they'd write back saying they'd seen the point.'

For his role as Father O'Malley in *Going My Way*, Crosby was voted actor of the year in 1944 by the Academy of Motion Picture Arts and Sciences and early in 1945 received his Oscar from the hands of one of his closest friends, Gary Cooper. Although it nearly didn't happen . . .

The presentations were to be a glittering affair at Grauman's famous Chinese Theatre on Hollywood Boulevard, where the paving stones at the entrance are studded with hand and foot-prints of the stars; a diamonds-and-pearls occasion with crowds and cops and searchlights criss-crossing the sky.

Bing knew that he had been nominated for an award, but so had several others and he rated his chances very slender. So much so that he had no intention of attending the night of the Oscars, when usually the names of the winners are a last-minute secret and are only known when an envelope is opened on stage.

But around six o'clock that evening, Paramount did get wind that Crosby was actor of the year. But where was he?

'My God!' cried a Paramount executive. 'Let's see if we can find him.'

'What do you mean, *if* we can find him?' echoed studio boss Buddy DeSylva. 'He's won an Academy Award—we've got to find him!' So the minions of Paramount set off in packs to scour the Los Angeles environs for their wayward star.

They found him playing the twelfth hole at the Lakeside course in his usual casual togs and sans toupée. And it was now well after six pm and the crowds were gathering outside Grauman's.

The Groaner was still not keen. He even suggested that the

studio call his mother and father and let them go instead, but Paramount would have none of it. And go he did.

When Gary Cooper handed him the coveted trophy Bing summed the occasion up: 'All I can say is that it sure is a wonderful world when a tired old crooner like me can walk away with this hunk of crockery . . .'

As Risé Stevens, his co-star, arrived at Grauman's and trod the traditional red carpet from the sidewalk into the theatre, a woman standing in the crowd behind the roped-off enclosure tugged at her arm.

'I want to thank you for being in this picture with Bing,' said the woman.

'Well, it was a great pleasure for me and I think he's a marvellous person,' said the actress. 'But tell me, why are you so interested?'

'I'm his mother,' said the woman . . .

The film went on to make more than seven million dollars for Paramount. In the Vatican Pope Pius XII watched several private screenings and wrote to Bing to say how much he had enjoyed seeing the priesthood 'humanised'.

Crosby was immediately signed to a new ten-year contract with Paramount, but still today waves a hand of dismissal over his Oscar.

'I'd been nominated, so I knew there was a chance, but I just thought it was a kind of popularity award. I'd done some charitable things, a lot of shows, benefits, I was a golfer and that was that. It was a war year and all the good talent was away and I figured they reckoned "give it to this guy—he's not a bad fellow".'

There were Oscars by the handful for *Going My Way*. Apart from one for the best song, there were others for Barry Fitzgerald as best supporting actor, Leo McCarey as best director and writers Frank Butler and Frank Cavett for best screenplay. The film also won the New York critics' Golden Globe award as best motion picture and kept Bing at the top of the box-office draw chart for the fifth year in a row.

Even before he had collected his Oscar he was rehearsing a follow-up role as Father O'Malley in *The Bells of St Mary's*, with Ingrid Bergman as a nun in the part of Sister Benedict.

'A marvellous girl and a tremendously gifted actress,' says Bing. 'We had endless gags all the time.' And the best of the many the two stars pulled during the shooting was no doubt one at the expense of the film's religious adviser, a dour priest named Father Devlin.

'We had to have someone from the diocese on the set all the time,' explains Bing, 'to see that nothing was done in any way that would reflect on the dignity of the priesthood or the Church. Father Devlin was a very serious, quite humourless but nice man.

'At the end of the picture there's a farewell scene between Ingrid and I and throughout the film there'd been a note of something more than just a priest–nun relationship. Father Devlin was watching us rehearse this scene the way it was going to be, then Leo McCarey said, "Now we'll take it." We got to the line where I had to say goodbye and I reached for Ingrid, took her in my arms, bent her over and gave her a real big soul kiss. I really hung in there!

'There was a shocking silence and when I pulled away Father Devlin was ashen. He was shaking and his eyes were sticking out a foot. Then, of course, everybody laughed and he saw it was a gag. He was so relieved, but for a moment it was really something,' says Bing with a twinkle in his clear blue eyes.

After these two films, he was faced for the first time with the problem of people identifying an actor with his screen role. Fan mail poured in addressed to 'Father O'Malley'. 'And it still does. People call me Father O'Malley when I'm walking around in a crowd or going to a football game,' says Bing.

'I was at a social some place, and it was a Friday and I ate meat. This lady was horrified. She said, "Father O'Malley— what are you doing eating meat?" I said, "That was just in a picture when I was Father O'Malley. I have a dispensation when I'm out socially." '

And there was the delightful aunt of Dixie's who was staying as a house guest when Bing had arranged a game of golf with Humphrey Bogart.

'Good Heavens,' she protested, 'you surely wouldn't play golf with such a man? I saw his last picture and he's the worst man you've ever seen. The idea of a priest and a gangster playing golf together!'

The long drawn-out shooting of *Going My Way*, spanning as it did 1943–4, was not allowed to intrude on Crosby's many other activities. He had now set up home in the fashionable San

Fernando Valley—an area where years earlier Bob Hope had bought large tracts of land and had now reaped the rewards when it became a built-up residential zone. To the Crosby house just before Christmas 1943 went top Hollywood song plugger Sam Weiss, bearing a number called, appropriately, 'San Fernando Valley', which had been penned by ace arranger Gordon Jenkins. Bing listened to it once and said, 'Hey! That's it!'

He recorded it on 29 December 1943, and within a week it was hitting throughout the country. Another one of those rare occasions when the Groaner had chosen a song for himself, although he had picked a real winner a few years earlier in 'Sweet Leilani'.

Bing had been on holiday with Dixie in Honolulu, at the Royal Hawaiian Hotel, where the composer, bandleader Harry Owens, played it nightly as his signature tune. The crooner was much taken with the melody, which Owens had written for his daughter Leilani—'Flower of Heaven'—and dearly wanted to include it in his movie, *Waikiki Wedding* then in preparation. But Owens wasn't all that keen to let the song move out of its natural environment into the great big world—even if it were going to net him a fortune with Bing's backing. Crosby managed to talk him into it after a session involving a fair number of local brews. But it wasn't going to be all that easy to get the song into the film.

'The producer was a man named Arthur Hornblow, who'd had some brilliant successes,' says Bing, 'but he was a difficult man. If he had something he thought should be done, you just had to do it his way. I knew a spot in the script where this song would go very well, but Hornblow said there was no chance, they had all the good songs they needed.'

Bing was not to be put off: 'I told him it was a hit in Hawaii and we had the benefit of knowing it to be a hit and it was likely that it'd become a hit in the States too, so why not take advantage of that? But again he said there was no chance.

'Finally we started the picture and we came to the scene that I had in mind. I raised the matter again with him and once more he said no. So, off I went to the golf course! I said, "When you change your mind, I'll be back." The picture was about half-finished and we stewed for a day or two—until eventually he said, "We'll put the damned thing in!" '

Not only was 'Sweet Leilani' a world hit. It won a best-song Oscar . . .

Golf was always the great escape route. During the war years NBC insisted that nobody should be allowed through the studio doors without an official pass. Even famous faces like Bing, a regular there to broadcast his radio show. Of course, he forgot his pass one day and sure enough they wouldn't let him in.

'If I can't get in,' shrugged the crooner, 'there's no use hanging around, so I'm going out to Lakeside to play a little golf.'

Writer Carroll Carroll rushed from the studio as Bing was heading for his car and said he would try to get him in on his pass. But that didn't work either. Carroll phoned the studio chief to try to sort out the impasse, but this only produced the comment: 'If I forgot my pass they wouldn't let *me* in.' To which Carroll retorted: 'If you forgot your pass you wouldn't have an hour of dead air between nine to ten o'clock tonight—because Bing is going to shoot some golf.' The studio head had to relent and guarantee that Bing was indeed Bing . . .

In that *Going My Way* year of '43 the Groaner made a rare appearance at the White House. Politics, along with religion and his private life, was one of the subjects he avoided getting involved with publicly. Unlike other show-business celebrities, he has never been photographed with Presidential candidates, nor has he been seen embracing incumbent Presidents at White House functions.

Not that Bing is without political opinions. The entire Crosby family have always been staunch supporters of the Republican Party, but Larry Crosby advised him against being seen to have political leanings.

'I had been a little in politics,' said Larry, 'in the State Legislature, but it was my idea that it is bad publicity to oppose either party—so we kept out of it. I told Bing that he'd got a lot of Republican fans, but he'd also got a lot of Democrat friends who were buying cinema tickets as well, so why antagonise them?'

But this was wartime and the invitation to the White House was to mark his appearance in a Navy show in Washington, D.C. With him was Bob Weitman, manager of the New York Paramount, and they were welcomed at the reception by Mrs Franklin D. Roosevelt, who was walking among the guests with a tray of cookies.

'Bing just walked over to the First Lady,' said Weitman, 'and asked her: "Mrs President, is that what we're going to get for lunch, cookies?" She smiled and said it was the best the White House can afford. That's the way Bing was . . .'

The year was marked by two other unrelated events that didn't rate world headlines but are worthy of recording.

The wide-eyed Joan Crawford, veteran of Hollywood epics since the old days of silent films, was struck with sheer terror when she appeared with Crosby on the Kraft show and had to be supported physically at the microphone.

Don Bingo, one of Bing's slow-coach horses and a half-brother to Ligaroti, won the 10,000 dollar Suburban Handicap at Belmont Park . . .

Life was definitely on the move, and not only with the War Bond drives with Phil Silvers; whistle-stop shows put on at any place in the country where an audience would gather.

The boys Over There in Europe were calling . . .

Chapter Twelve

The expectancy was everywhere, even in Germany, although there the feeling was coupled with fear. For this was 1944; the year that something had to give in Europe. The talk of invasion had long been on the lips of everyone in Britain and in France, now in its fourth year under the Nazi yoke. The only questions remaining were where and when would the invasion come? And Hitler was more worried about it than anyone else as his grey-green hordes fell back on the Eastern Front with Russia. But the Western Wall would hold, his people were told; the fortress Europa would remain intact.

It was pierced and began to crumble on the Longest Day, 6 June, when Allied troops landed on the Normandy beaches. The drive to victory had begun.

Bing Crosby—and the rest of California—would have heard the stupendous news of the landings the evening before, their clocks now nine hours back, due to double British Summertime. The Groaner had finished a day's work on a patriotic movie called *Here Come the Waves* with Betty Hutton, a light-hearted, flag-waving effort which had Bing in naval uniform with members of the WAVES.

In a little over two months he was to be at sea himself, crossing the Atlantic aboard the Ile de France, once a luxury liner on the Blue Riband run and now a drab, blacked-out troopship, on his way to Europe and the front.

Perhaps the best thing that came out of the film was 'That Old Black Magic', the Mercer–Arlen song that had been unceremoniously dropped from *Star-Spangled Rhythm* two years before. Paramount boss Buddy DeSylva, who had also been a songwriter of some considerable talent himself, remembered it and suggested that it should be given a new lease of life in *Here Come the Waves*.

But it didn't turn out to be exactly quite the same song. Mercer and Arlen had lost their original lyrics and had to start all over again with new lines . . .

Bing packed his bags after the film was securely in the can and set sail for the Clyde with thousands of American reinforcements for the war zones of Europe. Many of them were paratroopers, tough, dedicated fighters who weren't exactly enchanted by 'Sweet Leilani' and 'Love in Bloom'. He gave three shows daily during the voyage as they squatted row upon row in a liner denuded of much of its furniture and fittings. And they gave him a new nickname: Uncle Sam Without Whiskers.

He landed in Scotland on 25 August 1944, and headed for London. But even in the black-out he was recognised and a crowd gathered when he arrived at St Enoch's Station in Glasgow to catch the sleeper to town. As they milled round him seeking autographs Crosby noticed that one porter was taking more notice of him than anyone else and began to think that perhaps a button or two were undone in a vital area. Bing tackled him.

'I was just having a good look,' said the porter, 'because Bob Hope said you were a fat little man.'

Then women porters began to press the crooner for a song. But first he asked them to give him a chorus of the rousing 'I Belong to Glasgow'. In return, the Crosby tones echoed through St Enoch's with 'Where the Blue of the Night'.

It was his first-ever performance in Europe . . .

In London, he checked into Claridges but wasted little time before he was out again, strolling towards Marble Arch and Hyde Park, pipe in mouth, marvelling at how peaceful the capital looked this summer day.

On his way to the Serpentine a woman fan beseeched him to sing. 'I only sing in Berkeley Square,' he said with a mischievous Crosby smile, obviously thinking of the nightingale that was said to serenade there.

The nearest thing to excitement that London could furnish him with that morning was the sight of a riderless grey pony that made a mad dash from Rotten Row. It vanished into the trees before Bing could try to catch it.

When reporters caught up with him he was asked if he were going to do any shopping. 'I have no money and no coupons,' he confessed. 'Anyhow, I much prefer a quiet stroll around.'

He also revealed that he thought he was going to the Pacific, 'But they sent me over here instead. But I always wanted to come to England and now I'm here I want to see the things most people want to see, I guess—and that includes the Thames, Westminster Abbey, Ascot, Aintree and a few golf courses.'

He had much earlier received an SOS from the Pacific, where US forces had been having a tough time and the fighting had been particularly bloody. When General Douglas MacArthur and his men were marooned during the worst days on Bataan, MacArthur radioed President Roosevelt that the troops wanted to hear Crosby sing. They did, with White House co-operation.

Now in London, the Groaner, tie-less and in sportscoat, reported to American Army Headquarters where he was mobbed by officers and GIs alike. One lieutenant gave him a roll of one-dollar bills to sign, which he did, with the pen he kept at the ready in his jacket breast pocket.

Accompanying Bing on his tour were what he called 'my little company'. There were five of them. A guitar player and an accordianist to accompany Crosby, Gene Darrell, another singer, dancer Darlene Garner and a comedienne named Jo De Rita.

But London wasn't to be as peaceful as Crosby thought. He had arrived in the middle of the doodle-bug attacks on the city —jet-propelled flying bombs launched from occupied territory. When BBC executive Cecil Madden, responsible for light entertainment in Allied Expeditionary Forces programmes, called two days later to collect him for a broadcast he found the crooner standing on his hotel balcony watching the bombs go by. Alongside him was tough-guy actor Broderick Crawford, then a sergeant with the US armed Services.

The air-raid alert was still in progress when the three hurried into a car that was to take Bing to the Queensberry All-Services Club (actually the Casino Theatre) in Soho for a BBC Variety Bandbox programme. Despite the danger, crowds waited to catch a glimpse of Crosby outside the building.

Said Cecil Madden: 'Bing went very pale when he saw the tremendous numbers and thought we'd never get out of the car. American Military Police formed a passage from the car to the stagedoor. Broderick Crawford ducked and went first. Then Bing ducked and ran across. I forgot to duck and as the girls pushed all their autograph books forward all the buttons of my suit were mown off.'

The Queensberry Club was supposed to seat two thousand people, but for that edition of Variety Bandbox almost five thousand crammed in.

Pat Kirkwood was to sing duets with Bing, Geraldo was conducting his Concert Orchestra and Manning Sherwin who wrote 'A Nightingale Sang in Berkeley Square' played piano. BBC producer Stephen Williams chose Tommy Handley, Britain's biggest radio star of the day, as emcee.

'Oh, he's the chap that's got this very popular ITMA programme—full of catch-phrases, I believe,' said Bing when Williams told him about Tommy. He also fed him some of the catch-phrases.

'He made a few notes about them on his cuff,' Williams recalled, 'and said he'd remember them. Tommy did his act and towards the end of it he suddenly said "Now I've got a very pleasant surprise for you . . ." Unfortunately, in the wings one couldn't hear exactly what was being said. Bing slightly anticipated his cue and came on.

'The entire audience rose and shouted and shouted. They all recognised him at once. A Bandbox audience was normally quite easily controllable, but on this occasion it was absolutely hopeless and the din went on for at least three minutes.

'Tommy had been out the previous afternoon, and bought Bing a small pipe in a leather case. He produced it from his pocket and said, "I've bought this for you, sir." Bing picked up his cue magnificently and, in the words of ITMA's Dorothy Summers, said, "Oh isn't that nice!" '

Before the programme, old trouper Tommy Handley surprisingly became very nervous and wanted to rehearse with Crosby before they went on. The crooner wasn't having any of that and soothed the edgy Handley by saying: 'Just watch me go out and lay the biggest egg you've ever seen.'

The show, of course, was a complete success. He sang four songs, including the very popular 'San Fernando Valley'. On

'Moonlight Becomes You' he forgot some of the words but a couple of boo-boo-boos got him out of that one.

When the show was over, the audience refused to leave and demanded more. And got it. An impromptu show went on and on. When it looked as though there was a danger of running out of songs and material Cecil Madden hurriedly sent for one of Britain's youngest girl singers, Anne Shelton, to sing duets with Bing.

The Groaner had mentioned her earlier in the day, when he likened her to America's Dinah Shore. Anne was now at home relaxing. Her phone rang and a voice said: 'Miss Shelton, would you come to the Queensberry Club—Bing Crosby is waiting to meet you?'

'Oh I can't, I'm having tea with the King!' she said. And hung up.

Then the phone rang again and this time it was Cecil Madden, who repeated the request and managed to convince her it was no leg-pull.

A taxi rushed her to the club, where she was quickly hustled into the dressing rooms. 'And there he was,' she said years later, 'sitting on a table with a cup of tea in his hand and I couldn't see anything except those two big blue eyes. And he says, "Hiya, doll, I'd like you to sing with me."

'It was just ridiculous, I wasn't even sixteen and my knees felt like dough. He asked me to sing "Easter Parade" with him. We didn't rehearse at all, but we arranged a little gag: he said "Anne, what sort of a guy do you like?" and I said, "Oh I like Charles Boyer, because he looks into your eyes and flutters those long eyelashes." Bing's punchline was, "What do you want, love or air conditioning?" Then he said, "I bet you I can kiss you without touching you—I bet you two bob?"

'I had no idea he was going to really kiss me, so I told him to try. And he kissed me. "But," I protested, "you touched me." "So I did," he said, "and here's your two bob!" I still have that two shillings in a little plastic case.'

The duet was well-received, but one Press critic reviewed Anne's entrance thus: 'Anne Shelton walked on with a face like pre-war white flour . . .'

When the producers finally managed to clear the theatre, Lord Queensberry took Bing and the cast for a celebration supper at Kettners, a top Soho eaterie nearby.

'It was blackout,' says Bing, 'and it was awful foggy. Brod Crawford was with me and we were just kind of following the kerb and we fell in the gutter a couple of times. Of course we'd had a few belts at the bottle. Finally we got to the restaurant and quite a crowd gathered and they kept calling for a song.'

Air-raid wardens, worried about the size of the crowd and the bomb danger, went into the restaurant and pleaded with Bing to help. He did. He opened the first-floor window and, with the restaurant lights all out, swung his feet over the sill and sat on it. The police allowed two girls to shine torches on him and there he sat and sang.

Crosby was much concerned that the crowd, most of whom were disappointed at not being able to get into the Queensberry Club, would get into trouble: 'I told them they'd better disperse because it's illegal for any gathering of over two to three people due to the bombing. They said I'd got to sing something first. So I sang "Pennies From Heaven". They dispersed rather quickly—and I thought it was a form of criticism the way they took off.'

Pennies from heaven were more welcome than bombs . . .

For the record: The Variety Bandbox show was recorded on 27 August 1944, and broadcast the following week. Flying bombs were the reason why the programme did not go out 'live'. Explained producer Stephen Williams: 'We didn't want troops listening overseas to hear the sound of explosions in case it worried them about the fate of the people at home.'

A few days later, on 31 August, Bing was on stage crooning at the tumultuous opening of the Stage Door Canteen just off Piccadilly Circus. Fred Astaire was with him and, among others, Beatrice Lillie, Jack Buchanan and Nervo and Knox.

Mr Anthony Eden came from the war Cabinet to make the opening speech and talked about the doodle-bugs, saying, 'They are heading for the great round-up.'

Bing talked about Hope . . .

As usual, Crosby packed his days—and even became a secret weapon in his own right! From London he was persuaded to broadcast to Germany and particularly to the enemy soldiers. He talked and sang in phonetic German and expressed the hope that soon Germany would know the freedom that Americans and Britons enjoy. And the enemy fondly called him Der Bingle . . .

He travelled to an American military hospital to sing to four British children—the sole survivors of forty-one who were in an infants' school at Freckleton, Lancs, when a Liberator bomber crashed on it.

The children asked for 'White Christmas' and 'Easter Parade' and he couldn't refuse them.

He also squeezed in some recorded sessions with the late Glenn Miller and his orchestra, both in Bedford, where they were stationed for some months, and at the BBC's Paris Cinema studio in Lower Regent Street, London. Then these were broadcast on a Forces' network. Sadly, the public never got to hear them again. The recordings were stored in the BBC archives—but either vanished or were destroyed. There was a rumour that some misguided official got rid of them because 'neither artist was likely to sustain'. The fact is that the recordings are no longer there.

Cecil Madden—who was later to become the world's first television producer—invited Crosby to sing with Miller at the Paris Cinema, where his first song was to be 'Poinciana'.

'He rehearsed it once,' said Madden, 'and the person who got nervous was Glenn Miller. He was really quite shaky and said they must run through it again. Bing absolutely refused. He said, "What, and make all these boys tired? Glenn, dear boy, just wave your baton and I promise I'll come in." And, of course, he did it perfectly.'

Within a few months Glenn Miller would be dead, lost in a small plane over the English Channel on his way to organise dates for the band in liberated Paris.

After London, Crosby set off to sing to the troops in the field in France—and invaded enemy-occupied territory at the same time.

Not content with playing bases, he decided to go out and look for the guys who didn't get a chance to go to a concert. So off he went in a Jeep with his guitar player to sing to the GI Joes on duty in their foxholes.

The Special Services driver was told to follow the Forces' telephone cables along a road leading out of Cherbourg until they reached the American lines.

'But the advance was so rapid at this time that the troops would frequently get ahead of their lines of communication,' says Bing. 'The advice was that if you don't see our telephone lines, turn round and come back. Suddenly I noticed we were out of lines, but we pushed on to a little town and took a look ahead through field-glasses. We saw some strange-looking equipment some way away. Yeh, it was German . . .'

Jeep and Groaner made a smart about-turn.

That evening, the American Chief of Staff, General George C. Marshall, gave a dinner for Bing and asked him where he had been during the day. The crooner mentioned the name of the little town where the Jeep had halted. Startled, General Marshall walked across to a wall map and peered at it. 'We haven't taken that yet, it's still in German hands,' he said.

Bing's retort was classic: 'Well, we had it for a few minutes this morning!'

The Supreme Commander of the Allied Forces, General Dwight D. Eisenhower, affectionately known as Ike, had the Groaner along to lunch at his Versailles H.Q. They ended up getting together a barber-shop quartet with Ike singing baritone. He also lent Bing his five-star staff car for a few days and it was observed parked outside some of the joints that were normally not the haunts of five-star generals.

In France he met up again with Fred Astaire—who for some unexplained reason seemed to be better known than Crosby around those parts.

Says Bing: 'We met for breakfast a couple of times and the waitresses were French, of course. They kept looking at him, but didn't pay any attention to me. Finally, one of them came running over with an old magazine with a picture in it of him and Ginger Rogers—and pointed at him. Then they all shrieked and clapped their hands and jumped up and down. They never did dig me; I didn't get a tumble.'

There was little rest to come. The deadline for his return to the United States had been set at 1 November. A mountain of work awaited him, not the least an almost immediate start on *Road to Utopia*, fourth in the series with regulars Hope and Lamour.

It was the first to be made without writers Hartman and Butler. The screenplay was written by two of Bob Hope's former radio show writers—Norman Panama and Melvin Frank.

The only stipulation made by Paramount was that the film should be set in Alaska during the Gold Rush days. There was nothing else, and Mel Frank—who was to find fame in the 'seventies with his Oscar-winning Glenda Jackson film *A Touch of Class*—had the daunting task of explaining the writer's ideas to the big three.

'In those days,' said Frank, 'they were enormous stars; it's impossible to imagine the prestige of those three people. You really had to have their permission, even though they were under contract and technically could be forced to do what you wanted.

'First we had to sit down with Mr Crosby and tell him the story. And it sounded like it was going to be a Bing Crosby picture! Then we had to tell Bob Hope the story—so that it sounded attractive from his point of view. Then, of course, we told it to Dorothy Lamour.'

All three liked the Panama–Frank ideas. The basis of the 'Road' series was that the boys would be put into impossible situations and then somehow escape. And this script contained just the right ingredients, although some of the plans turned out to be a little too hair-raising.

One scene called for our heroes to share the stage with a rather grisly extra—a real live bear. It had been hired with its trainer and was kept off-set in a cage.

'In the scene,' said Bob, 'Bing and I had to be hiding under a carpet when this bear, now let off its chain, walked in looking for us. We had been told that after the director said "Cut!" we weren't to move until the trainer had the bear back on the chain and into the cage.

'We didn't realise how important that was until after the scene. During it, the bear walked over this lump—which consisted of Crosby and myself—and growled. Believe me, Crosby and I had a laundry problem right there! After the fellow said "cut" and the trainer had said, "Okay, I've got him back in the cage", Crosby got up and said, "Well, that's all with this thing! To hell with that! Don't ever ask me to do a thing like that again"—and a nurse carried me out . . .'

Next day the bear went beserk and tore its trainer's arm off.

Another scene decreed that the boys should be out in the cold wastes of Alaska. Hope still shivered at the memory of it: 'We were walking along an ice glacier,' he said, 'and if we'd have slipped off we'd have fallen fifty or sixty feet. In those days, we were numbers one and two at the box-office. Paramount didn't care—I guess it was another way of dropping your option.'

Worse was to come. 'Bing and I were climbing up the side of this mountain,' said Bob, 'and he was on the bottom. The rope broke and I fell back onto him, and he's had back trouble ever since—at least that's what he claims on the first tee!'

Despite the dangers, Bing remembers those days as being great fun: 'Oh! we had a ball. A million laughs,' he says. 'We always had directors that sort of swung with us and you could kind of suit your own schedule. If I had a big golf game, I'd say, "Can't you do something with Lamour, or with Bob?" And he'd do the same. If there was an important race at Santa Anita we'd take the afternoon off and go to the races and let them shoot something with some of the other people. You could just about do as you pleased.'

Hope too found the free-and-easy atmosphere of the 'Road' series most attractive: 'We were doing so many things. I was doing radio, had conferences with my writers in the dressing-room—or with my tax-man. And Bing would go over to the driving-range or somewhere, so when everything was ready to shoot a scene, there would be a shout "OK! Find them!" It used to take half-an-hour to find us. But when we made a picture where we had money involved we never left the set . . .'

The Crosby and Hope off-screen antics caused almost as much amusement to the film crew as the pair's on-camera patter. They couldn't even get to the studio first thing in the morning without clowning.

Jimmy Cottrell, the bumptious boxer from Spokane, remembered how a short bicycle ride was regularly turned into a virtual farce: 'Bing's dressing-room was close to Stage Five and Bob's was down an alley nearby. Neither would set-off for the set first; they always wanted the other to get there before.

'Bing would get his bicycle and start out, but he'd turn left and go clear round and return the back-way to watch for Hope. Then Hope, having seen Bing, would start-off, figuring well, Crosby's up there. He'd walk in to the studio and say, "Where's the Groaner? Where's Fatso?" But Bing was still back in his dressing-room.'

Possibly because of the continuing success of *Going My Way* and the scheduled *Bells of St Mary's* follow-up, *Road to Utopia* didn't reach the screens until 1946. But there was no shortage of Bing during that hectic 1944.

Somewhere along the line he was rather cheekily borrowed

by Warners along with the all-important word for *Road to Victory*, a one-reel propaganda film which featured Cary Grant and had Bing singing the title song.

And somehow he managed to slip away to a Sam Goldwyn production of Bob Hope in *The Princess and the Pirate* for a cameo role in the final scene in which, as a simple sailor, he wins the embraces of the lovely Virginia Mayo.

'Stick around son,' he says to Hope, 'something older may show up for you.'

'How do you like that?' snorts Hope. 'I knock my brains out for nine reels and a bit player from Paramount comes over and gets the girl. This is the last picture, I do for Goldwyn.'

There was a bit Bing had to do for another movie that went before the cameras that October—*Out of This World*, which starred Eddie Bracken and the peek-a-boo hair girl Veronica Lake. It was a satire on the bobby-sox cult that was being whipped up by a new boy being labelled as the Boney Baritone. A threat to the Groaner, some people were already saying and only time could tell . . .

Meanwhile, all Bing had to do was sing three songs for Eddie Bracken to mime to in the movie. The only screen credits Crosby received were a caption, 'Eddie Bracken's songs are sung by a great friend of his and yours' and the words 'Thanks, Bing' said by Eddie, looking into the camera, in the final scene.

There was a more tangible credit: the Groaner's fee was twenty-six thousand dollars . . .

And his four growing lads did not come off so badly, either. Gary, Dennis, Philip and Lindsay had feature roles in *Out of This World* and were said by the film company each to have been paid five thousand dollars. None was yet in his teens.

They were seen again almost at the same time in 'Duffy's Tavern', another of those large-scale, star-studded vehicles based on characters created by Ed Gardner for his popular radio show of the same title.

Bing sung a parody of 'Swinging on a Star' with a group that included Betty Hutton and appeared with the four boys—all wearing loud pyjamas that had become synonymous with their father—in a bed-time story sketch with humourist Robert Benchley.

Dad had always insisted that whatever work the boys did they should be paid the same rate as anyone else. It didn't always work out to their advantage. When they worked on his ranch in Nevada they got the same as an ordinary hand. But Uncle Everett frequently went into bat for them.

When Paramount once wanted Gary for a brief appearance they decided to be generous by upping the fifty-dollar minimum fee to seventy-five. When Everett found out he was livid. 'Are you kidding?' he asked the studio—and came away from the negotiations with a twenty-five hundred dollar War Bond for Gary instead . . .

Amid all this uproar that was in real life road-to-victory 1944, the Groaner was keeping a watchful eye on the Boney Baritone. In a gesture that might have been considered by some to be foolhardy Bing invited him to guest on his radio show on 16 November . . .

Chapter Thirteen

Francis Albert Sinatra was some fourteen-and-a-half years younger than Harry Lillis Crosby and says he was so skinny as a kid that 'my old man thought I was a clarinet'.

In his teens in Hoboken, New Jersey, he was inspired by the fantastic success story of Bing and wanted to be like him—but not a carbon copy. When he was a lean young man of seventeen he had a brief dressing-room meeting with the Groaner backstage at a venue in Newark, New Jersey, which was probably effected by the fact that Bing had been friendly with Sinatra's father Martin, a bantamweight who boxed under the name of Marty O'Brien, although he was a Sicilian. Thereafter, young Frank took the familiar road to stardom: studio warm-up singer, talent shows, big band singer with Harry James and Tommy Dorsey. The big pay-off came around Christmastide 1942 when he made the first of many knock-out appearances at the New York Paramount. For the first time in show business history, girls in an audience screamed and swooned. They made so much noise that it was difficult to hear the Benny Goodman band accompanying Frank. It was the birth of a new phenomenon that would endure right through to the Beatle days and afterwards. The Boney Baritone became the Swooner Crooner and the devotees in both Crosby and Sinatra camps were now talking about the battle of the Swooner v. the Crooner. The writers of the day had one recurring question for Sinatra: 'Do you think you will ever replace Bing?'

'Time will tell,' he answered modestly. But he did have this to say as well: 'I don't believe that any singer has enjoyed the unanimous acclaim of the American public as well as performers and musicians, as much as Bing. I know that I am indebted to him for the inspiration he has given me and I must admit that I'm probably one of his first and most enthusiastic rooters. He is truly the Will Rogers of song and I believe that he holds the same affection in the hearts of the public as that great man did.' (Rogers was an ex-cowhand who found fame as a home-spun philosopher, appeared in films and was killed in an air crash in 1935.)

Now, in the fading days of 1944, the inspirer and the inspired were to appear together for the first time on Bing's Kraft radio show.

After a lengthy introduction, Sinatra said for the listening millions to hear: 'Bing, I came here tonight because you can do me a big favour.'

'You know me, anything—just ask,' said the Groaner.

'Retire!' said Frank.

But it was just more fuel being added to a friendly feud that was being built up in Hope–Crosby style. Sinatra now had a radio show and the same man was supplying the gags for both programmes, the busy Mr Carroll Carroll, who said: 'Bing was the avuncular elder man who wanted to see a young man come along and make it; Frank was the impatient newcomer who wanted to push everything aside and get in there.'

Against Sinatra was his lack of height, which resulted in such wisecracks as: 'He looked up to everyone—because that was the only way he had to look.'

Among Bing's come-back lines were these gems:

'He weighed seven pounds at birth and has been losing ever since.'

'When he went to school he didn't dare turn sideways for fear the teacher would mark him absent.'

And asked if Frank was 'his boy' he would quip: 'Naw! Mine are all living!'

Much later in life, Crosby was to give this opinion of him: 'Frank's hot-headed. If he likes you, he'll do anything for you, but if he doesn't like you he can be the most ornery cuss you've ever known.'

And there was this letter that Bing wrote to writer George

Simon after Sinatra had emerged triumphant from a sad and lonely period in the doldrums around the late 'forties and early 'fifties:

'The most admirable thing about Frank is his great courage and determination. After a meteoric beginning he had every conceivable reversal and disappointment socially, professionally and privately. Very few people in our business can rally from something like this. But he did—and big! And all by himself. He made the moves and the decisions until now he's the biggest man in a wider scope of entertainment fields than any one we have. Something like this just doesn't happen accidentally. We know of his great talent, but he must have great taste and discrimination in addition. As a person he's a loyal devoted friend and an implacable enemy. But then he's a Sicilian, so what would you? He's awfully good company.'

But now, as 1945 approached and with it the defeat of Germany and Japan, it was on with the feudin'.

When Sinatra's first starring role for RKO in *Higher and Higher* was being prepared that year a cameo appearance was written in for Bing. The two singers had to ride bicycles past each other, then stop, dismount, stick their tongues out and ride on . . .

And in a one-reeler, *All-Star Bond Rally*, made for the War Activities Committee and the US Treasury Department, Bing sang 'Buy, Buy Bonds' and then watched from the wings—as if in envy—while Sinatra followed, singing 'Saturday Night'.

It was an anniversary year for Crosby; marking twenty momentous years since he had trekked to Los Angeles with Al Rinker in the battered Model-T. It was an opportune time for stock-taking. American magazines were estimating his annual earnings to be at least a million dollars.

For his Paramount movies the contract stipulated a minimum of one hundred and fifty thousand dollars a film. The average was two a year. It was sometimes more.

On radio he was picking up seven and a half thousand dollars a time for half an hour's work—the highest-paid performer on the air.

His record royalties for that year were to total four hundred thousand dollars from eight million discs sold. His take was five cents a record—twice what most other artists received.

In these three areas alone he was in the million dollar bracket.

In addition there were his investments, real estate, cattle-rearing and some added enterprises including Bing Crosby Productions Inc., which got under way with *The Great John L*; sponsorship of a touring water follies show; an interest in a fish-packing company and a boxer.

Despite the immense successes and the riches they brought, he remained basically the same old Bing, sloppy of dress and casual of manner.

For years he drove a decrepit 1940 Cadillac the eight miles from his home to the Paramount studios, where he usually arrived in a sportscoat that would disgrace a lesser being.

It was the same during the entire run of the Kraft show. He turned up in rumpled trousers, an assortment of gaudy shirts and invariably a golfing hat. His shoes, it was noticed more than once, were seldom new.

Not for him the trappings of a superstar. Record producer Milt Gabler had one day scheduled a nine a.m. session for the crooner and got there at eight-thirty, expecting to be early. 'But I saw this bicycle by the studio door,' he said. 'It was a Paramount bike and when I walked in there was Bing sitting reading his newspaper and waiting for every one to show up.'

There were times, however, when he had to dress-up; when it was considered bad taste to attend certain Hollywood dinner parties without dinner-jacket and black tie. Radio show announcer Ken Carpenter remembers what happened when Bing once reluctantly agreed to comply with tradition: 'One New Year's Eve, we happened to be doing a show and he was going to a formal party afterwards. So he appeared in full dinner-dress —but with no collar! But this didn't bother him or anybody else, because that was Crosby.'

Bing's dress-sense of course was greatly affected and hampered by his colour-blindness. As eldest son Gary remembers: 'Red and green look alike to him; he knows the traffic lights because one is on the top and the other is on the bottom. But I caught him one day coming out of the house and he was going to a pretty formal affair; at least to him it was formal—he had a tie and blue suit on. I looked down and he had on a pair of brown shoes, and that was back in the days when that was all wrong. I looked at him and said, "Dad, what colour are those shoes you've got on?", and he looked down, then looked me right in the eyes and said, "Dark".'

Another son, Dennis, also has fond memories of his father's difficulty with colours: 'I can remember,' he says, 'my mother used to yell at him as he was going out of the door, "You've got two different coloured socks on!", or his coat would be too bright and he'd say, "It doesn't look too bright to me! That's brown isn't it?" Of course, it wasn't. It was red, bright red.'

Richard Arlen once sent him a frightful polka-dotted shirt for a gag. 'It was purple and red,' said Arlen, 'but Bing thanked me for that "beautiful yellow shirt".

'I've seen him on stage in tuxedo—and brown shoes. It didn't make any difference to him. As far as he was concerned they were black.'

The only other member of the Crosby clan to suffer from colour-blindness was Everett. He managed to get into the Army during World War I only with the help of another recruit—who tapped him on the shoulder when Everett had his hand over the right button during a colour-sense test.

Bing has never really been too bothered about his eye weakness and even says there could have been a good side to it: 'I'd have been very useful in the Air Force,' he grins. 'They like colour-blind people as observers, because camouflage doesn't alter their view of what they see.'

Edith Head, the film industry's top costume designer with a battery of Oscars to her name, was responsible for dressing Bing in practically all his Paramount pictures. 'I just think he's allergic to fashion,' she said, 'even in his own personal clothes. Bing is famous for wearing a horse-blanket for a coat and an old cap for a hat. He has always had this complete disregard for fashion.

'In pictures, we've had to occasionally have him in full dress and he looks fabulous in clothes. But he hates dressing up, which is unusual because most actors adore it.'

Bing's allergy to fashion caused Edith problems, particularly in the 'Road' pictures, where there was usually a strong emphasis on fancy costumes. 'He didn't mind anything that was masculine,' said Edith, 'for instance a Scottish kilt, because he frankly admits he has pretty good legs! But if you tried to get him into something that was a little costumey, he'd say, "Don't these look a little ornate?" In *Road to Morocco* he wasn't terribly fond of the turbans and silks.'

Her worst moment was to come when Bing and Danny Kaye were called upon to dress in drag in the film *White Christmas*.

'In one part,' said Edith, 'the two main girls had to make an escape and the boys were to impersonate them. Bing flatly, definitely, absolutely refused. "I will not wear women's clothes," he said. So we had to fake it a little bit. He agreed to carry a fan, to roll up his trousers and cover them with a shawl. When he makes up his mind, he's like the stubbornest mule in the world and when you open a script with Crosby in it, you just pray that the clothes will be simple.'

Bing's constant wearing of a variety of hats was simply explained: it was the easiest way to cover a bald pate without the nuisance of having to affix a toupee.

'It just drives me crazy to put one of those things on,' he says. 'I have a whole team of them: curly, straight, ash-blond. I even have the *coup de soleil*—through the top. I have names for them; like *latkas*—they're Jewish pancakes—scalp doilys, rugs . . . all kinds of things.'

Bandleading brother Bob Crosby used to make gags in public about them until he found that a lot of people resented it.

Said Bob: 'There's an old Irish saying that "it's a poor bird that befouls it's own nest", so in other words I couldn't tell stories about Bing. Father O'Malley was too sacrosanct, but I could give the same joke to Bob Hope and it would get a laugh.'

One example of the type of gag passed on to Hope: 'Bing doesn't make personal appearances any more: he just sends a toupee. He's got three of them out on the road right now!'

Bing's unconventional attitude to dress was certainly no family trait. According to Larry Crosby their father was always a tidy dresser and 'Everett was considered a dandy and always pretty fancy. But Bing gave me orders to look like a businessman, so I don't go unconventional. He can come round in a sweater, but I've got to wear a coat.'

There was one more film to come in 1945 after *Bells of St Mary's* was completed in July. August saw the start of *Blue Skies*, which teamed Bing again with Fred Astaire. The movie was more or less an anthology of Irving Berlin songs and featured thirty of them (there were forty-two before cutting). Bing sang a massive total of sixteen of them, a feat he never equalled again.

During the summer break he would take the family on vacation up to Hayden Lake in Idaho, where because of the tight rein he kept on them, his four fast-growing sons dubbed him 'The Big Bad Wolf of Hayden Lake'. But, he admitted, he found the seemingly endless shouting matches and admonitions very tiresome.

Deservedly, he was awarded the General Dwight D. Eisenhower Medal by America's National Father's Day Committee for being the outstanding screen father of the year.

There were also to be some end-of-year results in the Crooner v. Swooner stakes.

In a poll of army camps conducted by the magazine Billboard, the Groaner emerged as top male singer with 1188 points, more than the combined total of his three nearest rivals: Sinatra (374), Perry Como (308) and Dick Haymes (308). The colleges of the nation also voted him top over Sinatra and Haymes again with more than their combined score. The same pattern was reflected in other ballots. And the BBC came up with the staggering fact that two-thirds of the requests for Forces Favourites programmes during the war were for Crosby records . . .

Bing's long association with the Kraft Music Hall came to an end in 1945. He left to plan a programme of his own and took John Scott Trotter and some of the musicians with him. But there was still fun and big names to be had in the dying days.

Gracie Fields, the lassie from Lancashire, was touring the States and called in to be Bing's guest. For once in its history, the show under-ran its allotted time and Gracie was asked to give an extra number. 'I told them I'd only got one with me,' she said, 'and they wouldn't understand it—"The Biggest Aspidistra in the World". And before I could try to explain they told me to get on and sing it.'

Within minutes the studio switchboard was jammed with complaints. Americans, unfamiliar with the plant, thought the song was vulgar. 'The biggest ass . . .' Bing repeated, trying to explain the thinking.

'Eventually,' said Gracie, 'I had to go on and say that it wasn't a rude song and that an aspidistra is the nearest thing to a rubber plant.'

Without doubt the biggest singing sensation of the Kraft show—apart from Bing himself—was the re-emergence from retirement in Florida of Al Jolson in the fading days of the programme.

It was an emotional and tremendous experience for Crosby,

who had idolised 'the greatest entertainer of all time'—as he had been called—back in boyhood days. Now here they were on the same stage, working together.

There were fears, however, that the show would not run smoothly, because Jolson had a reputation for giving musical directors a rough time.

'But that didn't happen,' said John Scott Trotter, 'because Bing was like he was. There was absolutely no temperament displayed around the Kraft Music Hall, because Bing didn't display it. He came in to do a job and he expected everyone else to do so.'

It was Scott Trotter, more than anyone, who saw the musical magic of the Crosby–Jolson pairing: 'It was a mutual admiration society and if you listen to early Jolson records, and then listen to the ones after the *Jolson Story*—when he became a regular guest with Crosby—you'll hear there's big a change in his style to Crosby's style of singing.'

One member of the Kraft team who did have trouble with Jolson was Carroll Carroll, who describes him as 'the most miserable man I've ever worked with'.

It was Carroll's lot to take the first script to Jolson's apartment for vetting: 'The first thing he did was to order dinner and he ate while he read, and I noticed him make a little notation in the margin. I sat there and watched him eat—which wasn't an exciting thing in itself—and finally he finished.

'He went over to the mantlepiece and got himself some candy, the most expensive you could buy, ate it and said "Okay kid"— that was the whole conversation. I couldn't wait to get in the elevator to see what the hell he'd written. In the margin, with no indication to what they referred, were the words "make better".

'Next morning my boss asked how I made out with Jolson. I told him about the "make better" note and he said, "Well did you?" and I said, "Yeah—I read it again this morning and it read better than it did last night." I didn't do anything to it and we ran it the way it was. The next time I went up to see him at his apartment I stopped at a bakery and bought myself a little bag of rolls to eat. He never noticed . . .'

Jolson never showed that side of his nature to his peers and reserved it exclusively for those he thought he could dominate. But there was at least one occasion when the tables were turned.

A young writer on the show had been trying to explain to Jolson where he was going wrong with a line. The singer was livid.

'You're telling Joly what to do! Come outside.' Outside the studio, Jolson asked the writer to point out his car—a Chevrolet.

'Well,' thundered Jolson, 'that's mine over there—a Cadillac!'

'Well, I've something you haven't got,' the writer stormed.

'What's that?' snapped Jolson.

'One friend.'

The writer who really managed to deal with Jolson on the Kraft programmes was the late Bill Morrow. He had an understanding way of coping with difficult guests. As Scott Trotter pointed out: 'Jolson was a very lonely and frustrated performer at that time, and Bill Morrow knew this and could talk to him. He also gave Judy Garland guest spots when she was at her lowest ebb with M-G-M and she actually made her come-back on the Crosby shows.'

When Bing refused to re-sign with the Kraft Music Hall the star chosen to take over for him as emcee was Al Jolson!

The Groaner took his new programme—simply called 'The Bing Crosby Show' to San Francisco for its start. He had become bored with Los Angeles audiences. He found them dull and felt that they had heard all the jokes before; that they had become so blasé they wouldn't laugh as much as they should. San Franciscans welcomed the move and later Bing took the show on the road around the West Coast.

He was under the Philco banner on ABC, America's third largest network, and when the first show went out over the air on 16 October 1946, it made history. It was the first national radio programme ever to have been recorded and was to change the face of American broadcasting, even though the technique, as yet, was rather primitive. It was also one of the most heavily promoted radio shows of all time. Extensive advertising proclaimed 'Wednesday is Bing's Day'.

The shows were put on to discs—three to each half-hour programme—and sent to radio stations throughout the country. For the first time they could decide themselves when a programme should be broadcast. Until then a 'live' show put on at 8 pm in Los Angeles would be heard at 11 pm in the East because of the zonal time factor.

The initial show was hailed as a tremendous step forward. The *New York Times* called it a 'portentous premier' and went on to enthuse: 'Mr Crosby has delivered a major, if not fatal, blow to the outworn and unrealistic prejudice against the recorded program . . .'

But in practice the idea began to sour a little. The discs were being pressed in a hurry and the quality was suffering. And engineers in some of the local stations were not particularly careful at putting them on and frequently spoiled the continuity. Before long the Crosby ratings began to slip and ABC had a major worry on its hands.

A back-room boy with Crosby Enterprises named John Mullin was on hand with a revolutionary remedy . . . magnetic tape.

Mullin had been serving with the Royal Air Force in Britain in 1942 when he discovered that the Germans must have a vital new recording system.

It was his duty to try to find signs of any development in enemy communications equipment. 'Germany was on the air all night,' he said. 'We heard beautiful music and you'd swear there was a live orchestra playing. It went on and on without a break and it was obvious that they weren't using 78 rpm records because there was no scratching or surface noise.'

He had to wait a few more years until the Allies marched into Frankfurt to find the answer. Tape . . .

With great foresight he dismantled two of the Radio Frankfurt machines and mailed the parts to himself at his home address in San Francisco along with fifty rolls of plastic tape.

'When I got home after the war, all the bits had arrived,' he said. 'I put them back together again and in April 1946, was able to give a demonstration to the Institute of Radio Engineers in San Francisco.'

Within a year, Mullin was demonstrating his captured, makeshift machines to Crosby programme producers and the first-ever show on tape was recorded in August and broadcast over the ABC network on 1 October 1947.

The two ramshackle machines, however, were not going to last for ever, so Bing Crosby Enterprises, then a tiny six-man company in San Carlos, on the San Francisco peninsula, formed an association with the Ampex company. John Mullin and Ampex engineers worked round the clock to produce the first and more sophisticated—machine, the Ampex 200.

It boomed and Crosby Enterprises were responsible for worldwide sales. The first customer was ABC with twelve machines—four each for studios in New York, Chicago and Hollywood—to transmit Bing's radio show.

Thus Mullin's souvenir of war—nurtured and encouraged by the Groaner—gave birth to a multi-million-dollar industry and spawned a new corporate giant in Ampex.

Tape would eventually revolutionise not only broadcasting, but the recording industry, films and television.

Bing's involvement with tape recording began some fifty years after the Danish physicist Valdemar Poulsen invented magnetic recording in 1898. Ironically, the crooner's songs of love and peace were taped on machines developed initially as weapons of war.

The Germans called them Magnetophons and they had been used by the Nazi war machine to broadcast Der Fuehrer's speeches and other propaganda throughout Europe at a time when Germany was crumbling.

The Gestapo had also used them for interrogation and were able, by judicious editing, to concoct confessions from tortured prisoners.

So it took a Danish physicist, a German madman and an American crooner to produce the device which changed the course of broadcasting.

Mullin went on to discover that he could tape TV and as early as 1951 called a Press conference to demonstrate what he called VTR (video tape recording). Aircraft were shown landing and taking off. Within a few months he was taping colour. But Ampex were working along the same lines and eventually outstripped the Crosby outfit.

'Their system was so superior to ours,' said Mullin, 'that we recommended to Bing that he stopped further development because we didn't stand a chance.'

So in 1956 he was to sell the electronics division of Bing Crosby Enterprises to the Minnesota Mining and Manufacturing Company—who in the early days had been asked to produce an alternative tape when Mullin's original fifty tapes were becoming exhausted.

Tape was a boon to Bing in the post-war 'forties. The show could now be recorded practically anywhere, cut, spliced, edited, pieced together. With audiences, or without. As happened when Rosemary Clooney, one of the biggest successes of his new show, became pregnant.

Rosemary, wife of actor José Ferrer, was confined to her Beverly Hills home for many months.

'I was allowed to come downstairs,' she said, 'and Bing suggested that we should try to find some place to record our part of the show in the house.'

The Groaner took a good look around and hit upon the basement den—where many years ago his old friendly rival Russ Columbo had accidentally shot himself dead . . .

'We were able to isolate ourselves there and got pretty good quality,' said Miss Clooney. 'Bing found it very comfortable.'

The home-recording sessions were long but spaced by two-month intervals. They would tape enough material—and commercials—to last for weeks.

Even when Rosemary was back on the road again, Crosby tried to find ways of cutting back on the amount of regular work needed to get the show on to the air.

The late Buddy Cole, a rare piano talent who had worked with Marlene Dietrich, was called in. Shortly before his death he said: 'I'd go in and record a basic track with Bing or Rosie with just the rhythm backing. I've done as many as twenty tunes in a day with Bing. Then, two or three days later, we'd play them back and add electric guitars, organ, kettle drums, chimes, or whatever.'

At one time, Buddy had canned nearly three hundred Crosby songs, two hundred of Clooney's and forty duets. They were to last until the show ended its run in 1955.

There was no cutting corners, however, with the oh-so-nervous but delightful Miss Peggy Lee. While the radio show was going out from San Francisco Bing spent a lot of time looking after her. He was, she said, quite a romantic.

'He took me out to dinner once and I got up nerve enough to tell him about how sad I felt at one movie when he didn't get the girl. I was so in sympathy with him that when he sang this song "Down By The River", I cried and cried.

'So he pretended that we were sort of sight-seeing in San Francisco and we went around to different little bistros until finally he found a pianist who knew the song and Bing sang it especially for me.'

Later, when Peggy's husband was seriously ill in hospital and not expected to live, the crooner showed his concern by phoning the hospital every morning to see how he was: 'And he offered me anything,' said Peggy, 'money, blood—even to sit with our baby. I'll never forget him for that.'

There were no short cuts, either, in the cutting of discs or the making of films in those bustling mid and late 'forties.

In 1946, America had some half-a-million juke boxes into which around fifteen million nickels a day were pushed—and every one had at least two Crosby records on offer.

America's radio stations were putting out about twelve hours of recorded music a day—spun by an estimated eight hundred disc-jockeys. And *The Musical Digest* calculated that Crosby records 'occupy more than forty thousand hours weekly of the eighty thousand hours given to the playing of recorded music on the air across the entire nation'.

In New York, an advertising executive announced his intention of auctioning off his entire collection of Crosby records. He invited bids—for the three and a half thousand discs—of a minimum of ten thousand dollars, which was the going price of an eight-roomed New York house at the time. He was reported to have held out for eighteen thousand dollars.

The collection included every commercial record to date (1946), both foreign and domestic, plus copies of broadcasts, Government-sponsored discs made during the war, records of movie sound-tracks and many personal transcriptions from the Groaner himself . . .

On the film front Crosby was reunited with Barry Fitzgerald for *Welcome Stranger*, in which they swapped their clerical garb of *Going My Way* for the white gowns of medicos. But they failed to recapture the magic of their earlier work.

It was the year too that Paramount tried to entice Greta Garbo out of exile to star opposite Bing in *The Emperor Waltz*. The lonesome Garbo still wanted to be alone and refused the offer. The lovely Joan Fontaine stepped in instead and was wooed by Bing singing 'I Kiss Your Hand, Madame', a number he first recorded and had a hit with in 1929.

The story, set at the beginning of the century, had the Groaner as an American salesman trying to sell the Emperor Franz Josef the new-fangled phonograph that looked very much like the one with the listening dog on the famous Victor label. Accompanied by his mongrel pet Buttons, the crooner whistled his way into the emperor's palace with 'The Whistler and His Dog'. Billy Wilder directed and the film was shot on location in Canada.

It was, of course and of necessity, a year that took him away from home and family and there were persistent rumours that his marriage to Dixie Lee was about to come to an end. It was reported that divorce proceedings were imminent and there was conjecture that they had avoided divorce earlier because of the effect it would have had on *Going My Way* and *Bells of St Mary's*. There was no divorce; the gossip died and the couple would remain married until death parted them . . .

But the Groaner had found a new interest in life—the Pittsburgh Pirates, the baseball team he bought into after giving up his holding in the Del Mar Turf Club.

Even as a child he was in love with the game and he once threatened his parents that he would run away to become a baseball player. He did, in fact, take the field as a semi-professional during his college days.

'I played for the Ideal Laundry, a very big institution in Spokane, who had a baseball team that they supported,' he says.

Now he had become the third largest stockholder in the Pirates, but his commitment wasn't just another show business tax-saving involvement.

First he set about getting the club better known and was photographed many times wearing the team cap or sweater, each emblazoned with a large P. He even managed to introduce their name into a couple of duets.

When the club trained in California in spring he would work-out with them in team uniform. And over the years he has bombarded the Pittsburgh Pirates about players he thought might make possible new signings.

'A tremendous fan,' said general manager Jo Brown. 'He wasn't able to get to many games in Pittsburgh, but in all my years he has never missed seeing us play when we have to go to either Los Angeles or San Francisco. He knows everything about our club, the players and their abilities, our minor league system, our methods and everything else.'

How good a player was Bing?

'I think it was obvious to anybody who saw him play that he had some ability,' said Jo. 'I don't think he had enough to play professionally, but he was more than a green hand. If you had to pick a position for Bing he'd either be a second baseman or a short stop. He has that kind of grace and body control.'

The accolade for baseball is to win the World Series, an

oddly-named competition since it is open only to American teams. The final, held between the two top teams from the two baseball leagues—the American and the National—usually lasts a week and is exciting enough to keep millions of Americans indoors by their television sets.

The Pirates repaid Crosby's devotion by winning the Series twice . . .

It was time, as well, to invest in his own talent.

When *Road to Rio* went before the cameras early in 1947 Crosby, Hope and Paramount each shared one-third of the financial responsibility. But it wasn't all that easy to raise cash for Bing's stake in the picture. His lawyer John O'Melveny found the Californian-based banks a little shy of the movie business at that time. The New York banks far removed from the Hollywood scene were more visionary and backed the Groaner instead. *Road to Rio*—fifth in the series—rewarded all the interested parties by making a substantial profit—although the new-found financial responsibility was not allowed to dull the Crosby–Hope sense of fun altogether. The comedy that was an integral part of the series still spilled over in the form of practical jokes, with Paramount boss Buddy DeSylva usually at the receiving end.

'We used to really fix DeSylva up at the rushes,' says Bing.

'Buddy and other executives used to look at these results of the previous day's shooting every morning—and we'd always put in a couple of scenes with special material just for them.

'They had no idea what was coming. We'd put in something very dirty and they'd come rushing out of the projection room and send us over notes which we'd ignore. We'd let them believe that we were going to use the scenes and were going to fight for them. Then they began to realise it was all just a gag.'

The exotic Miss Lamour was no mean hand in the prankster department either. When the Groaner's birthday came round during filming she and Hope once presented him with a cake bearing a solitary candle and the inscription: 'To save your embarrassment.' On one of Hope's birthdays she and Bing presented him with an old-fashioned rocking chair.

Crosby could be as relaxed before the camera as he was before the mike in the recording studio.

When he made *A Connecticut Yankee in King Arthur's Court* in 1949 with William Bendix and Britain's Sir Cedric Hardwicke, his leading lady was Rhonda Fleming, who saw just how free and easy he was. 'He was always pulling jokes and taking time to make people laugh,' she said. 'We'd just be ready to shoot a scene—I was ready to go like a race-horse at the starting gate —and Bing would be talking to the men up on the catwalks. He'd start to tell them a funny story—and I'm trying to remember my lines and also listen to the joke—and the director would shout "action".

'Bing would go immediately from the joke right into his scene. He didn't forget a line or a movement. The minute the director said "cut", he was back to finishing the story again—an incredible memory!'

Connecticut Yankee was the third film to be based on the classic 1889 Mark Twain novel *A Yankee at the Court of King Arthur*. It was first made in 1921 as a silent; again as a talkie in 1931 and finally by Crosby eighteen years later in colour.

It was quite a filmic year was 1949, with more new people to work with and a new dimension. Bing lent his voice to a Walt Disney full-length creation, *The Adventures of Ichabod and Mr Toad*.

'I thought it was a nice subject,' says Bing, 'and like everybody I admired Disney's things. One of the film's writers was a friend of mine, Larry Clemmons, who had worked on our radio show, and he asked me to talk to Walt about taking the voice of Ichabod.'

The story concerned the legend of Sleepy Hollow, a supposedly haunted cove on the banks of the River Hudson in the days before New York swallowed the village of Manhatten. Bing talked and sang for Ichabod and Basil Rathbone spoke for Mr Toad.

Top o' the Morning followed—and a reunion with Barry Fitzgerald. The story, set in Ireland, centred around the prophecy that one day the Blarney Stone would be stolen and disaster would follow. But it did give Bing a chance to sing 'When Irish Eyes are Smiling'.

Then Crosby signed for *Riding High*, the first of two movies he was to make with another of Hollywood's top names, director Frank Capra.

The crooner was extremely keen to make the picture because it involved horses and was undeterred by the fact that Capra had filmed the story fifteen years before under the title *Broadway*

Bill. But after the contract had been signed, Capra began to have second thoughts about the project . . .

'I began to hear all kind of stories about how uncooperative Bing was,' he said, 'how he needled directors; how he never came in on time and was always ready to go out and play golf and how he raised Cain with production schedules.'

Capra ignored the rumours and pressed ahead with his production, but on the first day's shooting Bing failed to show for the nine o'clock call.

'He showed up at about ten-thirty while I was filming other people,' said Frank, 'and greeted me with "I thought I was in the first shot?" I said "you were!" So we began shooting, with nothing said, and the next day the same thing happened. He came in at about eleven o'clock.'

Again he found Capra filming other people. Again he demanded to know why 'if I'm in the first shot did you start shooting at nine?' Capra was ready for him: 'Bing,' he said, 'I have forty days to make this picture and it's going to cost us at least a thousand dollars an hour and every hour I lose is that much money. Therefore I start shooting at nine o'clock with anybody who's here; if you're not here, we can't shoot with you!'

Crosby made no reply to the outburst—but next morning he was in at half-past nine and the day afterwards appeared at nine on the dot. He then began to question Capra about what time the director himself showed up on the set: 'I said "I come in at seven-thirty" and he asked "well, when do you see the rushes?" I told him at six o'clock in the morning at my house and several times he came to my home at six to see the rushes and was never again late on the set.'

Capra's reasoning with Bing was two-fold: firstly he reckoned the Groaner only played up people he didn't respect and secondly he thought him an astute enough businessman to appreciate the financial side of the venture.

This paid dividends later in the film when Frank was trying to fit three days' shooting—and thirteen pages of dialogue— into a matter of hours. It was a sequence at the end of the picture when Bing's colt—which he had reared and trained into a race-winning horse—had died and was to be buried.

Capra awoke early to find the wind and the scudding clouds just right and called Bing to hurry over.

'Holy smoke!' said Crosby. 'But whatever you say is fine.'

So the scene was shot. 'We did it and we did it fast,' said a grateful Capra.

By this time, Gary and twins Dennis and Philip were in their early teens and becoming interested in show business. And Lindsay, the youngest and known generally as Linny, was now too old for the bedtime stories that Bing used to tell, even though they were updated versions of traditional fairy-tales. When the Groaner told it, Little Red Riding Hood, for instance, was a jockey, the wolf a crooked race starter, and grandmother the racing commissioner.

So, in the late 'forties, Dad found a place for them in the radio show. They were heard alternately chatting with him between songs. And the going rate was much more than what they got on vacation when they worked as hands on the Nevada ranch.

The show was now costing twenty-seven thousand five hundred dollars per half hour, with Bing on seven thousand five hundred a time. Fifty million people listened in regularly . . .

In the recording field, Bing was to lose the man who had guided him along the golden path. Jack Kapp died in 1949 and was succeeded by his brother Dave. But the gap would take a lot of filling and one of Dave's first moves was to bring in record producer Sonny Burke. He had made a series of hits with Dinah Shore and had been an arranger for Artie Shaw, but was now going through a difficult time. So there was no dithering when Dave offered him the chance of taking over the Decca West Coast studio that had been built for Bing close to Paramount. And after four months working on Crosby numbers under Dave's supervision he was given his chance to produce the Groaner himself.

Their first meeting, early on a smog-ridden California morning, was far from comfortable. 'At eight, right on the nose,' said Sonny, 'Victor Young gave the downbeat and we ran through a number a couple of times. Then Bing said, "Okay—let's make one!" We started recording and very soon, I heard something I wasn't pleased with. It wasn't Bing's best. I had a fraction of a second to decide what to do. This was my first recording with him. Should I stop or let him go through it?'

Sonny decided to call a halt and sat back with a growing feeling of impending doom. There was silence in the control room and Bing said: 'What did you stop for?'

'Bing, it wasn't as good as I think we can get it, let's make a fresh start,' said Sonny.

'What do you mean? What's wrong with it?' asked the Groaner.

A very worried Sonny now had to decide whether to blame the orchestra or a technical fault, or tell the Groaner it was him: 'I elected to tell him that I didn't think it was as good for him as I thought it should be. There was a heavy silence in the studio—there must have been forty singers and musicians out there. And Bing said for all to hear, "Get a load of Mr Tin Ears!" My face flushed like a red ball. I thought, well, here's my first recording session with Crosby and I've rubbed him up the wrong way—and this is probably the end of my recording career and everything else.'

Crosby, who had arrived at the studio in a bad mood, now realised that he had embarrassed his new producer and, as they started to record again, looked for an opportunity to put things right.

It came, as Sonny Burke remembered with relief, during the next number: 'There was some question about changing tempo or making a cut and Victor Young asked Bing about it. Bing said, "Ask Sonny, he's the boss on the date; he's the producer, ask him." Victor asked me what I wanted to do and I decided to make the cut. Victor looked at Bing, as if to say "what do you think?", but Bing made the cut and suddenly everything was right again.'

There was another tempestuous morning in the Decca studio around that time.

Bing was already in place before the microphone, ready to air his magnificent lungs on the stroke of eight, when brother Everett blundered in in his big-business role with some contracts that had to be signed on the spot—or so he said.

The Groaner was livid. He took the contracts, strode across to a wastepaper basket and tore them into shreds.

It was to be at least half an hour and one row later before he cooled down enough to carry on with the recording session. But Sonny Burke, who had watched the whole incident, never did learn what the contracts were about or why Everett thought them so important.

Bing jumped on the wagon train that year and did battle with Frankie Laine on two big Western songs.

First came 'Ghost Riders in the Sky', which Laine recorded at a later date. But it was actor-singer Burl Ives who felt the full sting of Crosby's selling power. Burl had found the song and recorded it on Victor with an arrangement—strangely enough—by the crooner's guitarist, Perry Botkin. Bing liked this number and turned to him for advice.

'Do you think Burl will be hurt if I do the song?' he asked Botkin.

'Of course not,' said the guitarist, 'everybody else is doing it, so you might as well get aboard.'

Bing went ahead and Burl lost the sales race.

Then along came 'Mule Train', with which Frankie Laine was causing a stir. Sonny Burke decided to make a challenge with the Groaner.

'We recorded Bing's version at eight in the morning as usual,' he said, 'and had the record played on the air by twelve noon!'

The Crosby team even managed to include the famous whip-lash sound effects that were on the Laine disc—by spreading newspaper on the studio floor and thrashing it with a rope. When eventually the record returns were counted up, Crosby's sales were reported to be some two hundred and fifty thousand copies in advance of Laine's. Yet most people identify Frankie with the song and credit him with the big hit . . .

Orchestra leader and arch-arranger Nelson Riddle came Bing's way in the late 'forties. He was to find fame later in a fantastic swinging partnership with Sinatra, but now he was a lowly arranger and had been discovered by brother Bob Crosby sitting in an adjacent chair at a dentist's in New York.

Said Nelson: 'I talked to Bob about the possibility of my going out to California and working for him on some kind of salary—say two arrangements a week at seventy-five dollars a piece. He agreed and it was while working with Bob that I became acquainted with brother Bing.'

They met when the crooner recorded Riddle's arrangement of 'That's How Much I Love You', and for Nelson it was the realisation of a strange feeling he had experienced the day after he had joined the United States Army years before.

'I remembered the first morning that I woke up as a soldier,' he said. 'I looked up at the ceiling and there was this naked light bulb dangling on a cord, and Bing's record of "The Anniversary Waltz" was being played throughout the barracks. I don't know what the significance was, but I knew Bing was a very great big thing in my life.'

The record they cut together became a big seller and for that Nelson was happy, but he was slightly concerned by Bing's lack of warmth during the session; 'He's a very pleasant man; I have never known him to be unpleasant, but he has a certain reserve about him. This was also the case later on with Sinatra, but Frank was more evocative than Bing. Bing is a person who stands off a bit.'

As the decade that was the 'forties ended there was the joy of Christmas and family. There were more joys to come. But much sorrow . . .

Chapter Fourteen

There was always one sure way of shaking off the pressures of show business. Go chase a golf ball somewhere. And well Bing knew it. Only this time he would do the chasing more than five thousand miles from home and the sun-kissed courses of California. Clubs at the ready, hat at the right angle, he prepared to set off for Britain via France to do battle with the best of 'em in the Amateur Open Championships at the illustrious St Andrews links in Scotland in May 1950.

He almost didn't make it. Just weeks before in the March his appendix began to seriously grumble and had to be removed. Apart from anything else it upset his extremely tight schedule and resulted in a mad rush to tape sufficient material to keep the radio millions happy while he was away in Europe.

'There's nothing better I'd like than to play in the British championship,' he said sadly from his sick bed in Santa Monica. He recovered in time to make the journey and went first to Paris, with an entourage that included John Mullin, his wizard of the tape, a brunette secretary named Betty Hamilton and writer Bill Morrow.

They booked into the Ritz, dined at Maxim's and night-clubbed as well as recording a fifteen-minute day-by-day Crosby diary to the folks back home on radio for Bing's Minute Maid orange juice. While the rest of the party indulged in champagne, the Groaner stuck to his favourite 'cocktail'—Scotch and water—and readied himself for St Andrews with an occasional round at Chantilly or St Cloud.

Seen arriving back at the Ritz at one in the morning he told a reporter: 'I shall read a bit before I hit the hay. A chapter or so of a thriller. Boy, am I having fun!'

There was more on his mind than golf. From Hollywood it was reported that the Bing Crosby household was suffering from strained relations. Family lawyer O'Melveny put out a statement saying that the matter was 'in abeyance' until Mr Crosby returned from Europe in June. And in Paris Miss Hamilton, on Bing's behalf, officially denied to the Press that there was any strain.

As casual as ever, the Groaner went sight-seeing and sauntered one day in the sunshine along the Champs Elysées until he felt the need for a rest.

'All the benches were filled around the Rond Point,' he said, 'so I lay down on the grass with a newspaper over my face. I'd scarcely closed my eyes when I'm whacked on the soles of my feet and looking up saw three gendarmes looking very stern and pointing to a large sign that said "Interdit".

'I told them I was Bing Crosby. That laid an egg. Then I showed them the lining of my jacket where it said Bing Crosby on a label. Still no soap. The three of them started dragging me off.'

Then Bing remembered the gold bill-clip presented to him by America's Professional Golfers' Association—carrying in bold type the initials P.G.A.—and pulled it out. It did the trick . . .

In pidgin French he told them he was a 'police garde Americain'.

'They believed I was a cop,' he said, 'but they still have to figure out a question they asked and I couldn't answer: "How can a cop afford a vacation in France?"'

There would be no lying flat on his back sunbathing in Scotland. The wind was biting bitterly from the East when he drove off on the municipal course at St Andrews for a practice round. To keep warm he wore a canary-coloured poloneck sweater beneath a beige one and a magenta cardigan, and two pairs of trousers. On his head he sported a black and white knitted tam-o-shanter. The McCrosby Bonnet, the papers christened it (actually it had been given to him by a Red Indian tribe in Vancouver). Two thousand fans stampeded the course with him and had to be controlled by police. The first two balls he hit were picked up as souvenirs. And such was the crush that he was only able to play five holes.

There was a similar crowd—mostly women—the next day for his match proper against one of Scotland's top amateurs, a local builder named J. K. Wilson. In the betting Bing was a long shot at thirty-three to one. The favourite was Willie Turnesa at six to one.

Mr James K. Wilson was somewhat bewildered by the crowd as well as Bing's golf. More than twenty years later, he talked about his big day with Bing: 'It shattered me. I'd never seen the likes of it before and I was dead terrified, but I just had a dram and got myself down to the first tee. He started with two birdies. Then I was bunkered at the third hole and he got a four. It was a five for me. So I was three down out of three played. Before I knew where I was, half the crowd were laughing. However, not having played the course before, Bing didn't know it terribly well. I just scrabbled along and eventually beat him.'

Crosby lost three and two in drenching rain. The match was all over at the sixteenth, but Bing couldn't resist a small wager on the last two holes at a half-crown a time. They halved one and Mr Wilson won the other—but had to change a fiver from Bing before he could collect his winnings.

Oddly, Crosby's entry for the British amateur championship led to singer Donald Peers being pressurised into the contest. When it became known that Bing was going to take part there was criticism in the Press at there being no British show business personality to wave the flag. So Mr Peers rallied to the patriotic call. Donald always remembered the furore Bing caused with that first round.

'He did something which was outrageous as far as golfing history was concerned,' said Donald. 'Without having seen the course before, he waltzed off and opened with two threes, a four and then another three. He lost, as we know, but he startled everyone with that opening. When I arrived in the afternoon everyone was asking "have you heard about Crosby? He's burning up the course."

'He had a beautiful swing, long off the tee, but not so long with his irons. What I remember most vividly were the wonderful blue eyes and also the charm he had. Every now and then, if he hit a ball that wasn't quite straight, he'd sing a line from "Around the Corner" which went "hey! Round the corner".'

The game took three hours and when it was over, Crosby shook hands with Mr Wilson and with a smile was hustled off in a police van to his hotel still in his wet golfing togs.

At Christmas there was a card and a silver tie-pin shaped like a golf club from Bing for his opponent. They corresponded regularly but didn't meet again for twenty-two years, when the Scotsman received a sudden phone call from the crooner in 1972. He was about to visit St Andrews once more and would like a game . . .

It was a sport that would be with him all his days. As early as 1940 he had taken an unsuccessful crack at the American amateur championship at Winged Foot, in New York State, and for years he sponsored his own tournament, the Bing Crosby Open. He won his club championship five times and had wins at the Eldorado and Thunderbird Championships and the Jasper Park Amateur.

While the Groaner was acquitting himself well in the rain at St Andrews in 1950, the backroom boys of music were in a huddle in Los Angeles trying to come up with something new for him on his return.

Gary Crosby was nearing his seventeenth birthday and had already set his eye on show business, although so far he had been heard singing mainly around the house. Why not team him on record with father? It was a brilliant idea dreamed up by Dave Kapp. But they had to find the right song.

It didn't take long. Sam Weiss, who Bing called the elder statesman of song-pluggers, had now set himself up as a publisher.

'I'd only been in business about six weeks,' he said, 'when a songwriter friend of mine came in with a tune for me. He said he hadn't got a title yet, but that it was a duet. We ran it through together and I liked it. So he said, "It's yours Sam— Hey! That's a good title: 'Sam's Song'." '

Dave Kapp liked the song and so did Bing when he heard it on his return. And the idea of recording for the first time with Gary also pleased him.

All the family were on vacation at the Nevadan ranch and no one was more surprised than Gary when father came into his room one summer morning and woke him around eight o'clock.

'Come on,' said Bing, 'get dressed if you're coming with me.'

'Where are we going?' Gary asked, sleepily.

'We're going to make a record.'

Gary got up, got dressed and off they headed for Los Angeles and the Decca studio to make 'Sam's Song'. And Gary had not even seen the music . . .

When they started to rehearse Bing chose to do the patter on the record, then changed his mind and gave it to Gary instead, saying 'That's too fast—you do it.'

Says Gary: 'We ran the song through a couple of times, then recorded it. Afterwards we did "Play a Simple Melody" for the other side—and off we went back to the ranch.'

Irving Berlin wrote 'Play a Simple Melody' around 1910 and Bing chose it, because travelling home in the liner *Queen Elizabeth* he found himself 'bunking' with Berlin and Groucho Marx.

'We kind of buddied up for the whole journey,' says Bing. 'Berlin was a great epicure and we ate in the Verandah Dining Room—which was very elegant—and for a little man he was pretty good with the knife and fork.

'We had lots of laughs and I had known "Simple Melody" from when I was a kid and so we all did it together for the Captain's entertainment. Groucho knew all kinds of songs. He was a great barber shop quartet singer and loved to sing harmony.'

Sonny Burke was given the job of tracking down the music of 'Simple Melody'; no easy task because no one seemed to stock it any more. In the end he found a couple singing the song in a Los Angeles bistro from a tattered copy that was almost falling to pieces. They were reluctant to part with it, but Sonny managed to persuade them eventually.

Both sides of the disc topped the charts and sold more than a million, earning a golden record—one of the twenty that Bing was to notch up in a long career.

But Gary didn't know about the great success until after the summer vacation. At the ranch, in the remote north-east of Nevada, they could only get country and western programmes on the radio and 'Sam's Song' did not rate a play in those parts.

'When I got back to school,' says Gary, 'somebody told me we'd sold a million.'

It had racked up three hundred thousand in the first three weeks of release.

Jubilant with the rest of the participants in the making of the disc was Sam Weiss, with his newly-founded publishing business. He had gone along to the studio to watch the session. 'But Bing gave me one of his "stares",' he said, 'so I left. About two hours later I got a call to say that he wanted me to come along and hear the finished recording. He grabbed me as soon as I got in and said, "Hey! I think you've got a smash here!" '

It was disclosed that year in Los Angeles that the four Crosby lads had fortunes of more than $200,000 each. Gary was seventeen, the twins sixteen and Lindsay nearly thirteen.

Their financial status was made known when the Superior Court approved a contract which would give them a royalty of about three cents a copy on a record called 'A Crosby Christmas'.

Earlier it had been reported that each of them was collecting something like eleven thousand dollars a year from the Crosby Investment Corporation, a company set up for their benefit in 1942.

But the Crosby family life in reality was not always reflecting the happiness of 'Sam's Song' in the early 'fifties. The Groaner was still the strict father; the leather belt still hung threateningly on a hook upstairs at their home. But as the boys got older and bigger the corporal punishment diminished and Bing found other means to discipline them. His favourites were locking up the television for a week in a cupboard, banning movies and calling off baseball games.

He used to call Gary 'Fatso' or 'Stupid', which Gary admits 'didn't do much for my ego'. His father was so worried about keeping Gary slim as a child that he kept him on a rigid diet and weighed him each week. If he tipped the scales too heavily there was a taste of the strap.

Before reaching his teens Gary was also caned and confesses that he was always worried because his father rarely believed him and thought him a liar. Consequently, he seldom went to Dad with any problems. When he was living at home, Gary maintains, the only thing he really wanted 'was to get away'. But Bing says this was never really true.

Whenever Crosby had to be absent from home he left a set of rules to obey and a list of chores that had to be done. If any of the lads were disobedient or ignored their tasks, Dixie made a note and all the notes would be handed to Bing when he returned to the homestead.

Bing takes to the saddle at
Del Mar

Riding high at Elko, Nevada

Swing with Bing English style
—Cranbourne Court,
Berkshire

Swing with Bing American
style—Lakeside, Los Angeles

The crooner at St Andrews (Scotland) after losing in
the British Amateur Golf Tournament to Scotland's
J. K. Wilson (1950)

Crosby and Phil Harris clown on the practice putting green
during Bing's Pro-Am Tournament, Pebble Beach, California

Crosby, Silvers and Kaye

Jerry Colonna, Groucho Marx, Bing
and Bob Hope sing Barbershop

Cooper, Crosby and Gable with feathered friends

The boys visit Dad and director Frank Capra on the set
of *Here comes the Groom*

Lunch with Tallulah Bankhead and others

The swooner and the crooner

Kathryn Crosby and son Harry Lillis Jnr visit the
dynamic duo on the set and wonder who said, 'We had a
million laughs'

Going my way, son?

Bing with the Oscar he collected for *Going My Way* (1945)

Crosby, Leo McCarey and Barry Fitzgerald admire yet another
award for *Going My Way* (1945)

Comedian Red Skelton gives an award and admires a rare sight
—Bing in tuxedo

'This thing's bigger than both of us'

The best actor and actress, 1944—Bing Crosby and Ingrid Bergman

Mr Music becomes
Doctor Crosby—
Gonzaga University
(1937)

Doctor Music becomes Father O'Malley, with *Going My
Way* director Leo McCarey (1944)

From the film
Mississippi, complete
with girdle—his
first costume part (1935)

Dressed up again for a
television drama

Guess who?

A scene from an early Mack Sennett film—*Dream House*
(1931)

Bing and Kathryn—married at last (1957)

Mr and Mrs Bing Crosby—true love

Christmas television—Crosby style. Waiting to climb the
ladder: Kathryn, Nathaniel, Mary Frances and Harry
Lillis Jnr

'Because of this, we never got the feeling that he had deserted us or was never around when we wanted him,' says Gary. 'Mother always communicated through him, wherever he was, and word came back through her. So it was like he was right there really, even when he was away.'

The youngest of the four, Lindsay, was equally subject to the Crosby discipline, but he feels he may have got some sort of preferential treatment: 'I know the older boys got it a little worse than I did. I was the last one, so I kind of got away with murder. They had to be in bed pretty early, compared to other kids, and as I look back on it now I can see that it all makes sense and Dad did it for a reason. I know if I had something to do he'd let me do it, but he wanted me home at a reasonable hour.'

But when they holidayed at the big summer home at Heyden Lake, Linny wasn't always home at a reasonable hour. He shared, as did all the boys, his father's love for the good life and once, as brother Philip recalls, missed the curfew imposed by Bing.

'It was generally ten-thirty,' reveals Philip, 'but we'd come in, then wait until dad had got to sleep then sneak out again. One time, everybody made the curfew except Linny.

'It gets to be past twelve, and downstairs, in the basement where we had our little quarters, we couldn't go to sleep just waiting for the explosion to happen.'

It was a long wait. Linny, who was still in his early teens, didn't arrive home until a few minutes past two in the morning. 'He'd been out on the town drinking,' said Philip, 'and he'd gotten into a brawl and was in his cups a little bit. We heard him slam the door and Father heard it upstairs, and Dad's voice —when he was mad, or when he was acting—sounds like tremendous thunder.

'He shouted "do you have any idea what time it is?" and Linny says "yes". He said, "you are exactly three hours and thirty-five minutes late, my young son! What have you got to say about that?" But Linny said nothing, he just started to walk downstairs and the three of us started to look at each other. We were thinking, "God! Dad hasn't hit him! He hasn't thrown anything at him." And the only thing I could figure out was that Linny—by his blasé attitude—had Dad so shocked that he let him get away with it for a while. But he caught it the next day.'

There was another time, however, when Lindsay got away with it and Gary caught it instead.

One morning Bing ripped the bedclothes from Gary and told him to leave home because 'you sneak out every night and get your brothers into trouble'.

Gary packed his things and loaded them into his car. It was only as he was driving past the ninth hole of a nearby golf course that Crosby stepped from the bushes and stopped him.

'Go on home,' said Bing. 'I don't want to worry your mother.'

Philip Crosby, who is now married and has children of his own, has a theory about the reasons for his father's strictness. He feels it was entirely due to his own childhood and upbringing: 'I'm kind of the same way,' says Philip, 'I'm real tough with my kids and our father was that way because he had been raised that way. His mother was a very beloved woman, but she was a tyrant. She had the fear of all—my dad, his four brothers and my two aunts—up until she died. The aunts couldn't smoke in front of her and the boys weren't allowed to do an awful lot of drinking. She really ran that family and this sort of passed down. So Dad was very strict, but he was fair. Of course our mother was very strict too, because we were four very high-spirited kids. She'd let us have it and then when Dad got home that night she'd give him the story. And we'd get it again! It was always a double-header.'

Bing cherished great hopes for his sons and apart from teaching them the best of manners, to stand up when a lady entered the room and to call older men sir, he schooled them heavily in sports. His ambition was that all four should become All-American footballers, but it was not to be. All four were far too light and, although they played a lot, all sustained injuries and never really fulfilled his ambition. 'They were,' he says, 'very good high school athletes but never made it at college.'

The crooner's favourite jibe to his sons in those days was: 'You know what I'm going to do? I'm going to adopt me a nice great, big, tall fellow weighing 220 lbs—who can run the hundred in about nine seconds flat—so I can get me an All-American some way. I'm looking around for someone . . .'

Bing set his heart on the twins managing the ranch in Nevada and sent them to the Washington State College to learn agriculture.

Every summer for them was spent working the ranch. 'Most

people laugh when I tell them we worked,' says Dennis Crosby, 'but we did—from five-thirty in the morning. I can remember being in the saddle from five-thirty to ten-thirty at night, riding that range, and I got pretty good at it.'

At the start, both boys enjoyed the hard life as ranchers and Dennis even made quite a name for himself in local amateur rodeos. But in time the lustre wore off: 'Philip and I said there must be something other than cows,' says Dennis. 'There must be some girls at the beaches we're missing!'

Another of Bing's ambitions that didn't come off, as Dennis tells it, concerned Lindsay: 'He wanted Linny at one time to go for the priesthood and I said, "Dad, I don't think Lin's quite made out to be a priest!", so he gave up on the idea. One thing I'll say about Dad, in the trouble we did get into he was always there and was always giving us a helping hand when we asked for it.'

Crosby tried desperately to keep his family as normal or as ordinary as possible and went to great lengths to protect them from his widespread fame.

While they were very young, it was relatively easy, but sooner or later they had to find out. After twenty years of experience, each of his sons cast his mind back to try and recall the time when they first realised their father was someone out of the ordinary.

For Gary it came when he was in the third grade at school: 'Kids would come up and say "your father's so-and-so", either in a nice way or a nasty way. I guess I noticed that I wasn't asking them who their father was, so I figured they must know my father and the feeling was "how do they know my father?" '

Dennis became aware during high school: 'We knew he sang,' he says, 'but we thought he only sang in the house. He was always singing in the shower and had a great warm-up—up the scale and down the scale—but then when I got to high school kids would start to say who he was. It finally dawned that he was a singer. I think he'd taught us that it wasn't much of a thing; it was what put food on the table and that it was his job.'

Philip was nine years old when the truth dawned. The occasion was his father's 1944 Academy Award winning performance in *Going My Way*.

'It hit me that he was really famous, extra famous and had

reached the pinnacle of his profession,' says Philip. 'I remember it in the papers—of course there was no TV then—and the next day there were headlines. The house was just chaos with calls and telegrams. The kids knew about it in school and so did the teachers. It was the first time I really had the sense that he was a very famous person. If a kid of that age can have a pride in his father, I just thought to myself, "My God! I'm really proud of my old man. He's really done something." '

Lindsay was much more protected by Bing and was a teenager by the time he got the message. He says: 'We were very proud, but we led normal lives and when I look back I know how tough his schedules must have been. Yet he always made time for us, especially me as I got older. The other boys went away to school, so I was the only one around and he started me playing golf. I took a real liking to it then; I know he gave up a lot of his time to play with me. I think, probably, I never realised how big he was until my early teens.'

The realisation that they weren't just ordinary children was a blow to the foursome and brought trouble at school.

'We weren't ourselves any more,' said Philip. 'We were Bing Crosby's kids. It was a stigma. I think as early as about the fifth grade a kid came up and popped me one on the nose—a shattering blow and blood was flowing. I said, "What did you do that for?" and he said, "I just wanted to see what it would be like to hit Bing Crosby's kid." So I hit him right back and beat the hell out of him!'

Dennis also got his fair share of rough treatment on the football field according to Philip: 'Every time he took the ball and there'd be a pile-up, there'd always be a thumb in his eye or they'd rub tape across his mouth. One time they were really roughing him up in a pile-up when one boy came out screaming and yelling, claiming that Dennis had bitten him. The referee said, "What was your hand doing in his mouth?", and that was the end of that.'

If Bing was never at a loss for words when at home, there were certainly times when he was in the studio. Occasionally he would forget or fluff a line in a lyric. As these recordings with errors on them always stood a chance of finding their way into the world outside as collector's items and eventually could turn up on radio, Crosby used to try to lessen the risk by throwing in some pretty risqué language on the rest of the take. Four-letter words and others that were longer were fairly common on a messed-up disc.

Patty Andrews, of the hit-making Crosby–Andrews Sisters partnership, suggested that he used this kind of language 'because he was a dirty old man', but she did laugh when she said it.

'If he made a mistake,' she added, 'he would just keep going with anything that came to mind. It was really hilarious.'

But despite his efforts, a number of spoiled recordings have popped up on the air throughout the world.

BBC Radio 2 put out this fluffed version of 'Wrap Your Troubles in Dreams' during their fourteen-part biographical series on the Groaner:

> When skies are cloudy and grey,
> They're only grey for a day,
> So wrap your troubles in dreams,
> And dream your troubles away,
> Until that sunshine peeps through,
> There's only one thing to do,
> Just wrap your troubles in dreams,
> And dream your troubles away.

> *Music break, during which Bing whistles*

> Whistle and dream your cares away,
> Castles may tumble,
> That's fate after all,
> Life's very funny that way . . .
> Sang the wrong melody,
> We'll play it back,
> See what it sounds like,
> Hey, hey,
> They cut out eight bars,
> the dirty bastards,
> And I didn't know which eight bars,
> he was going to cut,
> Why don't somebody tell me,
> These things around here,
> I'm going off my nut . . .

Crosby has a great love for the English language and used to carry a copy of *Roget's Thesaurus* around with him during the early years to look up words and their antonyms and synonyms —and confesses that he enjoyed 'trying them for size'. There is always a book at his bedside.

He describes duets as 'the crossing of cadenzas' and calls himself 'a raspy rattler'. A group of college girls are 'a covey of culture-vultures'. When he sang for an audience he was 'tossing the folks a few notes' and if he pleased them he was 'crumpling the folks'.

The Crosby–Clooney partnership was renowned for the liberties they took with lyrics. Their version of 'How About You?' contained a whole series of ad libs. Rosemary started it by throwing in the line 'Frank Sinatra's looks give me a thrill' (the original words referred to Franklin Roosevelt's looks). To which Bing replied, 'Helps you, huh?' Time for Rosemary to say 'yeah' and Bing's in again with, 'Well now, Bob Hope is more my style, hokey nose and all. He's stuck with it.' And he managed to get all that in before the next line of the song.

There was always great rapport between the Groaner and Louis Armstrong, who had a vocabulary all his own and was a frequent guest on radio with Crosby. Bing had been a life-long fan of the great jazz trumpeter and always tried to see him perform whenever he could.

'It was a great coup, I thought,' says Bing, 'to get him on my show. I used to see a lot of Louis and he always used to send me postcards from his tours. He called me "Pops" and a card he sent me from Sweden once read: "Hiya Pops! Everything over here is *skol* and I'm the skol-iest cat there is!"'

But the fall of 1950 brought sad news. Bing's father died after a heart attack at the beginning of October. Bing and the rest of the family were at his bedside. Only brother Ted was unable to get there on time. The passing of 'Hollywood Harry' made front-page news around the world as the Crosbys mourned.

Soon afterwards tragedy struck again. When the 1950 radio show began its winter season that October, Bing asked John Scott Trotter to book Al Jolson, who had just returned from entertaining the troops in Korea.

Said Trotter: 'I talked to Al on the phone and asked him what numbers he wanted to do. He said, "I don't know, we'll just do something we've already done. I'm tired, I've got a bad cold and it was a rough trip." The show was recorded on the Monday night, but about midnight on the Sunday Jolson passed away at the St Francis Hotel in San Francisco.' The date: 23 October.

A few days later brother Bob Crosby was called in to top the bill on the Bing show . . .

Chapter Fifteen

There were two things that Bob Crosby never wanted in life. He never wanted to be a singer, but was for a time. He never wanted to lean on his famous brother, although he once sought advice and once tried to borrow money—with surprising results on both occasions. He stood alone and never became a part of the Crosby empire with its tentacles reaching into so many fields. He worked *with* brother Bing on radio in the recording studio and in films—but not *for* him; not in the sense that the rest of the family did.

True, the younger Bob owed his show business break to the illustrious name. It was a humble beginning and it began with the arrival of a telegram while Bob was picking strawberries and cucumbers—as Bing had done years before him—for twenty-five cents an hour.

The family were still living in Spokane and Pa Crosby had a huge smile on his face when he took the wire along to Bob in the fields. It was from a bandleader named Anson Weeks in San Francisco and it said: '*Offer you a hundred dollars a week to join me at the Palace Hotel*'.

Pa Crosby was now laughing out loud and Bob asked him why.

'Well,' he said, 'you can't sing!'

'Anything's better than picking cucumbers,' said Bob. 'Let's get hold of brother Bing and find out if he's got an extra tuxedo and we'll take the job.'

'But you can't sing!' Dad protested again.

'I'll learn . . .'

Neither Anson Weeks nor anyone else in the big band business had ever heard Bob sing. It transpired that when Weeks was searching for a new singer he asked a colleague: 'Who can we get that's a name?'

'There's a guy named Crosby,' said the colleague.

'We can't afford him,' growled Weeks.

'No—not that Crosby. He's got a brother . . .'

And off went the telegram.

Filled with enthusiasm—it was in the depressing 'thirties and a hundred dollars a week was no mean pickings—Bob headed West to Los Angeles to seek out Bing and get hints from him on this singing business. But the crooner wasn't exactly forthcoming. Every time Bob tried to put the question, Bing made an excuse and said 'see you later'.

Finally the Sunday arrived when Bob had to catch his train to San Francisco. Bing was just about to go out as well. 'Listen,' Bob told him, 'I came all the way down here to find out how to sing. I've got this job and I want some pointers about what I should do.'

Bing tapped him on the shoulder and said: 'Just stay in tune, kid!' Then walked away.

Bob was hurt by his brother's apparent indifference and stormed off to the railway station.

'Later on,' Bob admits, 'I realised he did the very best thing he could do for me. He was not going to teach me to sing in two or three days and in effect he was trying to tell me to stand on my own two feet. He did this in many ways and I'm very appreciative. He never let me feel that I had a crutch.'

The younger Crosby proved to be a good pupil. He learned the singing craft well enough to move from Anson Weeks to the Dorsey brothers' original band as a vocalist.

'That was quite a group when I look back on it,' said Bob. 'Glen Miller on third trombone, Ray McKinley on drums, Charlie Spivak on trumpet and of course Tommy and Jimmy Dorsey.

'Out of that came some pretty good schooling, but I found myself being compared to Bing and I wanted to create some niche of my own. So, when I had an opportunity to form the Bob Cats and The Dixieland Jazz Band in 1935 I took it immediately, and that became my kind of music—and still is.'

But the first date brought a crisis and resulted in an SOS for financial help from Bing.

Bob's band was engaged for two weeks at a ballroom in Georgia, with a third week at another in Carolina. The outfit would need the money from the first two weeks to travel to the next venue.

But three nights after they opened in Georgia the owner of the ballroom came storming out of the blackness of the dance floor and said: 'Who's the leader of the band?'

'I am,' said Bob.

'Well lead it the hell out of here! Saturday you're through!'

A telegram was hurriedly sent to big brother in California. The reply that came back read: '*You can't reach me stop regards stop*'.

'That,' said Bob in later years, 'was the only time I ever wired Bing for money.'

Again Bob was very annoyed, but he was to discover that the Groaner was not as hard-hearted as it seemed.

In Georgia, Bob lifted the phone to take a New York call. On the other end of the line was a music publisher saying that he wanted to buy a number of his orchestrations. The fee was one thousand dollars, which arrived in time for the band to push on to Carolina.

'I found out only many years later,' Bob revealed, 'that it was Bing who had contacted the music publisher. He told him he'd got a kid brother stuck down in Georgia and could he phone him and say he was interested in some of his orchestrations and Bing himself would send a thousand dollars to the publisher.'

The early years for the Bob Crosby band were tough, even though the bookings rolled in. Bob couldn't escape from the inevitable comparisons with his brother and almost had a succession of nervous breakdowns.

His friend and saxophone player, Gil Rodin, was distressed by what he saw: 'Bing's success was something I always regretted for Bob's sake,' he said. 'He always had this big shadow there. "Bing's brother, Bing's brother"—he could never get away from it. He didn't know which way to go and became a meek little fellow instead of really doing something on his own. They tried to compare his singing; they tried to compare his talking. It was always "well, Bing is so much greater". It was a spiteful kind of thing.'

Bob stood firm and overcame the drawbacks of having a famous brother. He moved from triumph to triumph. His Dixieland jazz became a rage and at one time he was even allowed to fill brother's shoes as master of ceremonies on the Kraft Music Hall programme. 'I had Victor Borge and Mary Martin and did what Bing did—only not as well,' said Bob, 'because it was more demanding on the singing and I had given up singing.'

He wasn't a great success on the Kraft show and made no secret of the fact that the band was his real love: 'The one thing I didn't want to do was sing. I wanted to be a leader. I wanted to have the best Dixieland jazz band in the whole land. We had quite a few great singers in the outfit. In fact we started Doris Day, Gloria de Haven and Kay Starr. The very first jobs they ever had in their lives were with our band, because I didn't want to sing. I didn't want to be compared with Bing. I didn't want people to say his brother Bing sings better than he does. I knew darned well I had a better band than he had!

'Of course, he didn't even have a band. I don't think Bing was ever interested in leading a band. I think probably the one trait that would concern me about brother Bing would be his lack of responsibility. He is a loner; he likes to take care of Harry Lillis Crosby and he does take care of Harry Lillis Crosby.

'I don't think he would have ever been happy standing up in front of sixteen to eighteen musicians and having to be concerned with whether they were going to show up on time, with the proper uniform and in a condition to play. I don't think he would have liked to be bothered with that. I think Bing did exactly what he wanted to do.'

There were some things, however, that Bing did *bother* with.

He encouraged Bob to play golf as well as tennis—so much so that one year he won the crooner's own annual Pro-Am tournament. But Bob has his own secret about the game.

'Every time I hit a golf ball,' he said, 'I guess I'm hitting the trombone-player who hit a meatball in an arrangement last night. It was an outlet, because when I'm on the bandstand and someone in my band makes a mistake I never turn round. I never look at him. I've found with musicians that to do this inhibits them to such a point that they can't play. So I would take it out on the golf ball.'

Now, as the first year of the 'fifties folded, brother Bob was up there with the high and mighty of the show business fraternity, the Astaires and the Garlands, topping the bill on Bing's show.

For the Groaner himself, the pattern of the immediate future was scarcely different from the past. He went to work with Frank Capra once more for *Here Comes the Groom* and had with him Jane Wyman, Dorothy Lamour and his close friends Phil Harris and Louis Armstrong. Bing thought it was a 'funny film' and certainly there was some fun in the making. Crosby was no longer the problem boy for Capra, but there was a rooster that refused to toe the line.

The idea was the rooster crowed at the right time during a musical scene. To try to get him right on cue, the resourceful director put the bird in front of a mirror and let him fight his own image—then pulled the mirror away at the exact moment, expecting the rooster to crow in victory. Instead he took fright and hid under a bed.

Capra tried again with the same result. Then he called in a bantam hen to help get the rooster a-crowing. Nothing. And the hen chased the rooster all over the lot. By which time, Crosby and the rest of the cast were themselves cackling away.

A trainer was enlisted. He took the rooster into a corner and had a man-to-man with it and reported, 'Now he'll crow.'

'So he crowed,' said Capra. 'I timed him with a stopwatch and he crowed every twenty-two seconds. The trainer said he could get the bird to crow any time. And he did. But he never told me the secret.'

The movie was memorable for a song called 'In the Cool, Cool, Cool of the Evening', by Johnny Mercer and Hoagy Carmichael. It had been written for a Betty Hutton movie called *The Mack Sennett Girl*, but somehow was never included.

When Crosby and Capra heard it they scooped it into *Here Comes the Groom*—even though the rest of the score had been written by two other songsmiths, Ray Evans and Jay Livingstone. A shrewd move: it waltzed away with the Oscar for best film song of 1951—the fourth and last Crosby song to receive the award.

If Evans and Livingstone were embarrassed by the inclusion of the rogue number in the film, they were equally put out by the changes Bing made in one of their songs that did get in. Once more he was getting the line of a lyric wrong, and they asked the musical director to tell him so. He refused.

'They were all afraid of Bing with no good reasons,' said Jay Livingstone, 'except he does have a way of looking at you—he kind of freezes you—until you get to know him. So I asked Frank Capra to tell him and Frank said "you tell him". I walked up and told him. He looked at me strangely—and sang it wrong from then on . . .'

The cameo appearance was now an expected and popular fleeting feature in movies and Bing made several around this time, notably in *The Greatest Show on Earth*, in which he and Hope simply had to sit eating popcorn while they watched a circus performance. Then Bing turned up in Hope's starring vehicle *Son of Paleface* and was shown driving his car home from the studio during Hope's opening scene. 'What's this?' asks Bob, who goes on to explain: 'This is an old character actor on the Paramount lot who we try to keep working. He's supporting a large family, but I guarantee this fellow won't be in the picture tonight!'

Two starring roles were scheduled for the Groaner in the first six months of 1952, *Just for You* and the more important *Road to Bali*, bringing the series to six and the first to be filmed in colour. Paramount, Hope and Crosby shared the million-dollar cost. But this time, although it was a Paramount production, Bing Crosby Enterprises and Bob Hope Enterprises held the copyright as well.

An expensive film, making extensive use of trick photography and described at its première as 'A pantomime for grown-ups'. Bogart and Jane Russell had guest roles and Paramount president Adolph Zukor was later to reveal that a long and expensive water ballet scene had to be scrapped 'because it was so boring . . .'

Typical sample of the sort of Crosby–Hope nonsense that went on in the film: when Bing is about to croon, Bob makes an aside to the audience, saying, 'He's gonna sing now folks—now's the time to go out and get the popcorn!'

Road to Bali was all wrapped up in August and it was time once more for the Groaner to pack his bags and leave the family. Awaiting him in Europe was a charity golf match at Temple course, near Maidenhead, partnering Hope against Donald Peers and comedian Ted Ray in a foursome to raise funds for the Duke of Edinburgh's National Playing Fields Association; and a movie called *Little Boy Lost* based on a novel by Marghanita Laski to be partly shot in France.

Bing arrived at Plymouth at dawn on 18 September in the French liner *Liberte*. Within eight hours he was tee-ing up on the first hole at Temple for a practice round. He had motored from Plymouth, snatched two hours' sleep—but still managed to go round in 76 and easily beat Mr J. E. Perkins, Paramount's managing director in Britain. Nevertheless, Crosby blamed 'a bad case of sea legs' for his four over par.

He wondered if the links might be a bit too strenuous and hilly for Hope and crooned 'Some Day I'll Find You' while he was looking for a ball at one stage.

The charity match itself, played on a Sunday, was a near riot. Thousands of spectators turned up and stampeded the Temple course. The National Playing Fields Association benefited well, but the occasion did nothing to further the cause of the game.

The memory has long lingered with Bing: 'It was quite an experience,' he says. 'They'd never tried this sort of event in England before and they had no conception of what kind of gallery it would attract. It was a blustery day and we could hardly get down to the tee for crowds. They stood right in front of us and Hope said, "We're going to drive-off down that way", and they said, "We don't care, go ahead!" '

Ted Ray admitted to being a little scared by it all: 'The first part of Temple is downhill,' he explained. 'It was like looking down a black keyhole! Eighty per cent of those people had never seen a golf course before; they didn't realise that a golf-ball leaves a club at about a hundred-and-eighty miles an hour —or in my case a hundred-and-ten—and can cause an awful lot of damage.'

Worse was to come. The marshalling got completely out of control, children started building sand-castles in the bunkers. Women wearing stiletto heels walked casually on the greens. Bing was getting extremely upset and Ted Ray described him as being 'pale with fear' at what might happen. Hope stayed his usual self, cracking gags continuously.

But Ted Ray wasn't really joking when, just as he was about to swing, he said to one woman in the pressing crowd: 'Excuse me, madam, would you mind either standing back or closing your mouth. I've lost four balls already.'

Balls vanished like magic into souvenir hunters' pockets. Finally, the foursome were forced to abandon most of the eighteen holes and make a mad dash to the last one in a car to try to get ahead of the crowd. It was a classic scene that might have come from a 'Road' film: a big black limousine, with Bing and Bob bouncing around in the back seat and Ray and Peers standing on the running boards like Keystone cops, trying to cling on as the car bumped perilously across the undulating English countryside.

Ted and Peers won the match, if it could be called that, by one hole—the last. Hope blamed himself for pulling a seven-iron shot when he and Bing were still in with a chance.

Donald Peers, talking about the debacle not long before his death, said: 'I was a little overawed by the whole thing because I had never been in such wonderful company. At that time I was shy; I had only been in the public eye for three or four years and was still conscious of being the boy from the provinces. We all acknowledged that the big attraction was Bing Crosby—simply because so few people had seen him in person before. And I heard someone say that even if the Duke of Edinburgh had been there he couldn't have had more attention than Crosby had that day.'

Ted Ray had to hurry off to Heathrow to catch a plane for Korea, where he was due to entertain the troops. Waiting for him at the airport was a telegram from Hope, which read: *'Bing and I challenge you and Donald to a return game in Hollywood stop With just a few of your relatives present this time stop All the best stop Bob stop.'*

After the chaos at Maidenhead, Bob persuaded the Groaner to make his one and only theatre appearance in Britain—at the Stoll in London's Kingsway at a charity show in aid of the Clubland Settlement in Camberwell and the Midwife Teachers' Training College. Jack Buchanan emceed the first half, Hope the second. And there was a touch of chaos again about Bing's part in the proceedings.

As the late Denis Goodwin, a scriptwriter for Hope for many years, saw it: 'During the interval I went backstage with a couple of extra lines and Bob told me, "Bing is in the pub over the road! I'm going to go and get him out of there." After the interval, when Crosby suddenly appeared, it looked as though he'd been pushed on stage. But he was marvellous and did about an hour. I know by the time he finished the pub would have been closed.'

As Donald Peers, who also appeared on the bill, saw it: 'I

was on fairly early in the first half and nipped round to the back of the stalls afterwards to watch from there. Bob Hope came on and did some gags—talking about "dad" Crosby—and suddenly the spotlight moved from Hope and there was Bing, with his pipe, leaning against the scenery.

'The applause was something like you'd never heard. It was just fantastic. He did some songs and there were lots of titles shouted at him from the audience. He would start one or two, but not having rehearsed them would get so far and then say, "Well, that's enough", or "I can't remember the rest of the words".'

Not surprisingly. During the interval, Hope had taken Bing to the rehearsal room on the top floor of the Stoll and sent for pianist Pat Dodd. But there was no chance of a run-through. 'Reporters and photographers were there in swarms,' said Dodd. 'There were flashlights going and people talking to him and I didn't even get a chance to try anything, let alone ask him what he wanted to sing.'

For the record: the date was 21 September 1952.

The Groaner sped off to France the next day for location work in and around Paris on *Little Boy Lost*, a straight, serious role that would demand more from him than *Going My Way* and *Bells of St Mary's*.

Director George Seaton had fallen in love with the Marghanita Laski story of *Little Boy Lost* and had adapted it for the screen himself. 'And,' said Seaton, 'I always wanted to work with Bing, because I think he has a lot more talent than he is willing to admit. He could play a serious role, although he always said of himself, "I'm a crooner, I'm not an actor."'

Miss Laski, however, was not as enthusiastic as Seaton.

She had originally sold the film rights to actor John Mills, but he resold them to Paramount and she was concerned that the leading character—an unhappy British intellectual—should be changed to—as she put it—'a singing American' (after seeing the film, she admitted that Bing had done a remarkable job with a very demanding role).

But now, not only had Bing to convince cinema-goers that he could play a straight part: he had to try to hide a very personal tragedy.

The crunch came, director Seaton revealed, during the

shooting of a minor scene: 'It was just simply Bing walking from a small-town bus to the railroad station. We were lining up for the shot and someone came out from the hotel with a letter for him. Bing sat and read it, and I said to him, "Sorry Bing, we're ready now—the light's right."

'He put the letter in his pocket and the shot was to be merely him getting off the bus carrying a suitcase, having left this child he wasn't going to adopt because he was convinced it wasn't his. The walk wasn't more than thirty yards. But the way he carried that suitcase. He had the whole weight of the world on his shoulders. When he got to the platform I yelled "cut" and looked around to find half the crew were crying.

'It was so beautifully done. I went up to him, put my arms around him and said, "Bing, that's the most magnificent moment of film that I've seen in years." And he took the letter out of his pocket. It was from his wife's doctor. He'd just found out that Dixie had cancer . . .'

Dixie had already undergone an abdominal operation in July and her condition was now terminal. But when Bing arrived back in Hollywood in October after the *Little Boy Lost* location shooting, Dixie dressed up in her best outfit and was driven to the station to meet him. In a last defiant gesture of togetherness she left her sick bed against doctor's orders. There was a relapse and she went into a coma.

A priest administered the Last Rites and the crooner and fourteen-year-old Lindsay kept a vigil through most of the night at her bedside. Gary flew home from Stanford University. The twins flew back from Washington State College. But it was a losing fight for Dixie Lee Crosby. She died on 1 November 1952. On her forty-first birthday . . .

She had been an enormous influence on Bing's life and there were those who said she changed and tamed him. 'Certainly,' says the Groaner, 'her love and the family she gave me slowed me down very much.'

But Gary Crosby believes that any changes his father made in his way of life he made voluntarily.

'I don't think she asked him to change in any way. But he did change and I think he enjoyed the change. He became a married man and kind of settled down. He gave as much of himself as any man with a wife and family can do while in a business that constantly kept him away.

'Mother was great,' he went on. 'She could really put him on. She used to call him "the romantic singer of songs you love to hear". She would kid him, but she would always give an honest opinion of what he did—good, bad, or whatever. She always said what she thought and he listened to her. You could see it going in there; he'd analyse it and weigh it up. I think he appreciated that she would never con him.'

Bob Crosby had this to say about her: 'Dixie was a magnificent woman; the catalyst for what happened to Bing Crosby would have to be Dixie Lee. First of all it was a great love affair and secondly she was a very knowledgeable, wonderful and understanding person.

'I think when he lost Dixie he lost a great deal. That's evident by the problems that the family had. There was a great love and great motivation; she was intelligent; she was smart; she was understanding; she was attractive; she was generous; she was a helluva woman.'

Dixie was never told that she had cancer. Bing nursed the tragic secret on location in France and finished the scheduled shooting there. If he had flown home instead she would have probably sensed that some thing was seriously wrong with her.

'She was as sharp as a razor,' said Gary. 'You couldn't get anything by her. He had to go and do that picture at the time my mother was dying. He was away at a time which was very important to him, because he loved my mother very deeply and wanted to be home . . .'

In 1975, Bing paid this tribute to Dixie: 'She was a very fine woman. I was devoted to her. She was very timid, terribly shy. It was awfully difficult to get her to make any kind of public appearance and that was the reason she never did anything more in show business. She just hated the exposure and the necessity to work with strangers and people she did not know. When she did get to know anybody she was a marvellous friend and a great deal of fun. And she could really sing, too, and I often regretted that she didn't sing more. She had a great style and a marvellous voice, a voice that was terribly pleasant to listen to.

'She was interested in everything the children did, was very severe with them and they all loved her very much.'

At the graveside the family stood sadly together, the four sons with their tearful father. Bing leaned heavily on Gary's shoulder . . .

Chapter Sixteen

Bing lived out a period of intense loneliness and soul-searching in his huge Holmby Hills mansion after Dixie's death. Lindsay, who would be fifteen in the coming January, was now—with his brothers back at their studies—a real life little boy lost. The Groaner's mother Kate, in her eightieth year, moved in to comfort them both.

For Harry Lillis Crosby life was again at the crossroads. There was that feeling, as there had been twenty-seven years earlier on Wheeler's Ridge when the Model-T spluttered to a halt, that one had to pick up the pieces and press on. A far more tragic situation now, but needing the same perseverance and endeavour. Perhaps he should have found ways to spend more time at home with wife and family, but the difficulties and pressures were immense; there had been so many other facets of his life that made heavy demands on his time. Perhaps, perhaps, perhaps . . . Now was too late. The marriage had endured for twenty-two years; an astonishing length of time by Hollywood standards. Many had been the rumours of partings and divorce, but Bing had always maintained that there would never be any split. And rightly. There had obviously been difficult patches as there are in most marriages. Yet theirs, in fact, was a great love story—right to the end, when Dixie proved to the world her devotion by meeting Bing on his return from Europe. It was the last time she was seen in public.

Now, as the days mounted towards Christmas, there was little but emptiness for the man who had everything . . . almost.

He had to return to work at Paramount to finish 'Little Boy Lost' and this no doubt helped him along the road to normalcy. The picture was concluded by February, but there would be no other vehicle for him that year. His only other screen part in 1953 was another brief cameo appearance with Bob Hope in a Dean Martin–Jerry Lewis comedy called *Scared Stiff*.

Hungry columnists of the day seized upon this and speculated, wrongly, that the Groaner was on the road to retirement . . .

Towards the end of the year, however, the old Bing was back—in more ways than one. He agreed to star in a new musical based on his biggest hit—'White Christmas'. And during rehearsals showed that he still had some zest for life.

He was leaning in the doorway of his dressing room when a cute little nineteen-year-old walked past with a tennis racket beneath one arm and a bundle of petticoats under the other. She was on her way to return the petticoats to a wardrobe mistress and then to keep a date on the court.

Her real name was Olive Grandstaff, which would never stand a chance of getting into lights, and she was now known as Kathryn Grant. She hailed from Texas where she had been a beauty queen and now she was a Hollywood starlet with an ambition to get to the top.

'Hi! Tex,' he said. 'What's your rush?'

'No hurry at all,' she stammered, dropping the racket and two petticoats.

Remembering it all now, she says: 'I just skidded to a stop, turned and received full voltage from those robin's-egg-blue eyes. We exchanged pleasantries and I was invited in to tea. I forgot my tennis date, became very confused and very comfortable all at the same time. That was our first meeting . . .'

By the following year they were in love and dating regularly. Eventually she would become his second wife, but the courtship would have a lot of ups and downs along the way.

She was five months younger than Gary . . .

Meantime, columnists had been pairing Dad off with a few other lovelies. One was actress Mona Freeman. When it was reported that he was going to marry her the Groaner had to step in with a denial: 'I don't know how these rumours started,' he said. 'Mona is an old and very dear friend. I have known her since she was a child.'

Another gossip had him making a play for Mary Murphy, who was described as being 'a luscious eyeful in any man's country'. Again untrue. He had been seen on dates with a number of beautiful actresses, in restaurants, on the golf course, but there was nothing serious.

It was true that he had some admiration for Rhonda Fleming—but the romance didn't happen, as she confirmed years later: 'I liked him and he liked me,' she recalled, 'but at that time I was going with a young man. He was pretty much a steady in my life. One day I had a phone call from the columnist Hedda Hopper and she said, "Rhonda, honey, you have a man who admires you very much." I said, "Who's that?" and she said, "Bing Crosby."

'Well, I was very involved with this other young man and there was a possibility I might marry him—but I didn't. I've thought of it so many times, because Bing probably would have been a delightful companion.'

By the time Rhonda's affair was over, the crooner was interested in another . . .

While his romance blossomed with Kathryn Grant, despite the fact that there was an enormous age-gap of thirty years between them, the Groaner went before the camera twice in 1954 to make two of his greatest successes—*White Christmas* and *The Country Girl*.

Like other Hollywood hits, *White Christmas* was decidedly fragile in its infancy. The money was there all right. Paramount, Bing and Irving Berlin, emerging from a ten-year retirement, were sharing the bill.

The songs were there, too. Berlin, in a great burst of enthusiasm penned eleven new numbers, nine of which would be used eventually along with those hardened veterans of the jukebox, 'White Christmas' itself and 'Blue Skies'.

But the script was missing on some if not all cylinders.

The original idea was said to have cast Fred Astaire and Crosby together again. But Astaire is reported to have taken one look at the script and turned it down.

Perhaps Donald O'Connor might step into Fred's vacant dancing shoes? Donald said he would love to work with Bing again (he was only twelve when he appeared with the crooner in 1938 in 'Sing You Sinners' and sang 'Small Fry' with him). But observers at the time recall that he had back trouble and couldn't work.

Danny Kaye was then approached and agreed to join Crosby—provided writers Mel Frank and Norman Panama improved the script. They did. And the movie got under way— the first to be made in the VistaVision process.

Irving Berlin paced the sound stages and was glad to be back on the scene. 'I thought I was finished,' he said. 'I thought I'd had it as a songwriter, but I was just tired. The longer I didn't write the worse I got. I had spells of great depression and the only thing that could get me out of it was going back to work. It was as simple as that.'

A frail, ageing figure, he still paid much attention to detail. Leading lady Rosemary Clooney said that he looked quite worried when he listened to the first take of Bing pre-recording 'White Christmas' and began to pace up and down.

Crosby, noticing it, shouted: 'Irving, why don't you go back to my dressing room and sit down and wait. We'll play the tape to you when it's finished. It'll be all right, because you know I did record it a long time ago—I really know the song!'

'And Irving did just that,' said Miss Clooney.

There was a gremlin about as well. After three days of work on one particular scene it was discovered that there was something wrong with a camera. 'Bing was furious about that,' said Mel Frank.

Then director Michael Curtiz tried to pre-choreograph a Crosby–Kaye scene while the pair looked on from the sidelines.

'What the hell is this?' Bing demanded. 'Where's our creativity going to come into it?'

'Look,' said Curtiz, 'we've got just so much time to do it and this is what I want you to do.'

They did.

But there was time for the studio to try to impress some VIP royal visitors, though Miss Clooney, like everyone else, refuses to say who the couple were. The Royals were coming along to watch the finale of the film. The snag was that the scene had been shot in the morning and the visitors were due in the afternoon.

Director Curtiz was undaunted. 'We'll re-do what we did before lunch with no film in the camera,' he said.

Said Miss Clooney: 'We had ballerinas, we had soldiers; the snow was there and we were all dressed in red satin for the scene that morning. We had everything but fireworks and everybody was singing "White Christmas".'

Despite everything, the movie went on to become one of Bing's biggest money-makers.

But he fought against going into *The Country Girl* a little later with Grace Kelly and William Holden. When he was asked to play the role of an alcoholic actor fighting to make a come-back, Crosby said: 'No! Absolutely not! I'm a crooner.' And was protesting once more to director George Seaton.

But Seaton, with whom he had made *Little Boy Lost*, was not to be put off. He pointed out how convincing the Groaner had been in *Little Boy Lost*. And in the end he persuaded Bing to take the role. But that wasn't the end of Seaton's problems.

'Come the first day of shooting,' he said, 'and at nine-thirty there was no Crosby; ten o'clock, no Crosby; ten-thirty and still no Crosby.

'At eleven I had a call from Wally Westmore—who was head of the make-up department—and he said, "You'd better come up here, I think you've got big trouble on your hands!" '

The trouble was Bing. Beforehand, George had agreed with the crooner that he should wear a different toupee for *Country Girl* so that he would look more his age.

'When I walked in,' said Seaton, 'there sat Bing with his *College Humour* wig on! The wavy one he'd worn in all those early films, and he was very defiant. He said, "I've just decided that this is what I'm going to wear in this picture".

'I reminded him that we'd already agreed he had to play the character and that he couldn't play *College Humour* all over again. He said, "Well I've got my audience to think of. I don't want to look like an old man on the screen" (he was fifty-three). I said, "You won't—you'll look your age—but there's nothing wrong with that, you're playing a character part." '

Then Seaton realised what the real trouble was. 'I said, "Bing, let's be honest, you're frightened," and he almost started to cry and said, "I can't do it." I said, "Please have faith in me, I'm frightened too, so let's be frightened together." We threw our arms around each other and walked on to the set and from then on there was no problem at all.'

Crosby admits to having been nervous about his role in *The Country Girl*, which was based on a Broadway play by Clifford Odetts.

'I was worried about the songs (there were four by Ira Gershwin and Harold Arlen),' he says, 'and whether they would weaken the strength of the story, because I'm a singer and everyone would think here he comes singing again.'

George Seaton called for extensive rehearsals. And for realism he suggested that Bing should peel off his toupee in one dramatic scene. But the crooner was resolute and absolutely refused to take off what he sometimes called 'The Crosby Curse'.

It was Seaton's theory—and he told Bing so—that Crosby in his films usually came out playing Crosby. In this film Seaton was simply trying to get him to emerge as the character the script called for.

The rest of the cast were also aware of his worries. Grace Kelly particularly so, because it affected their relationship right from the start. 'I think Bing was a little nervous about doing that part,' she said, 'I was certainly nervous about doing my part. It was a wonderful opportunity for me and I was very anxious, but we didn't pay much attention to one another and we really didn't get on too well during the first week we were working.

'After the first rushes the strain sort of came through and George Seaton said, "Look, we're going to shoot this all over again." We did—and it started to work from then on. It was a very happy picture and took only five or six weeks to make.'

During the shooting one of the Hollywood gossip-writing ladies suggested in print that Grace and the Groaner were having a raving affair. They weren't.

Crosby was most memorable in *Country Girl* in a scene where he was supposed to be in a Boston jail after an all-night binge— something he had first-hand experience of. Cinema audiences saw a perfectly hung-over Bing, with half-growth of beard and eyes practically bleeding from lack of sleep.

Few of them realised the effort and preparation that went into that segment. And it wasn't, as Bing's son Dennis revealed, an actual case of hitting the bottle hard: 'I can remember that very clearly, because he made Philip and I stay up with him the night before he did that drunk scene. He wouldn't go to sleep so we walked with him and kept him up. He usually liked to go to bed early and get up early, but that next morning his eyes were all red and he looked like he'd been drinking. I think when he wants to act, he can act.'

Bing's mother traditionally never visited the film set, but on the day they shot that scene she decided to make an exception. 'Bing just looked awful,' said Seaton, 'it was perfect for the scene and Mrs Crosby brought three women friends with her who were very straight-laced. She came in and looked at Bing, who was sitting at a table exhausted, and said, "Harry!" Then she walked right off the set, sure that he'd been drinking. I had to chase her down the street and assure her this was not the case, but she didn't come back.'

Grace Kelly was voted best actress of 1954 for her performance in the film. Bing was nominated, but faced fierce competition from Marlon Brando in *On the Waterfront*.

Crosby lost out and George Seaton was disappointed. 'I thought Bing's performance was outstanding, because he went beyond anything he had ever done before. Brando gave a magnificent performance too, but it was still within his own range.'

There was some consolation. Bing was elected actor-of-the-year by the American National Board of Review of Motion Pictures.

Towards the end of that year Mrs Dixie Lee Crosby's will was published. She left a gross estate of $1,332,571 but debts, taxes and the cost of administration would reduce the sum to $550,000.

However, the most important date of the year proved in the passage of time to have been 30 October 1954.

Bing proposed to Kathryn, she said yes, and a wedding day was set for 7 February the following year.

During their courtship he had held her hand and crooned to her among other songs 'You'd be so Easy to Love', which resulted in her toes going numb. She remembered it well, because, 'curiously, I'd never had numb toes before,' she said.

'Yet I never was a fan,' she confides, 'I never collected Bing Crosby records. I never saw Bing Crosby movies. I fell in love with the man. Although I think, probably, the man I fell in love with is the man that comes across on the screen. You see, his speaking voice and singing voice are the same and they're quite wonderful. When he says something to you, it's irresistible.

He's very naïve about his charm, but I think it's very real and it's a very lasting thing.'

One member of the Grant family who did find the Groaner resistible was Kathryn's uncle Walter Raspberry, who lived an hour's drive from Hollywood in Topanga Canyon.

In the early days of the romance she had gone to stay with him for a holiday and simply left a telephone number for Crosby. Uncle Walter, a plumber and described by Kathryn as a very direct kind of man, was unaware of their association. So that when Bing called, her uncle asked, 'Who's this speaking?'

'It's Bing Crosby,' said the crooner.

'Yeah? And I'm Harry S. Truman!' said uncle, banging down the phone.

A worried Kathryn said later: 'I thought my whole future had been wrecked and that I would never hear from Bing again. He thought it was very funny.'

There was a laugh soon afterwards for Kathryn too. When Bing visited her flat and failed to find an ashtray he emptied the tobacco remnants into his trouser turn-ups.

'It keeps the moths away,' he explained with some embarrassment when she discovered what he was doing.

But there were more serious things to discuss. She had been a Baptist before she met Bing and became a Catholic—sharing his faith—not long after they first fell in love.

It was no token gesture, she says, and in fact her conversion helped her through the difficult time of courtship.

When the romance became public there were the fans and friends who pointed an accusing finger at the immense age barrier, a fact that the couple were themselves very conscious of. But wagging tongues had nothing to do with the cancelling of their February wedding date.

Crosby became troubled with kidney stones and went into hospital to have them removed (he was to have four such operations during the 'fifties and his doctor commented that he only wished he would be as fit when he reached the crooner's age).

At the same time the studio sent Kathryn tearing around Europe to publicise a movie. So a new wedding date was set for 2 May—when Bing would be about through making *Anything Goes* once more, although it would bear little resemblance to the production of some twenty years earlier.

This time he did have with him song-and-dance man Donald O'Connor, plus Mitzi Gaynor. Donald was—and still is—impressed by Crosby's dancing ability: 'He's not a Kelly or Astaire and he would be the first one to admit it, but as far as doing the basic steps—what we call hoofing and laying-down-the-iron—he can do any of those things. Primarily, that's not his bag you know, but he can go in and fake it very well.'

Yet for Donald the making of the movie brought a personal problem. He was in awe of Bing to such a degree that he appeared to be aloof. The crooner noticed it and mentioned it to a friend of Donald's. 'Do you like Crosby?' the friend asked O'Connor a day or so later.

'I adore the man both personally and professionally,' said Donald.

'Well,' said the friend, 'he feels you don't like him and it's hard to get to you.'

What had happened was that during the years that separated their last film together Donald had grown up and now knew Crosby for the superstar that he is. O'Connor explained it like this: 'In 1938 I'd played his kid brother and he was protecting me all the time. But when I did *Anything Goes*, we were to be buddy-buddys of about the same age and it was very difficult for me to relate to Bing at that time.

'I had become really enamoured with him, starstruck, which I'm not prone to do with people; but with Bing yes. Maybe it was because I had this great admiration and respect for him. But after that talk with my friend we got along beautifully and in the few times that we do see each other, it's a nice happening.'

O'Connor's admiration was such that for some time he had been trying to imitate Bing's crooning style. A fact that didn't go unnoticed during *Anything Goes*.

'I was doing a scene with Mitzi Gaynor,' said Donald, 'when Danny Kaye happened to walk through the set while I was singing. He stopped and said, "Why is it that when they make a picture with Bing they all sound like Crosby?" It was a snide remark, but I didn't take it so.'

Miss Gaynor, who was just becoming a name, thought that Crosby moved very well in the dancing routines, but described him as 'a waist-up dancer'.

Mitzi obviously moved very well, too. 'Phil Harris played

my father,' she said, 'and we were going through a scene when Bing looked at me as I was walking away from them and said, "Hey! Phil. Doesn't she walk like a little Brook Trout going right up a stream?" From then on I was known as Brooky.'

Mitzi Gaynor's fondest memory of *Anything Goes* was the recording of the soundtrack album. The studio call was for eight in the morning and she had been up since half-past five to get to the studio by ten to eight. 'Bing had been there since about seven-fifteen,' she said, 'talking with the musicians and all warmed-up, and ready to go. Billy May did the arrangements for us and he came roaring in like a bull at one minute to eight.

'His hair was standing in rats' tails, he was still in his pyjamas and bedroom slippers, and had on a big old funny coat and big funny hat; he was running around and was supposed to give the downbeat at eight o'clock. I was a little kind of dopey—but we got it all done and I was out of there by nine-thirty.'

About this time, the British comedian Norman Wisdom was making his first visit to Hollywood and was scheduled for an audition at Paramount. Bing was relaxing in a studio deck-chair when Norman went into his singing-and-dancing routine. Afterwards, the crooner left his chair and ambled across to Norman, saying: 'Gee! That's a swell dance. I wish I could do that.'

Crosby explained that in his picture he had to perform a sort of soft-shoe eccentric dance and asked Norman if he would show him how it was done.

'I was with him quite a few hours,' said Norman, 'showing him the steps. And he did them, too.'

Now the wedding bells should be ringing out for Kathryn and the crooner . . . But come 2 May she lost her nerve and, it transpired, so had he. They set a third date for 10 September 1955, up at Heyden Lake, where Crosby still had his summer home.

Meanwhile, there was much to occupy the Groaner—notably the fast-developing medium that was television.

His radio show came to an end that year and it was the passing of an era; the finale to a historic career that had lasted twenty-five years—eighteen of them at the top.

He moved immediately into television, but not to the same extent as radio, with some good reasoning. 'Anybody who allows himself to appear on television once a week,' he said, 'is out of his mind. Exposure like that devours you.'

He felt that television would eat up talent and material faster than it could be developed and that people who appeared too frequently would eventually lose their appeal.

Consequently his TV début was an all-star affair in the traditional American form of a one-off special. Appearing with him were Frank Sinatra, Louis Armstrong, Rosemary Clooney and the growing Lindsay Crosby.

A great deal of rehearsal went into it with Bing always present even if the rest of the cast weren't. 'Frank Sinatra didn't rehearse as much as we did,' said Miss Clooney. 'Bing and I knew our parts perfectly by the time he showed up. And I must say that Frank kind of came off the best, because he was looser than everybody else.'

Musical director Norman Luboff thought Crosby was very nervous about the show. 'You must remember it was a whole new medium for him,' he said.

The Groaner's diligence paid dividends. The show was a walloping great hit and soared to the top of the ratings. The networks saw the obvious attraction of pairing Crosby with Sinatra and when Frank was given his own special, Bing was a natural star guest choice. With him were Dean Martin and Mitzi Gaynor and the show was entitled 'Frank Sinatra, Dean Martin and Bing Crosby present Mitzi Gaynor'.

Because of film commitments they rehearsed at night. Dean Martin was going through his Crosby phase of crooning and was uninhibited that the Groaner was there to listen to him.

'How'm I doing?' Dean would ask him.

'You seem a little tense,' Crosby would kid him. 'A little sensitive . . .'

The show won three awards and kept millions round the box . . .

In those mid-'fifties Bing lost another old and close friend. Songwriter Johnny Burke—who had been with him since 'Pennies from Heaven' days—died. But the show had to go on and the lively lyricist Sammy Cahn replaced Johnny in the Jimmy Van Heusen partnership.

Most of the Cahn–Van Heusen numbers were penned in a small white bungalow on the Paramount film lot in Hollywood. It was affectionately known as The Blue Goose Café: 'At five o'clock the piano was closed,' said Sammy, 'the typewriter covered and the booze brought out. At which Bing used to say,

"Well, so long brothers—I'm too old for Mr Van Heusen after five!" And it was true, because when Bing and Jimmy were younger they used to swing a little. At the Blue Goose, Crosby would say, "When the sun goes past the yardarm, you avoid Van Heusen like a plague." '

The Groaner's recordings were fewer now along with his appearances in the hit parades, but the output was still considerable. To mark his twenty-one years with them, the American Decca company came up with a brilliant idea—a bumper anniversary collection of his big songs on five albums packaged in a box. It is now an accepted marketing style, but in 1955 it was a remarkable innovation and another first for Bing.

The discs had him singing eighty-nine songs spanning more than the twenty-one years he had been with Decca, for the selection included material he had waxed earlier.

He re-recorded the whole lot with the Buddy Cole Trio—and took only five minutes a song, each with a commentary from Bing about its history.

In Britain it was thought that a reasonable sale of the package would be five hundred. By the 'seventies, eleven thousand had been sold.

But 10 September 1955, wasn't going to turn out to be an anniversary. Kathryn arrived at Heyden Lake all right. All seemed well until, a few hours before the marriage ceremony was to be performed by a Catholic priest, she announced: 'Bing, I think I'd better get back to the studio now . . .'

Crosby, it appeared, kept his cool and agreed, although a little earlier he had told her: 'I'm not going to let you go home this time. You've traipsed around long enough.' But it was he who drove her to the airport.

Within weeks he was enmeshed in *High Society*, along with such friends as Sinatra, Satchmo the Great and Grace Kelly. The film was a musical version of *The Philadelphia Story*, which became a Hollywood classic in 1940 with Katharine Hepburn, Cary Grant and James Stewart. It was Sinatra and Crosby's first major film together and it was the last to be made by Grace Kelly before retiring to marry Prince Rainier and become Princess Grace of Monaco. Cole Porter wrote the score and it marked his return to the Hollywood musical scene after an absence of ten years.

Princess Grace still talks with great enthusiasm of her fare-well movie: 'I'd always longed to do a musical and, of course, working with Bing Crosby and Frank Sinatra was simply mar-vellous. They create a certain excitement and are two very strong personalities. So it was fascinating for me to be in the middle—watching the tennis match go back and forth from one to another with tremendous wit and humour—each one trying to outdo the other.'

Bing was also delighted to be working with Grace Kelly again. After their initial problems on *The Country Girl* they had become good friends: 'She's a great lady,' he enthuses, 'with great talent and kind, considerate, friendly with everybody. She was great with the crew and they all loved her. She used to bring gifts for their children's birthdays or anniversaries. I adored her and thought she was one of the nicest women I knew, and ever worked with.'

The big song to come from *High Society* was the ballad 'True Love', duetted by Grace and Bing. It sold a million, earned them a gold disc and put the Groaner back in the charts round the world.

'I'm very proud of my gold record,' said Princess Grace as she talked in her Palace at Monaco where the award now hangs. 'Of course Bing really pulled me through. My brother once made a very unbrotherly remark by saying that he thought my voice on a golden record was one of the "modern miracles". But I was very delighted about it.'

Her brother's comment about the Kelly voice was also shared by M-G-M. Says Bing: 'I had a great deal of trouble with the studio. They didn't want her to sing on the record; they thought it should have a better voice. Of course, I was determined to have Grace on a record that I thought had a chance to be a gold one and we had quite a squabble about it. She didn't know anything about it; she didn't care whether she sang on it or not, but she was delighted when she did. Every time I see her—or hear from her—she says something about it.'

'True Love' was Bing's twentieth gold disc and Grace's first and only one. The recording scene was—she reckoned—a bit of a mystery to her: 'Bing was so easy, because he's used to it and you know he can record with his pipe in his mouth! I found it quite a worrying experience to be recording with a big orchestra, but Bing made me feel very relaxed and helped me through. He has a very deep voice and my voice is rather thin and high, and it was a problem for this recording. I was supposed to sing the melody, but there was too much difference in our voices and I finally had to sing the harmony instead.'

Those few harmony lines that Grace Kelly sang on 'True Love' have earned her at least fifty thousand dollars in record royalties over the years.

High Society was completed in March 1956, and was Crosby's only film that year.

His romance continued to blow hot and cold and there was one more attempt to go through with a marriage ceremony up at Heyden Lake. This time Bing was scared off when he found batteries of cameras being set up on his lawn and the Press there in battalion strength.

'Bing has a very private feeling about life, and marriage and death,' says Kathryn. 'He doesn't like to share certain things . . .'

Crosby had a discussion with the priest who was to have married them and said later to Kathryn: 'Father Corkery and I talked at great length today. Maybe we are wrong. Maybe the world is trying to tell us something . . .'

The Groaner chased some of the blues away by busying himself in a ninety-minute television drama, an adaptation of the Maxwell Anderson play *High Tor*, which concerned a small-town American newspaper publisher who, fed up with all the bad news, intended calling his paper *Wonderful World* and printing only good news. In the tele-play there was a romance between Bing and Nancy Olsen and another between him and the ghost of a Dutch girl in the shape of Julie Andrews. Seven songs were written for the production by Arthur Schwartz and some critics thought these and Bing's singing of them were the best thing about it.

In the *New York Herald Tribune*, John Crosby (no relation) pointed out that this was hardly enough to pull the show through. He wrote: 'So the problem of what to do with the national asset named Bing Crosby remains unsolved, at least as far as television is concerned. I'd like to see him wander through a live show some time, but the chances are pretty dim. "I've watched those poor fellows on the live shows, the sweat pouring out of them," says Mr Crosby. "Not for me." '

High Tor was shot in twelve days—and looked like it, said some professional film-makers in Hollywood, who would have spent at least three times as long if it had been their baby . . .

It would be a year before the Groaner and Kathryn saw or spoke to each other after the Heyden Lake debacle. Kathryn ran away not only from marriage but also from her work. When she could no longer stand the monotony she called Harry Cohen, her boss at Paramount and told him she was coming back.

'When I arrived at his office,' she says, 'he rose—the first time he'd ever stood for anybody, I'm sure. He said, "How can I help you, Miss Grant?" Then I cried. Because he had the reputation of being a very mean man—and yet he was the most gallant person. He asked no questions; he simply threw me into picture after picture.'

Bing threw himself into *Man on Fire* for M-G-M as 1957 began, playing an industrial tycoon. It was his first totally non-singing role. To try to keep this identity, the Ames Brothers recorded the title song to be played over the credits. Crosby also recorded a version for his faithful followers throughout the world. When producer Sol Siegel heard it he changed his mind and had Bing singing at the opening of the film instead.

Crosby entered for the British Amateur Golf championship once more in May—but scratched and had a tilt at the French championship at Chantilly the following month. Nonchalantly, it was reported, he swung his way to victory in the first match, beating Frenchman Pierre Bouchayer four and three. But no stampede this time. A gallery of less than fifty was made up mostly of women and photographers.

Despite this public show of nonchalance, he desperately longed for Kathryn and bombarded her with letters. Not that they simmered with passion or really said anything definite.

'He wrote letters like weather reports,' says Kathryn. 'Like, "It's now cold and clear up in Pebble Beach; the golf is good and the skies are blue . . ."' They went unanswered.

And no one would give him her phone number—not even Aunt Mary, who wasn't a blood relation but a long-time friend of Kathryn's in Texas.

'So I scoured around and used every device,' he says. And even went so far as to invent a lawsuit.

He wrote that he was being sued and needed a deposition from her explaining where he had been on a certain September day—actually they had been trying to dodge reporters on one of their non-wedding days. So she rang him. 'Yes,' she said, 'I will be happy to help you with the court case, but I won't see you.' Then she left to make a film in Spain.

Still determined, Bing fired off another salvo of letters; again they went unanswered until suddenly he found himself on target with a proposal. Kathryn was astonished.

'He actually came out and said on paper that he loved me,' she revealed—'and that was quite a blow.

'I called Aunt Mary in Texas and said, "I think I'd better answer this one"—and he happened to be on the other line to her. So she talked to him for me. We flew to Las Vegas that day and were married there the next morning. I'd not spoken to him really for a year until we were married . . .'

Bing moved fast. To try to keep the marriage a secret he dreamed up a story about having to visit his dentist in Las Vegas and called up his old boyhood pal Leo Lynn, now his personal assistant and companion. They arranged to meet in Vegas that evening in the Sands Hotel, one of the bright-light casino-hotels on the glittering Strip that is the backbone of the gambling mecca; a twenty-four-hour-a-day town that boasts no public clocks. Leo was going to be best man, but as yet he didn't know it.

'When I got there,' said Leo, 'he told me, "I'm going to get married! I'm going to marry Kathryn Grant and I want you to go and get a wedding ring and to find out where the licence bureau is." '

Bing also asked Leo to arrange for some flowers and told him the wedding was to take place at St Anne's Catholic Church. It was then eleven o'clock at night—but Vegas stays up late. 'So I went down,' said Leo, 'and first found the licence bureau and told them I'd got a friend who might be getting married and asked if they were open all the time. They were. So then I checked the street for parking zones.'

Next, Leo reconnoitred the route to the church and made a dry run to find the best and quickest way there. Getting the ring was no problem. Las Vegas is well used to late shoppers and caters for marriages around the clock.

Getting the flowers was not so straightforward. 'To get a

corsage,' said Leo, 'I found I had to go to a wedding chapel. They wanted to know who was getting married. 'Well,' I says, 'it's my brother,' but they asked me to bring him in. I said "I'll try and persuade him, but I have to have the flowers for the girls and he'll probably just come here for the wedding." ' So he got the corsages.

Leo snatched a few hours' sleep before collecting Bing, Kathryn and her matron of honour Mary Banks at seven-thirty the next morning.

Running to plan, their first stop was at the licence bureau. 'But as soon as we walked in they recognised Bing—and vooom!' said Leo.

The bureau buzzed with excitement and confusion and—as if by magic—the Press appeared.

'A reporter came up,' says Kathryn, 'and asked, "Are you getting married?", and I turned on my heel and walked out. Bing grabbed me by the elbow—which was a very positive step—and said, "Yes, we're going to Yerington to get married." I'd never heard of that place and thought that's interesting, but kind of in a fog. I didn't know where Yerington was or if we were getting married! (Yerington was a town some 350 miles north on the road to Reno.)

'I didn't care actually, because I was going into a movie and had a costume fitting at ten o'clock that morning, and if I got the next plane I could still make the fitting. So I started out of the building, because this was what had happened before. The reporter bolted out to tell all his friends to go to Yerington. We drove two blocks down the street to St Anne's and were married at last!'

The date was 24 October 1957. Monsignor John J. Ryan officiated at the ceremony and reluctantly agreed to the church doors being locked at Bing's request 'so we won't be bothered'. The only members of the public present were the two altar servers who assisted Monsignor Ryan at the service and at the nuptial Mass that followed.

Kathryn was in a white suit and wore a Spanish mantilla on her dark hair. The crooner looked spruce in a dark pinstripe. None of Bing's four sons could be there; two were in the army, two at college.

Asked if the marriage was sudden, before the couple left for a honeymoon at Bing's Nevada ranch at Elko, Crosby said: 'No,

I decided long ago, but it was a matter of selling her on the idea. Now I must phone the boys and tell them the news.'

After four tempestuous on-and-off years they were at last man and wife. They were fun years to look back on but no laughing matter at the time.

'I think there were as many complications in our romance as most people have in a lifetime of marriage,' reveals Kathryn. 'As a matter of fact our courtship was so traumatic that I think any problems of marriage are simple by comparison. There were a lot of things. I was young; Bing felt he was older. He didn't know whether I would like the kind of life we live, but its the only kind of life I've ever known and it's what I really love—taking long walks, early to bed, early to rise and that sort of thing.

'The long delay was very good, because, by the time we did marry, I knew that I could live without him, though I wouldn't have been as happy, certainly. I wouldn't have had the fun that he means to my life, but I could have made it on my own as an actress and as a person. I think that's very important for every woman to know before she decides to join her life with another individual.'

There is no doubt that the thousands of 'you've no right to do this—you're too young and he's too great—you've no right to marry each other' letters that she received from Bing's fans played a major part.

Kathryn took them very much to heart and was even deeply hurt by some of them: 'Maybe they were right,' she says matter-of-factly, but I thought if they were right, then they had the right to be all the way right. So we wouldn't date, we wouldn't go to dinner, we wouldn't do those things. If our relationship wasn't going to progress in an honourable fashion, it was going to stop completely. I changed my phone number and that seemed to be a little frustrating to him.'

Bing reflects on the courtship with a smile. 'We were going to get married three or four times and then I'd lose my courage,' he says. 'I was fearful that there'd be a lot of criticism. I was a bit timorous about it, but finally I figured that if I could just do it secretly and privately, and then let the news come out, it would be all right. Her mother was furious. She said that I married Kathryn for the publicity,' he says with a definite twinkle in both eyes.

The difference in ages was great, but with Bing and Kathryn there was a meeting half-way. He was a man both physically and mentally younger than his years and she was a girl who liked more mature people and who had a more mature view of life. One doesn't have to be around them very long, to see that the gap isn't wide at all.

Back home in Hollywood after the honeymoon Kathryn was surprised and not a little shocked to find that a blanket cover on their double bed bore the initials of his previous wife— D. L. C. And in a bathroom there was a portrait of Dixie with the inscription 'To my angel Bing'.

Kathryn confessed that she was jealous and thought of calling her mother, but she was convinced that mother would say that now she was married she would have to work out her own problems.

Instead, Kathryn consulted Bing's mother. There was a new blanket cover on the bed that night . . .

Like her predecessor, Kathryn retired from the screen after her marriage to Bing, although later she returned to the stage but still faced the inevitable questions about regretting giving up a promising movie career: 'I haven't given up anything really,' she replied, 'I've gained everything; I've gained three lovely children, although I never particularly wanted to have children. They just popped up—one, two, three—and they're the most exciting young human beings I've ever known and it's lovely,' she said proudly.

The three children came all in the space of four years. Harry Lillis Junior was born on 8 August 1958; Mary Frances—his one and only daughter—on 14 September 1959, and Nathaniel Patrick—Nathaniel after Bing's great-grandfather the mariner —came along on 29 October 1961, twenty-eight years after the birth of his first son and making him a father for the seventh time at the age of sixty.

But it wasn't going to be the stay-at-home life for the second Mrs Crosby. She went out on tour for ten seasons, taking lead roles in well-known plays and starring in such productions as *Pygmalion* both as a musical and straight play. 'In fact,' says Bing, 'she was busier than I was. The only person busier than Kathryn is Bop Hope!'

The second marriage and subsequent family brought about a marked change in Bing. In the years preceding it there had been many newspaper reports about the crooner's dissatisfaction with life in general and Hollywood in particular. Army Archerd, one of America's top show business journalists with twenty-five years' knowledge of Bing, sees the marriage as a turning point: 'I think it was the rebirth of his life and a new impetus for him to continue in show business. I doubt whether he would really have gone on—as successfully as he had in this second-half of his life—had he not married again and had this wonderful second family. I think he got the urge to be Bing Crosby again.'

He also had the urge to leave Hollywood and at the first opportunity bought a mansion in the San Francisco suburb of Hillsborough and moved up there lock-stock-and-pipe.

But he denies that he was turning his back on the film capital. 'I had no dissatisfaction with life or Hollywood,' he says. 'Of course, a new wife and family gave me some inspiration and great pleasure, but it had nothing to do with my zest for work. Nor did it change my life style. We moved north because I had many dear friends there; it's a better climate; there are better schools there and more of the things I like—and only one hour from Hollywood and work.'

Although he wasn't working as hard as when he was bringing up his first family, the Groaner still travelled widely and—bearing in mind that he spent little time at home with his first four sons—made a great effort to be with the new children as much as possible: 'I think I'm with them a lot more, you know,' says Bing, 'because I'm not working that much and when we do travel we take them with us. Kathryn has a teacher's certificate and she takes their school work with us and has a little session with them every day.' (She has a Bachelor of Fine Arts degree from the University of Texas.)

The three Crosby children have seen the world with their parents—Africa, Europe, South America, Hawaii and Mexico every year—and the airlines consider the crooner to be somewhat of a modern jet-setting gypsy when he regularly turns up with wife, children and mountain of luggage.

For a year and a half the busy Kathryn Crosby has been appearing on a morning CBS television show that goes out locally five times a week. She interviews personalities such as authors with new books; artists, gardeners, doctors, cooking experts, and the rest. A time-consuming calling. 'She is up at a quarter to seven,' says Bing, 'and doesn't get home much before five pm.'

There is a lot of preparatory work for the programme—but Kathryn still manages to be very active in various charity works. And two or three times a week goes to ballet class 'for work-outs.'

As with her own family, and Bing's first, his mother Kate—until she died in 1964 at the age of ninety-one—made sure she was around to keep an experienced eye on the upbringing of her youngest grandchildren. 'When I first met Bing's mother,' says Kathryn, 'she was a very lovely lady of about eighty-five. When the children were little, I did what most mothers will do—I made mistakes. Harry put his hand in his oatmeal and I patted his hand, and he thought it was a game. So I patted it harder and then he realised it really wasn't a game, and mother was hitting his hand to hurt it, because she didn't like what he was doing. He bellowed.

'But instead of snatching him up from the table and running, as my mother would have done, Bing's mother said, "Well, there's nothing wrong with his lungs, is there?" and she was always my dearest friend, and greatest ally.'

Through the years, most of Bing's fervent female admirers have considered him to be a very romantic man, mainly because of his film roles. Kathryn is able to shed some first-hand light on Crosby the lover: 'Bing has said all the lovely words to the very lovely ladies on the screen, but he had very good writers! Innately, he's very sensitive and I think when it came to saying words that would commit him, he would be doubly reticent—without his script.'

Between having babies, the second Mrs Crosby spent five years training to be a state registered nurse. When she took her finals she was first in the Los Angeles area and fourth in the State of California.

While the first-born of the second union, baby Harry Lillis Crosby, was cooing in his cot, Bing's first family were really making a noise. And not only singing . . .

Chapter Seventeen

The Las Vegas audience liked them and the applause was generous. The Crosby Boys—as they called the act that was led by ex-soldier Gary with the crew-cut hair—seemed mightily pleased with the night's work and the reception it received.

'Well, that's pretty good for four boys trying to get ahead without the old man's money,' Gary told the rows of smiling faces at the supper tables.

Then he said: 'That's the biggest hand we've had since we told Dad we were leaving home.'

Later in a dressing-room interview he told a reporter: 'Dad and I just don't get along. You take it as long as you can. I'm not taking guff from anybody. You might as well handle your own troubles, because nobody ain't gonna do it for you. We're just a bunch of crazy Irish and we lead our own lives.'

Life, however, was beginning to turn a little sour . . .

It was really inevitable that the four Crosby boys should eventually follow their father into show business. He had done exactly what his parents had and actively encouraged music around the house. After dinner most nights the boys were allowed to sing with their father and even develop their own acts for their parents. 'We always fooled around with songs at home,' remembers Gary, 'kidding and singing together in harmony. No big thing, but he'd be singing something and I'd sing a top to it or a bottom to it or the other way round.'

Being the eldest, Gary got the show business bug first, but he found Bing neither helpful nor unhelpful: 'He always asked me what was going on in my head. Then he'd just kind of look at me and would give me a few hints—"If you're going to be in the business, do this or do that." He never pushed me towards it and he never pulled me away from it.'

Gary made his motion picture début with father in September 1942, a brief appearance in *Star Spangled Rhythm*. He was thrilled, but regrets that he wasn't old enough to take real advantage of his initiation into the business. 'I was standing outside the studio,' says Gary, 'bouncing a ball against a wall. Betty Hutton comes up and was supposed to ask me where Bing Crosby was and I was to say "in there". Then she picks me up and kisses me—which I thoroughly loathed at that age. That was disgusting!'

But he enjoyed that first picture. For a start, three days off school was a welcome bonus and then there were the stars— forty-three of them, including Gary Cooper, Bob Hope, Mary Martin, Dick Powell, Frederic March and William Bendix. 'I can always remember sitting in a corner,' says Gary, 'watching all the biggies walking around and talking like they're regular human beings.'

Gary was eighteen when he set out to try to conquer the business on his own—and found all too soon that he was simply living in the shadow of his famous father.

'They tried to make a second Bing out of me,' he says. 'They put me with Sammy Davis Junior to make a second "Bing and Louis" (a celebrated album by Crosby and Louis Armstrong), then they put me with a sister group to make another Bing-and-Andrews Sisters sort of thing. I guess they figured people would buy an imitation, but at eighteen I knew they wouldn't.'

For Gary there were tours with Armstrong and with the Les Brown Band. Then the Army called him and he served 730 days. When asked how long he had been in uniform he would reel off the precise number of days, hours, minutes and seconds he had served. He detested the Army but thought the discipline was 'nothing compared with what I had to endure at home.'

When he returned to civilian life to pick up the threads of his career, he was to find his father married to an actress who was younger than Gary himself.

It was Gary's idea to form the four-brother act and call it

'The Crosby Boys' (the music business dubbed them the Bingettes).

Says Dennis Crosby: 'I was a disc-jockey at ABC radio in Los Angeles. The other boys were just getting out of the Army. Gary got us together and started to push us. Dad kind of stayed in the background and said, "If you want to do it, go ahead, that's fine with me". But he never pushed us.'

Bing's reaction to his son's nightclub act was not what one would expect from a proud father, but—says Dennis—it was characteristic of him: 'He was surprised the first time he saw us. He said he didn't think we'd be that good and he was a little nervous. In fact the first time he saw us was at the Moulin Rouge in Los Angeles, but instead of coming down and sitting with us and taking a table he went way up in the light booth! We didn't know he was there until the middle of the act, when he came backstage and said in his usual manner "not bad, not bad", and then he walked off.'

'The Crosby Boys' were to have four years of success, but they travelled a tough and rough road along the way. They squabbled, they fought each other with their fists. They rowed in restaurants, at parties, in nightclubs—even on stage—and they got their names in the papers and on to the police files with drunk-driving charges. There was it seemed, a fair share of the Crosby strain in them.

In Las Vegas—the family marriage ground—Dennis wed a divorcee showgirl named Pat Sheehan, who was three years his senior and already had a son of six years. There, too, twin Philip found Miss Sandra Drummond, also a showgirl. Both ladies were high-kickers in the Tropicana Hotel chorus line.

The Groaner, talking to Hollywood columnist Joe Hyams, commented: 'They married nice girls and that's the important thing. A lot of showgirls are pretty wonderful people. I would have been upset if the boys had married too young, though. I think a boy or girl of 23 or 24 is old enough to get married, but I don't like to see anybody 19 get married; even a girl then is too young.'

It was to Hyams, that Crosby made his oft-quoted confession about having failed his first family: 'I think I failed them by giving them too much work and discipline, too much money and too little time and attention. But I did my best and so did their mother.'

Then he admitted that he did 'get out of patience' with them now that they were grown-up. He said: 'But the jury isn't in yet on what kind of citizens my boys will make. I just want them to be nice guys. I don't care how big they are or how important. I'd just like them to be the kind of people you like to have around and that other people would like to have around. I want them to have good friends, but not necessarily important ones. And I want them to be thoughtful of other people; I hate thoughtlessness, rudeness and arrogance . . .

'I know I could help the boys if they'd listen to me. I could make it much easier for them. But ten minutes after they leave me they've fallen in with somebody else who undoes everything I've done.'

The Crosby Boys went on their merry, roistering way. In Montreal there was a report of a vicious fight between two of the brothers at the El Morocco Club. A management spokesman said that the boys had been most uncooperative. One night they put on only a two-minute show instead of the usual forty-five minutes. Then they decided to terminate the engagement. Gary, it was said, was having throat trouble because of the Canadian weather. Their manager said there had been a temporary split and the brothers were taking a lay-off for five or six months.

Eventually dates became fewer and transportation costs soared alarmingly and the Crosby Boys called it a day. 'We found we were losing money,' said Philip Crosby, 'so we just split and everybody went his own way.'

Philip is now the only one of the quartet still singing—entertaining the customers in the plusher bars of the big hotels. But says he hasn't found comparisons with father troublesome.

'I never really thought of having them forget that I am Bing Crosby's kid,' admits Philip, 'because I know that there isn't anything I could do or say, or any disguise I could wear; they would still know its Bing Crosby's son up there. So I don't take him out of the act. I talk about him; I use him; I use him a lot in comedy; I bounce off him. Its very well meant and I do sing some of his hit records, which are received tremendously. But that's about as far as I go; I don't try to imitate him any more than that.'

Gary and Lindsay are actors and much of Gary's spare time

197

is devoted to voluntary youth work. Dennis quit the footlights and now has a sound equipment business.

Since Bing's move to San Francisco the four only see him when he visits Hollywood for television shows or when they call occasionally at his Hillsborough mansion.

Chapter Eighteen

It was time to put on the priestly robes once more, time to complete three pictures in one day—and to take to the road again when he got his breath back.

This time he became Father Conroy in *Say One for Me*, made by his own production company and co-starring Debbie Reynolds and Robert Wagner. But Bing's re-entry into the priesthood was anything but solemn or ceremonious. When he arrived on the set for the first scene Father Crosby tripped on his cassock and fell flat on his face ... to a great accompaniment of laughter from the rest of the cast.

'I forgot you had to hitch these things up,' said Crosby, picking himself up. 'It's been so long.' It was December 1958, and it had been thirteen years since he played Father O'Malley in *Bells of St Mary's*.

He spent four months as Father Conroy and managed to stay the right way up. Then it was time for family, for fishing, for hunting, for travel, for golf, for a television spectacular— they usually took some ten days to make and therefore did not cut deeply into his now more prolonged periods of leisure.

Not that his leisure was leisurely. He would fish streams, fish the seas off Alaska or Mexico; travel miles in search of game; fly to Europe for a three-day recording session.

But the crooner has always kept a low publicity profile about his shooting activities. He doesn't like photographs of himself with guns or dead animals, because he feels that it would draw unnecessary attention to firearms and also stir up animosity amongst anti-blood sport groups. But he has been shooting for years and an early partner was one of the best shots in the United States—actor Robert Stack, known to television millions in *The Untouchables* series. 'Bing shoots a twenty-gauge double and he shoots it very well,' said Stack. 'And he's a little better than average,' added Crosby's old buddy Phil Harrris.

Mainly, Bing confines his hunting activities to his male friends, but he did and still does occasionally involve Kathryn: 'I love to walk the fields with Bing,' she says, 'and I take a very little gun that I can carry all day without bothering him. I love being out in nature and Bing is very comfortable in the world of nature; it's a man's world and I'm very grateful that he's shared it with me.'

Kathryn has always been used to being around hunters and therefore finds nothing strange in Bing's occasional bachelor trips into the outbacks of America: 'My father was a hunter. He came from pioneer stock in Louisiana and I was accustomed to my daddy disappearing at the beginning of the deer season and coming back when it was all over,' she says.

Yet, amidst all this sparetime activity, Crosby considered himself to be lazy—and still does.

'Well,' he says, 'golf is a kind of desultory past-time; there's no activity involved there. You walk round, you hit a ball, you talk with your friends. Its just a walk in the country, belting a ball about.

'Fishing's a very relaxing activity. You fish a stream, in the quiet and the woods, and you're trying different kinds of flies to attract the trout and you get so involved and so engrossed in what you're doing. Time flies and first thing you know, you've walked miles up some stream and then you have to walk home and it's getting dark.

'Hunting's much the same. If you're working with hunting dogs you get engrossed in that too and it's a very relaxing past-time. So, those are the three things I do most—hunting, fishing and golf. They're all relaxing and maybe that's the way I'm constructed.'

But it was back to work now in the new year that was 1960 and into a film aptly titled *High Time*. It has previously been provisionally called *Daddy-O*, which was equally appropriate with Crosby as its star.

It was a story that had originally been written for Spencer Tracy and now had to be adapted musically. And it gave Bing an opportunity to work with another top Hollywood director, Blake Edwards, who later married Britain's *Mary Poppins* star Julie Andrews.

Co-starring with Crosby were pop singer Fabian and the up-and-coming Tuesday Weld. And once again our hero was late on parade.

'We were on location in Stockton, California,' said Edwards, 'and Bing had an early call. He didn't show up and I was forced to shoot something else. There was no word from him and when he did show up he was typical Bing; very easy-going and not going to explain anything.

'This made me even madder and I said something like "Okay, where the hell were you?" and he replied, "I was locked in a closet with twenty-four wild gypsies and a hot guitar!" Now, how can you be mad with anybody who delivers a line like that? I tried very hard to have a very tough face about it, but I broke up and laughed.'

There was another delay too—the Hollywood actors' strike that cut into production for five weeks during March and April.

It was *High Time* that gave us the Sammy Cahn—Jimmy Van Heusen standard 'The Second Time Around'. The song was nominated for an Academy Award but lost out to 'Never On Sunday'.

On the final day of shooting there was no time for Bing to join in any end-of-picture celebration; hardly time even to put his feet up to enjoy a pipe.

He hurried across the 20th Century-Fox lot to another studio to make a guest appearance in the Marilyn Monroe movie *Let's Make Love*, which had a part in it for British singing star Frankie Vaughan.

Then he had to pop down the road to Columbia for another guest spot in *Pepe*, with the Mexican comic Cantinflas and Dan Dailey. Thus he completed three films in one day and must qualify for a mention in the records somewhere.

Guesting with Bing in the Monroe film were Gene Kelly and Milton Berle, the comedian. But their presence was due only to the actors' strike. Fred Astaire, Jack Benny and Frank Sinatra were originally cast as guests, but the strike so delayed the productions they were in that they weren't available when the time came.

Gene Kelly flew specially from Paris to make his one-day appearance. And asked for his expert opinion on the qualities of Crosby as a hoofer, he replied: 'There's nothing to criticise; he moves very well, but he never seriously tried to dance. You know, it's a laugh. He always made joke of it. So I don't think I could do anything more than Bing does himself—just kid about it. But if he had tried harder at it he could have done a lot more.'

Bing, after his marathon movie day, danced off on vacation for a month in search of game, large and small.

Then it was off to London with Kathryn, on their way to Rome for the 1960 Olympic Games and his first audience with the Pope.

In London the couple checked in to Claridges with its memories of his wartime visit and the doodle-bug bombs. He showed Kathryn the sights and answered the increasingly popular question: Why did a man of his wealth still go on working?

'It's kind of hard just to pull out, you see,' he said, pulling on his pipe. 'You have obligations to people, you get tied up in contracts. Besides, I like it . . .

'It's flattering to see that there are still people around who remember you.

'I don't work anything like as hard as I used to. I reckon I've just about got things worked out right now, with about four television shows a year, a few records, a film. Gives me plenty of time for golf, fishing and travelling.'

Asked about his four sons of his first marriage, he said: 'They are all provided for. They needn't do another thing if they don't want to.'

He bought five suits from his London tailor and called in on 'my old pal Jock Whitney, the American Ambassador'.

Said Bing: 'It was a funny thing; I just walked all incognito and unannounced into the embassy and asked to see the ambassador and the guy at the door says just go up to the secretary's room, but the secretary's room was empty so I just walked through a door and there was Mr Ambassador himself. He was kind of surprised . . .'

When he returned home Bing cut an album of one hundred and one songs in three days!

'We do it quick,' he explained, 'because the musicians get 'golden time' after six hours' work.'

Which left him time for more leisure, the celebrating of Christmas—'that's a three-week project by any standard,' he said—the annual Crosby golf tourney, and a fishing trip to Mexico to land tuna and swordfish and another to Canada to snare the wary salmon.

But there was work in the offing. In fact preparations had been going on for a year setting up *Road to Hong Kong*—seventh and last in the series that had begun more than twenty years earlier and the first to be made outside Hollywood.

The film went before the cameras in Britain's Shepperton Studios on 2 August 1961 and took four months to complete.

Bing brought Kathryn with him and young Harry. Bob Hope brought his wife Dolores and his son Kelly, then fifteen, and daughter Nora, then fourteen.

Again, the Groaner and the comic each had a third share in the financing of the film with Mel Frank and Norman Panama, who wrote *Road to Utopia* in 1944 and were now producing and directing *Hong Kong* as well as having written the screenplay.

It was the first 'Road' film without Paramount—and the first without Dorothy Lamour as leading lady.

Brigitte Bardot had been the first fancy for the role. Bing was all for it. 'I'd like to see Bardot in the part most of all,' he had said some months earlier. 'Mind you, I think she might be a little on the young side for Hope.

'Filming is kind of difficult for someone at my time of life. I'm too old to get the girl and not old enough to be her grandad. But still I'd sure like to work with Bardot. I only saw one film of hers, but it made a deep impression. Pretty good lines, I'd say . . .'

His next choice was Gina Lollobrigida. There was also a production discussion about getting Sophia Loren. But in the end the leading feminine role went to Britain's Joan Collins.

Bob Hope thought that Lamour was the lady for the part and was indignant when he found that she had been offered only a small 'sop' part.

This she herself turned down initially because in the scene her song would be ruined by a comedy sequence.

The production team had reasoned that Miss Lamour was no

longer the sexy sarong girl of years past and that a younger actress would be the natural choice. Finally, after a direct intervention by Bop Hope, she was persuaded to make a brief appearance as herself.

A bigger headache for producer Mel Frank, as filming neared, was finding somewhere to park Crosby and Hope and families for four months. Ideally, he wanted them near the Shepperton studios, but this proved difficult and with London at the height of the tourist season both families had to stay in different hotels in town.

Hope soon tired of the arrangement and so did the Crosbys. Kathryn and Mrs Hope went in search of alternative accommodation somewhere out of town. Apart from having Harry with her, Mrs Crosby was also heavily pregnant for the third time.

Mel Frank luckily came up with a winner for the Hopes— Cranbourne Court, a stately country house at Winkfield, Berkshire, with twenty-five acres and twenty-two bedrooms; the Wentworth and Sunningdale courses close at hand and Shepperton only minutes away. Complete with a traditional Wodehouse-type butler named Pope. The only snag being that the rent was £400 a week.

Producer Frank took Mrs Hope out to see the house. 'She fell in love with it at once,' he said. Then she drove immediately to Wentworth where Hope and Crosby were playing eighteen holes. The news was big enough for them to forget golf for once and they dashed off to give Cranbourne Court the once-over.

'Jeez, it's too big,' said Hope. 'Twenty-two bedrooms.'

'Why don't we both live in it?' suggested Bing.

So the families moved in under the one roof—the only time this had ever happened to Crosby and Hope, despite years of working together.

Bing went in search of a nanny and hired a £100-a-week Rolls to commute to the studio.

'It was delightful,' said Mel Frank, 'they were like two little boys going to school every morning.'

They stayed at Cranbourne Court for two months, until Kathryn went home to give birth to a bouncing 9 lb 2½ oz boy to be called Nathaniel. Whereupon the Groaner handed out cigars all round to cast and unit at Shepperton. Hope sent

Kathryn a telegram: '*You can tell there was a lot of Texas in this Boy*'.

Mrs Hope flew home a week later to prepare for Bob's return at the end of the picture. Bob moved out into a country hotel within studio distance; Bing moved back into London.

There was still some fun and some golf to be had. Like the day when, for a harem scene in the film, Hope had his finger- and toe-nails painted red—only to forget about his feet when he and Bing scurried off to Wentworth for nine holes after the director called 'cut' at five o'clock.

Bing remembers it well: 'We sat down to change our golf shoes and there were two elderly English gentlemen—typical Colonel Blimp types, with the luxuriant moustaches, the tweed coats and the knickers—sitting across from us. I saw one of them's eyes fly to Hope's bare feet. He gave a shocked look, then nudged his partner to look at these red toe-nails. Hope was unaware of this scrutiny and then they looked at me with a kind of unspoken query. I just shrugged my shoulders, like I couldn't believe it either. Hope then saw that he was being surveyed, looked up at them, then down at his feet. One of the gentlemen said, "Mr Crosby, is your friend in the ballet?" Hope put on his shoes and socks and rushed out! That's the first time I ever saw him stuck without a retort—he was half mad, half embarrassed.'

A couple of weeks later the script called for the boys to travel to the Moon by rocket and to be showered with confetti on their return. 'They threw confetti on us all day,' said Bob, 'and I went back to play at Wentworth again. It was very warm and I decided to take a shower before I went home. I walked in, took off my shorts in front of two Scotsmen who were present— and confetti fell out of my shorts! They looked at me like I hadn't had a bath since New Year. Around Wentworth I was known as the fellow with red toe-nails and confetti in his shorts. I was a rare novelty in those days,' the comedian chuckled.

Road to Hong Kong—which co- and guest-starred, among others, Dean Martin, Robert Morley, David Niven, Peter Sellers and Frank Sinatra—was a box-office smash. The magazine *Films and Filming* rated it as the fifth most successful film at the box-office in 1962 and it was also claimed that both Crosby and Hope would pick-up two million dollars apiece from the receipts.

So at the age of twenty-two the 'Road' series reached the halt sign. Years later the two principals had the final word about this considerable slice of cinema history.

'I used to love it,' recalled Bob, 'because I enjoyed working with Bing. He was such a pro and it was all great fun. Bing is what you call a sympathetic comic and straight-man. He has a good sense of comedy, but he also knows more about feeding a line than anybody. I'm the best straight-man for anybody, because I know how I would like to be fed a straight line.'

Bing reciprocates the compliments, but feels Hope was the better comic: 'He's too good. I couldn't cope with him—he's a master! In the "Road" pictures I did about break even, because I'd have a few zingers to my bow. And we had a gag-man who watched the action and gave me a few things to say.'

For the statistically minded: Although the series-proper started in 1939, with *Singapore*, there was an eighth 'Road' film. It was in fact the first, made without Hope and Lamour in 1931, and was called *The Road to Hollywood*. Made by the Astor Picture Corporation, it was a compilation of the first four Crosby–Mack Sennett comedy shorts and told the story of the crooner's early rise to fame.

For the Record: The word 'love' at the end of the song 'Let's Not be Sensible' on the original soundtrack recording from *Road to Hong Kong* was not sung by Bing and had to be dubbed on by somebody else.

In the film itself there was some sort of visual distraction, which meant that Crosby never sang the last note. But the record couldn't be issued without it. Bing had hurried home to join Kathryn and the new arrival and it was too late to get him back. There was only one alternative: get somebody else to do it. Mike Sammes, of the Mike Sammes Singers group, was working on the album and was called in to supply the missing word. Bing wasn't told and co-writer of the song Sammy Cahn had no idea of this technical drama until the author played the record for him in his Hollywood home.

The Groaner went back to his life of less work and more play, which was slightly interrupted at Christmastide when he suddenly felt ill after dinner. It seemed to be something very serious and he went off to hospital in a wheelchair and Kathryn spent the night at his bedside. By morning the doctors knew it was nothing more serious than stomach influenza, but it was a worry for a time.

By March he was in such fine form that he was taking on the President of the United States at golf. The late Jack F. Kennedy was Bing's guest at his Palm Springs home—not a great distance from Frank Sinatra's magnificent spread. The visit was almost secret and received little or no publicity. But Sinatra, then deeply entrenched in the Democratic camp, knew about it and was reported to have been upset that Kennedy didn't come knocking at his door as well. Especially as he had built a presidential suite in his sprawling compound, complete with accommodation for Kennedy's Secret Service guards.

But Bing recalls that there was possibly an easy explanation.

'Frank told me,' he says, 'his place was thought unsuitable because it was in a thickly populated area right next to a popular golf club and my place sat alone on a hilltop where all approaches could be controlled and the necessary security could be achieved. I'm sure this is the right reason.

'Jack Kennedy was at my place twice for a week each.'

It made no difference, however, to Sinatra's relationship with Bing. They still saw each other and were filming together within a few months in *Robin and the Seven Hoods*.

Crosby, in fact, was an early member of the much publicised Clan. It was usually thought that Sinatra had always been king of the Rat Pack—as the group became known in the Press —and that his main courtiers were Dean Martin, Sammy Davis, Tony Curtis and Peter Lawford. But there were some other big names in the set-up when it began.

Sammy Davis talked about it: 'Bing was a member based upon the fact that the Clan really started with Bogart and Betty Bacall. Crosby, though he wasn't at every party, would be there at certain times; he'd leave early if he had to go fishing or somewhere but he'd have dinner.

'So, all the people who were involved in what the papers later called the Clan, he knew on an intimate basis and was friends with. He was a member and he made no bones about how much fun he was having. He used to say, "Do you guys live like this all the time?" '

The Sinatra-led faction of the Clan got together for the making of *Robin and the Seven Hoods*. Frank himself produced and starred in the picture, with Dean Martin, Sammy Davis,

Peter Falk and Barbara Rush. Bing only took one of the main parts when a film he was hoping to make fell through.

Robin and the Seven Hoods was a tongue-in-check look at the wicked Chicago of the Roaring 'Twenties and Edward G. Robinson—who started it all with his portrayal of a gangster in the 1930 film *Little Caesar*—made a spoof guest appearance in his immortal role. One of Bing's sons, Philip, also had a one-line part; offering his father a chair and saying, 'sit down, Pops!'

It wasn't one of Bing's best films, nor Sinatra's either, but there were reasons why.

'I just took the part for a lark,' said Crosby. 'I thought, gee, this will be fun working with these guys like Sammy Davis and Peter Falk, who's a great actor—we'll have a lot of laughs. It was a good part with some good songs, but I don't think they got involved enough. It was right at the time of Jack Kennedy's assassination and there were a lot of delays. We didn't feel like working for a few days and for some reason the co-ordination fell apart.'

Bing played an unwitting part in the lack of co-ordination too. Sammy Davis explained it like this: 'I'm working with three of the biggest guys in the business—so I can't wait for that first day when we all get around the piano to rehearse a song called "Mr Booze".

'In this there are so many Crosbyisms, all the things that we and millions of people have loved him for. And I'm standing there, and I missed my cue five times because I'm watching him. Frank said, "What the hell is wrong with you?", I said, "To hell with you, Frank, I'm listening to Bing Crosby!" Everybody just broke-up.'

That night when Sinatra, Davis, Martin and Crosby recorded 'Mr Booze' the sound stage at Warner Brothers was packed with people.

'Hey, we're drawing pretty good!' said Sinatra.

'They ain't come to see us, they came to see Bing Crosby!' said Sammy.

Working in the same studio as Bing during that film was one of Britain's best-known actors, Wilfred Hyde-White: 'The place started shaking,' he recalled, 'and I thought it was an earthquake, but it wasn't; just the boys marching in to make *Robin and the Seven Hoods*.

'Sinatra would turn up with three or four Karmen Ghias. The doors would open and bodyguards would march down, but Bing would turn up in a little car, stop at the gate for his dressing-room key and then park it himself! The difference was rather marvellous,' said Wilfred, a Crosby fan of long-standing.

'Bing was God to me, and when I came to Hollywood in 1959, to make *Let's Make Love* with Marilyn Monroe and there was to be a guest appearance by Bing Crosby I couldn't believe it. When he actually said "Good morning", I couldn't answer him.'

When four years later he had overcome his wonderment, Wilfred spent a lot of time talking to Bing during the making of *Robin and the Seven Hoods*. Their mutual interest was horse-racing and the Groaner often used to drop into the English-man's dressing-room as he arrived for work—*Robin* was shot mostly at night on Sinatra's insistence—and Hyde-White was preparing to go home.

Their first chat got off to an embarrassing start: 'I was in my little bathroom,' said Wilfred, 'washing my face, when I heard a knock at the door. I shouted, "I'm in the bathroom, won't be long. Who's that?" A voice said "Bing Crosby". "Oh," I said, "don't bugger about!" I thought it was the assistant director coming to tell me to get in at seven the next morning instead of eight. I said, "To hell with you! I'll be out in a second." I wiped myself off, went out—and there was Bing Crosby.'

There was only one more film to come. The long and glorious career on celluloid was approaching the final fade-out. But it was a farewell on a big scale on the giant screen.

Bing's last motion picture was made in Hollywood in 1965 for 20th Century-Fox. It was a Cinemascope remake of the classic John Ford western *Stagecoach*, which made John Wayne a star at last. Bing was cast in a non-singing role as the drunken doctor; the role that gained Thomas Mitchell an Oscar in 1939.

Many actors would have thought twice, or even more, about taking part in the remake of a triple-Oscar-winning classic such as *Stagecoach*. Bing says he didn't even think once: 'It was a chance to do a character and I wanted to try it. They had a big cast and I knew it had been a success before. There were some people who thought we were foolish to make the picture, because the original one was such a legend. I went to see it and great as it was it really isn't much of a film to look at any more. It's more dated than any picture I can recall ever seeing.'

John Ford was none-too-pleased about the remake of his masterpiece either, but it was backed with five million dollars and filming started in July of 1965, with Ann Margret, Alex Cord, Red Buttons, Van Heflin, Stefanie Powers and Keenan Wynn in supporting roles.

Keenan Wynn, like most of the cast, was also aware of the dangers of comparison with the earlier production and feels that Bing succeeded in overcoming them: 'Immediately you are placed in that sort of situation, you are going to be compared. I got the vision that Bing was doing his best to stay away from any preconceived opinion, which is what a pro will do. He was following an actor who had done it all before, so he wanted to do it completely differently.'

Red Buttons found the Groaner a good audience: 'He loved dialect stories,' said Red, 'and old vaudeville jokes. One story I told him became a running gag between us. It was about a Yiddish actor on a Yiddish stage on New York's Second Avenue who dropped dead during a performance. They pulled the curtain and the manager went out and made an announcement. "Ladies and gentlemen, Mr Lew Finklestein is dead!" And a guy in the balcony yelled out "give him an enema"; and the manager yelled back, "It wouldn't help"; and the guy yelled back, "It wouldn't hurt!" And this has become our punch-line throughout the years. Whenever he sees me, he yells, "It wouldn't help, but it wouldn't hurt." '

Stefanie Powers, the English-born Hollywood-based actress, has a different rapport with Bing. 'We never ever really discussed anything more than horses,' she said. 'My step-father bred horses, Bing loved race horses and we had some mutual friends in racing. So we'd bring in *Thoroughbred Magazine* and tout each other's horses. But he got into his part with the greatest of ease. He would get his make-up on, get his wardrobe on and walk right into *Stagecoach*. He just seemed to be the doctor.'

And so Bing pulled the curtain on Crosby the film star, although in 1972 he claimed he hadn't officially retired. He would, he said, return to the screen 'provided the part was right'. Having just turned down the umpteenth script, he explained what he meant: 'If one came along, and it wasn't dirty or pornographic, or lascivious, or full of smut and was a good role, I'd do it. But I don't think there are many of those films around, unless you get one with Disney.'

Bing followed this with an uncharacteristically strong attack on the film industry of the 'seventies: 'I really think its disgraceful what they're doing on the screen now,' he scowled, 'and they're starting to do it on television too. I think the entertainment media has got a lot of things to be responsible for.'

Crosby is no prude and is prepared to tell the raunchy joke with the best of them, but he believes—and his Catholic upbringing may have something to do with it—that the sexual act is a very private and loving thing: 'These films are commercial, I guess, and they sell,' he will tell you. 'I must say I I haven't seen all these things, but I read about them and I've seen a couple of them. How the hell are you going to raise children to be good citizens if they have to be exposed to things like these?

'They see actors and actresses whom they adore involved in the seamiest capers and they feel it's the sophisticated or chic way to behave. They see marriage and the family debased and derided and every license glorified. I'm sure it's agreed that no other medium in the history of the world has had such a profound influence on manners, dress, coiffure, speech or behaviour as the motion picture. And now they are selling, furiously, moral irresponsibility. I think it's wicked . . .'

Bing didn't always turn down films because of their moral content. Between 1935 and the early 'sixties he rejected at least twenty firm picture projects for a number of reasons.

By far the most significant was his absolute refusal to consider the Universal Pictures suggestion that he should star in the *Bing Crosby Story*. He said he would take part in 'anybody else's' life story and in 1960 he was asked to take the role of Jimmy Durante's partner in *The Jimmy Durante Story*. He agreed and Frank Sinatra was to play the other partner with Dean Martin as Schnozzle, but the actors' strike meant the project had to be dropped.

Two further 'Road' films were proposed, *Road to the Moon* and *Road to Bombay*—the first to co-star Marilyn Monroe—and it was thought in the early 'sixties that Bing could form a new screen partnership with the ageless and effervescent Lucille Ball. Neither were available and the suggestion never materialised.

Bing also turned down the starring stage role in *The Music Man*. Robert Preston had a film smash with it in 1958. Bing also failed to choose the 'role he wished' in *The Brothers Grimm*; and a suggestion that he get together with Frederic March and Sophia Loren as the lead in *The Devil's Advocate* in 1962, failed to materialise.

Other notable 'misses' included his non-availability to star in Otto Preminger's *Advise and Consent*—because he was committed to making the *Road to Hong Kong* in England—and the failure of negotiations to place him with Judy Garland in *By the Beautiful Sea* in 1961. He also failed to capitalise on his hit record album 'How The West Was Won'. M-G-M offered him the chance of co-producing and featuring in the film, but he turned it down and the company went on to produce an all-star epic. Considering his record inspired the film it was a big mistake.

In the early 'sixties, Crosby used his apparent wealth to try to buy the rights to two film stories: the first wasn't important—except it carried the title *Never Too Late*. But when he failed to get *The Rainmaker* in 1963, he was 'grieved'. With good reason, for Burt Lancaster won an Oscar with the role.

By far the most sensible decision the Groaner made during his long film career was his insistence on never being billed as the star. He always had it written into his contracts that the billing should be equal amongst the named actors. His logic was simple: if the movie died a death, he alone wouldn't be blamed; and if he was good, the credit would be even more effective. Nowadays, when one of his films is featured on television, he gets star billing. Yet when they were originally released, it was always 'Bing Crosby and . . . star in . . .' His publicity people said it was 'modesty', but he himself admits it was 'self-preservation'.

It preserved him in the top ten movie star ratings for a total of fifteen years in a row . . .

Chapter Nineteen

Home for Bing Crosby is a fourteen-roomed mansion set in three acres of plush grass and tall trees at Hillsborough, some seventeen miles outside San Francisco. Sharing the house with the Old Groaner, his wife and their three children, is a staff of four—including an English butler, his wife who acts as maid, another maid, a cook and a couple of lively labrador retrievers.

The front door is oak and opens on to a huge hall where a genuine Ming vase usually has one of Crosby's many hats draped over it. The house is light and airy and has a library stacked to the ceiling with books on every subject. The paintings which hang where there is space are by the great Western artist Charlie Russell. There are also two fine Munnings.

In the living-room there is a piano that Bing cannot play, French windows and paintings by Corot, Vlaminck and Laurencin.

Crosby's study is panelled in rich, dark wood bought from the William Randolph Hearst estate and said to have been originally part of a sixteenth-century monastery. Around the walls are mementoes and sports trophies.

Missing from view throughout the house is the considerable collection of paintings of Bing himself by artists known and unknown. They are all in the attic.

The traditional Crosby day starts early. Bing is usually up and around by seven o'clock. After making himself a cup of coffee in the kitchen, he retires to his study to read the morning paper and, as he puts it, 'await breakfast with Kathryn and the children'.

Breakfast is a seven-thirty ritual. The munching of cereals and toast is punctuated with searching questions from the head of the family to his children: 'Have you made your beds? Are your rooms clean? What about your homework?' and so on.

Bing, still a strong disciplinarian, admits to being a Victorian-type father. The questions about beds and rooms are important to him. The children must obey a substantial chore-chart, which is upstairs, and the jobs they have been given to do are ticked-off daily. If they aren't done, then 'their allowances are docked, or they are denied privileges,' said Bing sternly.

Another main topic at breakfast-time is the coming day's activities. Bing's contribution is usually vague because, as his family will tell you, 'nobody knows what he is going to do—he seldom knows himself.' Kathryn sometimes discusses her dramatic activities or her plans to visit the local ballet school where Mary Frances has been a student for the past nine years.

If the children are going to school, Bing talks to them about their forthcoming lessons, school activities and homework. He might help them a little with their schoolwork, but confesses to having difficulty with the modern techniques of teaching mathematics—the subject he says he never did well in when he was at school.

Breakfast over, Bing heads back to his study to attack his considerable mail bag. Most of it arrives from his Los Angeles office the afternoon before. Letters come from all over the world. Some concern business deals and there are notes from his business manager Basil Grillo; there are film script suggestions, offerings from song-writers and record producers, social invitations, a great deal of fan mail and letters from sporting friends.

Bing dictates all his replies on to a Dictaphone machine and the tapes are despatched to his personal secretary in Los Angeles, Lillian Murphy, who has been typing them out and returning them for signature for the past twenty-five years or so. There is also an occasional request from a fan club or radio show presenter for a personal taped message from the Groaner. These he ad libs on to his own tape recorder.

With the mail chore complete Bing usually turns his attention to a variety of things—meetings, phone calls, a trip into

San Francisco to film or tape appeals for charitable causes. When he isn't grabbing a bite of lunch at home, the crooner heads for San Francisco where he either meets personal friends for lunch or sometimes meets business-men, when he discusses more serious matters as he eats.

When time permits there is always the golf course but, whatever happens, Wednesday afternoons are exclusively reserved for playing golf. So too are the weekends, when Bing is usually out playing with Harry and Nathaniel at his local course—which is only a quarter of a mile from the boys' school. Both Harry and Nathaniel have taken after their father and are good and keen golfers. Often Bing is seen scurrying to the course in the gathering dusk of a summer's evening intent on running them off the course and back home for dinner.

The crooner calls Hillsborough 'the village' and shops there almost every day. It has a tiny main street and the usual stores plus an icecream parlour.

'He's so independent,' says the butler, Alan Fisher. 'He would never ask me to pick up a book for him or to buy half a dozen rolls of film. He goes out and gets them himself and if he sees the icecream parlour not too full he'll pop over and get himself a double-dip or whatever is his favourite of the moment. Everybody leaves him completely alone. They just say "Hi! Bing" or "Hi! Mr Crosby" and everybody feels he belongs to them, because he's lived there for so long.'

The main meal of the day takes place at around six-thirty, when the whole family gather for dinner. Bing shows a great interest in what everyone has been doing during the day, but usually manages to angle the conversation to sporting issues.

Kathryn, who is wholly unenthusiastic about such talk, says that it's usually youngest son Nathaniel who rises to the bait first: ' "Now, on the first tee I hit a big drive," ' she reports him as saying one dinner-time, ' "even with the big tree on the right side of the fairway. You know the one, Dad? Then I took a seven-iron and then I kind of chipped it in low, but it hit the trunk of a tree. You know, the one on the left, Dad," and I'm sitting saying, "pass the potatoes please!" We're going to have to make a rule about that!'

Frequently Bing and his sons hold hole-by-hole inquests into their rounds of golf over the dinner table. 'We go from the tee-off to the ninth hole during the soup,' says Kathryn, 'then from nine to sixteen on the main course; and sixteen through eighteen and into the clubhouse over dessert.'

When the golfing talk really gets too much for her, Kathryn resorts to discussing her theatrical activities. 'This,' she says, 'drives all my family right up the wall, and usually does the trick.'

To an outsider, the Crosbys at dinner can seem rather formal. Suburban San Francisco's strictest parent has always insisted that his children be called by their full first names—Mary Frances is never simply Mary, Nathaniel never Nat and Kathryn definitely not Kathy or Kate.

After dinner, Bing and Kathryn like to sit and relax in front of a blazing log fire. Entertaining is rare. Bing only has the occasional overnight guest, holds a small dinner party now and then and only two or three times a year has anything which could be called a sizeable function. A life-style far removed from that normally associated with the wealthy. Several times a month they might dine out at the home of neighbours or at their favourite local restaurant.

He and Kathryn have few personal friends. Says Alan Fisher: 'Kathryn's life is centred around her husband, the children, her theatre work and the dogs. She doesn't play bridge; she doesn't go to cocktail parties; she never goes out shopping—she never goes into a shop of any description from one year's end to the next.'

Sometimes in the evenings the Crosbys watch television, but Bing—who mainly likes sporting events—monitors the programmes carefully. Television is out for his children while they are at school and, anyway, they only get to see the things that he considers suitable.

In keeping with their simple life style, the lights in the Crosby household go out early. Bing and family are usually in bed and asleep soon after ten o'clock each night.

The man who really runs the Crosby home is Alan Fisher. He deals with the fans who occasionally knock on the front door and it is he who usually answers the telephone which rings constantly from morning to night.

He was formerly the late Duke of Windsor's butler and joined the Crosbys in 1963 after unsuccessfully applying for a job with them during the making of *Road to Hong Kong* in England. At that time, they couldn't agree on wages but

Kathryn Crosby wanted Alan and he eventually travelled to Hillsborough to become Bing's first gentleman's gentleman.

'It isn't a butler as such that the Crosbys need,' explains Alan Fisher, 'it's purely a man to live in the house, someone that they can rely on. It's different from working for anybody else in the world. It's not like working for an ordinary rich American, because Mr Crosby—although a very wealthy man —lives the utmost simple life.

'There's no edge to him at all. If the fire's lit and goes out, he's the sort of man who would go out and get a log of wood and bring it in or ask one of the children to do it. He isn't the sort of man to ever ring a bell. I don't think he knows where they are.'

After five years, Alan tired of the simple life with Bing and left: 'It was very dull,' he says. 'I liked the Crosbys enormously, but they never entertained from one end of the year to the other and stuck to their daily routine of having breakfast, lunch and dinner with the children and then going to bed about ten. I thought I was young enough to have a little bit of excitement.'

Alan took a job with the multi-millionaire American race-horse owner Charles Englehard. He was impressed by the man's reputed wealth of between two hundred and fifty and three hundred million dollars; 'I knew there was going to be a lot of excitement,' he says, 'and I worked for them for exactly one year. They had people coming in through windows, the back-door and even out of the wallpaper, because they just entertained everybody worth knowing.'

At Hillsborough, Alan was replaced by his brother-in-law, but he stayed only a short time. The Crosbys couldn't find anyone else suitable and Kathryn decided to try to lure Fisher back. He didn't need much persuading: 'Mrs Crosby rang and said, "Look, when you left us, I told you you were just going on a vacation to get away from us and were coming back. So how about coming back?" I just jumped at the chance.'

He is now quite happy with the way the Crosbys live and has even adopted some of Bing's attitudes towards entertaining and overnight guests. 'He hates it,' says Alan, 'and I've got to hate it even more than he hates it! They've made me like that and I think if I wanted to come to England for good, I'd have to retire because they've just ruined me for anybody else.'

Bing has a second home in New Mexico. It's one of a handful

of Spanish-Mexican hacienda-style houses perched on the side of a mountain at Rancho Las Cruces on the tip of the Southern Californian peninsula of Baja and fronting on to the Bay of Cortez. Bing keeps his fishing yacht *True Love* down there and describes the place as 'remote'. The only way into the Crosby hideaway is by boat or plane—which lands on a rough dirt-track runway—because the road over the mountains is perilous. He used to have two planes but has now sold them.

The remoteness of his New Mexico home and the simplicity of Hillsborough, combined with the freedom of semi-retirement from show business, has enabled Bing to devote much more attention to his second family. His efforts impress his wife greatly: 'I think he's a heavenly father,' coos Kathryn. 'He does lovely things with the children and thinks a great deal about them and their welfare. He wants good things for them; he wants them to do well and he encourages them in the most positive way.

'He's very fond of the boys and is very comfortable with them and has been since the very first breath they drew. Mary Frances was quite a different matter! He thought she was very frail and very red, and used to ask, "What does one do with a little girl that screams a lot?" She's had him confused ever since she was born and I suppose that's how it should be too.'

Handling the boys was always easy for an old-fashioned disciplinarian. When they stepped out of line, a gruff 'Shape up, or there's going to be some head-knocking around here!' was usually enough. All the Crosby sons have felt the crooner's reprimanding cuff round the back of the head and until Mary Frances reached the teenage years, she too felt the heavy hand of father. But when he suddenly awoke to the fact that she was 'thirteen, going on twenty-four' a whole new approach was called for.

At fourteen, she was an inch over five feet tall with long brown hair and very much a young woman. She had the Crosby shyness and never smiled much, especially when strangers were around—because of the braces that banded her teeth.

Mary Frances is a serious student and often studies late into the night. One of her best subjects is Latin, which delights Bing because he loved it so much at Gonzaga. She has also long been in ballet school, starting at the age of six or seven—but is an incorrigible tomboy.

She is highly competitive with both Bing and her brothers —even to the extent of playing baseball with them—and when the family went on safari in Kenya she not only shot more birds than Bing did, but bagged a thirteen-foot-long man-eating crocodile as well. Fishing down in Las Cruces, she caught a massive, vicious moray eel and was most disappointed when Bing wouldn't allow her to have it mounted and hung in her room.

'Teenage girls are difficult to understand,' says Bing, who is confused by Mary Frances's ability to turn on the tears during a reprimand. He now finds that the best way of handling her is to simply not talk to her, but Kathryn says that the silences don't last long and on the whole Mary Frances manages to 'take Bing in' more times than he realises.

Crosby doesn't like miniskirts or blue jeans. He has delivered many a lecture to Mary Frances about modern fashion and prefers her in full-length dresses. This irks her, but she does obey him!

Both Bing and Kathryn realise that their biggest worries will come when Mary Frances starts dating boys regularly. She's allowed to go to dances and parties, but is chaperoned carefully. Bing allows his daughter to invite her girl-friends to Hillsborough for the occasional overnight stay and is well aware that many of the giggles he hears are to do with boys they know, but says that he could be 'a little unreasonable' when boys start hanging around the house.

Being the only daughter, Mary Frances receives special attention from father, but only gets the same monthly allowance as her two brothers—about twenty dollars—and must do the same chores as them. Bing is very close to Mary Frances— although he is both embarrassed and pleased when she shows him real affection. But he is not her confidant. She goes to her mother with any real problems.

The three youngest Crosbys have all inherited Dad's love of sports along with some of his talent. Harry plays the guitar and piano well, is studying harmony and composition and plans to go to a leading music college. Mary Frances openly talks about becoming an entertainer. Bing says she gets this from her mother, 'who is a consummate ham', but—as with the first family—although he actively encourages them in sport, there's no pushing on the show business side.

His views on the subject are strong. 'If they're any good', he'd like them to have a go, but if they're not he thinks 'they should be directed otherwise.'

'I think it's frustrating for a person who is really determined to be a success in show business and who just doesn't have it. They may have great training and a good start, and may be attractive in every way, but if they just don't have that certain something that makes people successful it really can be a destructive thing to a young person.'

Mary Frances listens carefully to Bing's advice. She dances and sings well and has already appeared in school stage productions. Those who have seen her, claim that she is going to make a very fine actress one day.

Crosby hums and croons around the house a lot and his children join in. They also appear with father and mother in an annual Christmas show on television, but unlike the first four boys they have never sung on record with him or co-starred in a movie. Although Mary Frances has appeared in a television play with her father and also took a part in a partially animated film about Goldilocks.

The Christmas season has always been something special to the crooner and Rosemary Clooney has been witness to it. 'He knows every Christmas carol known to man,' she said. 'He used to carol with his first four sons and then he would carol with the younger children later on. He would carol in front of friend's doors and then they'd go in and have cookies and milk with the children and sit down and talk. It was a lovely thing around the festive season.'

The first four Crosby boys are now all married and bringing up children of about the same ages as their half-brothers and sister. They live more than four hundred miles from their father, but still keep in touch. They understand why Bing chose to leave Hollywood—and approve of the vivacious Kathryn and the young family.

Gary Crosby had this observation to make: 'Naturally, Kathryn is the more modern mother. She's gone into Dr Spock to a certain degree; not all the way, because they are not what I would call permissive. But I see him sitting back. He takes a lot more. You can see him looking at them sometimes like he'd like to give them a shot in the back of the head—but he kind of holds himself back a little and listens to them a little more.

Whatever mistakes he thought he'd made with us, he is making sure he's not going to make with them. But I think he's also careful he's not going to go too far the other way.'

Butler Alan Fisher summed up Crosby the family man very neatly: 'Once he enters his front door, he forgets he's Bing Crosby. He's just the father of three children and two dogs.'

Chapter Twenty

There were cries of delight from the family Crosby as they tore the colourful wrapping from their Christmas presents round the Yuletide tree in their Hillsborough mansion. Bing beamed a fatherly smile as he looked upon the scene with a great inner happiness. But always intruding was the nagging thought that there might not be another Christmas . . .

For some time he had not been feeling well and it was a situation that had to be faced. A fever and severe pains in his chest had been getting worse. Preliminary tests had failed to diagnose the trouble and he knew that in the New Year he would have to enter hospital for more extensive probing. Already he had been warned that there was the possibility that he might be suffering from cancer.

'We both thought it was cancer, but we never mentioned it,' said Kathryn. Instead, as they sat together around their comfortable fireside that Christmastide of 1973, they talked of other things and mostly about their children.

On the morning of New Year's Eve he felt so ill that he knew the time had come to stop putting on the brave face. Reluctantly he packed his bags and with a last wistful look at the festive home allowed Kathryn to drive him the few miles to the hospital at nearby Burlingame.

Soon the little drama was big news and all the world wanted to share the anxiety with his wife and family.

The first statements issued said that the crooner had been

admitted for pleurisy. Then it was reported that he had developed bacterial pneumonia, but the truth was that his personal medical adviser, Doctor Stanley Hanfling, was carrying out a number of vital tests for lung cancer.

On 8 January, Hanfling announced that a biopsy had been performed and doctors had inserted medical instruments, including a tiny electric light bulb, into Bing's left lung. 'They have found an abscess,' Dr Hanfling told a press conference. His patient was expected to recover, however, with only drug treatment.

Asked about tests for lung cancer, Hanfling said: 'They have been negative so far, but there is still a possibility that a tumour might be an underlying cause of the abscess.'

This public statement came as a complete surprise to Kathryn, who had thought that the likelihood of cancer was to be a well-kept secret. The statement made the front pages round the globe and brought a torrent of telephone calls into the Hillsborough mansion.

During the next two days the drama continued. Bing's condition worsened and the doctor admitted to being 'very concerned'. A further test for 'a lung disease' was announced, but Dr Hanfling said he wouldn't know the results for a couple of days. And he gave an ominous warning: 'There is a possibility of bad news, but I don't want to say anything prematurely.' A remark that had the news media everywhere scampering to its files and thousands of journalists hurriedly banging out glowing obituaries of Bing Crosby on their typewriters.

On the evening of 12 January, doctors at the Burlingame hospital revealed that the abscess on his lung was massive. Indeed, it was 'the size of a golf ball' and growing. A 'decision', they said, 'on whether to go ahead with surgery' was to be made later in the week.

Bing was described as being comfortable and was still able to read many of the thousands of get-well-soon letters and cards that were deluging into the hospital. He was also fit enough to make and receive a number of telephone calls. But what was worrying his doctors most was the tremendously rapid growth rate of the abscess. Since his admission twelve days before, it had enlarged at an alarming pace and had stubbornly refused to respond to treatment.

'Medically, it is an unusual problem,' Dr Hanfling told

anxious reporters. 'We must choose between a wait-and-see policy or direct surgery.'

The choice was made soon afterwards. Within a few hours Dr Hanfling was helping to rush Bing down the long antiseptic corridors to the Burlingame operating theatre. Shortly before the surgeons wheeled him off, Bing had a few moments alone with his wife. His last drowsy words to her as the pre-med injection took effect were 'see you later'. Then she left to attend 6 am Mass with her children at the tiny Catholic church in Hillsborough.

Four top surgeons led by Dr Paul Kennedy gathered round the hospital's main operating table and the terse command 'scalpel, please' from Dr Kennedy heralded the start of three-and-a-half hours of critical surgery.

As the pale January sun saw millions of Californians off to work that morning, the operating team discovered that the abscess had grown to the size of a 'small orange'. To remove it, they had to cut away more than two-fifths of the left lung—leaving the Old Groaner with effectively only one wholly workable breathing organ. And the threat of never being able to sing professionally again.

Sometime before ten o'clock, the last stitch was in place and the marathon operation over. Bing was wheeled carefully to the hospital's intensive care unit and the surgical team were reasonably confident that their patient would pull through. Dr Hanfling, who informed the world of the extensive lung operation a few minutes later, told journalists: 'Mr Crosby tolerated the surgery very well,' and then he added tersely 'his condition is satisfactory.'

Hanfling also revealed that a preliminary study of the tissues removed showed that the cause of the abscess was a very rare fungus infection and, apart from one final test, lung cancer had been discounted.

Although his doctors had been optimistic, it was revealed later that Bing had been very 'close to death' and had faced what he himself described as the 'worst crisis' of his long life. He spent two days in the intensive care unit before he was well enough to return to his small private side ward, where Kathryn was a constant visitor with the children.

The doctors finally diagnosed that Bing had contracted a rare fungus disease called noearchosis during his world-wide travels, but admitted that the crooner was very fortunate to pull through.

Within ten days of the delicate life-or-death operation, Bing was out of bed and walking gingerly around his hospital room, promising his concerned nurses that he would be out very soon and would sing for them before he left. Despite his doctors' entreatments to 'take it easy', he discharged himself from Burlingame on 26 January, just thirteen days after the surgery, and announced that he was planning a fishing trip as part of his convalescence.

But it was a very weak, thin and pale Bing Crosby who was welcomed home to Hillsborough that sunny Sunday afternoon. He soon realised that it would be a long recovery and resigned himself to leading a quiet life pottering around his half-million-dollar estate. For once in his life, Bing was forced to follow the easy-going image so carefully fostered in the minds of his public. He progressed to a daily routine of brisk walks, each a little longer than the previous one.

It was to be two months before he was fit enough to make the fishing trip he had promised himself. On 11 March, in a letter to the author, he gave a clear indication of how hard he was finding the road to recovery: 'Thanks for your sympathetic expressions about my surgery and convalescence,' he wrote. 'Coming along pretty good now, but it will be some time before I can circulate as before. Standard, in cases such as mine, I guess.'

Four weeks later Bing was on a plane to his desolate retreat in New Mexico, for the long-awaited fishing holiday. He made a remarkable recovery and celebrated his birthday in the health-giving sunshine of New Mexico—and began tentatively to test his voice with a few scales.

Amazingly, he found it still strong, with the familiar mellow Crosby sound very much intact. Further practice showed that —like the time nodes on his vocal chords silenced what was to be his national radio début in the 'thirties—he could sing even better than before. This, combined with the special awareness that comes with a close brush with death, gave Bing a completely new outlook on life.

During the summer of '74 he was back at Hillsborough busily involving himself in a number of projects. Decca in Britain wanted to release a whole series of his classic radio shows; MCA, through the World Record Club, planned an August '75 release in Britain of a seven-album set of the hundred best songs of Bing Crosby; and he quickly got back into the recording studio for a three-hour session to tape jazz songs accompanied solely by a pianist and at his own expense.

Then the independent British record producer Ken Barnes—with ninety-five albums to his credit—came up with a suggestion for a major project on disc. Barnes, who had just completed two successful albums with Bing's songwriter-singing friend Johnny Mercer, wanted the Groaner to travel to London to record twenty-six songs for two fiftieth-anniversary albums.

Bing listened to the material Ken had recorded with Johnny Mercer, liked it and sent for the producer. With top British arranger Peter Moore, Barnes travelled to Hillsborough and discussed the idea in detail. Before the end of the year, Bing had whittled a suggested list of seventy-five songs down to the final twenty-six and the British arm of United Artists had come up with 'the most expensive' package deal the company had ever proposed to any single artist—although they are not prepared to say how much they paid Bing.

In a letter to Ken Barnes before he arrived in London he wrote: 'I do hope that you'll avoid any sort of news release about my being there and that when we're recording the studio will be absolutely clear of everybody except those directly connected with the recording itself—and I include the control room.

'Just you and Pete, the engineer, the band and myself. I find we get a lot more done that way in a lot less time . . .

'It's just not possible for me to concentrate when there are people watching from all sorts of vantage points.'

On 14 February 1975, Bing kissed Kathryn and his children goodbye at San Francisco Airport and boarded a plane to Chicago, where he caught another bound for London.

In one respect, it was a sad journey for him. A week earlier his elder brother and publicity director Larry died of cancer at the age of eighty in a Los Angeles hospital after being in a coma for two months. Bing stayed just long enough to bury him before flying off to tackle one of the toughest assignments of his long career—twenty-six songs in six three-hour recording sessions.

Ken Barnes was at Heathrow to meet him when he arrived

at 7:30 am and suggested that they should get together after the crooner had rested for twenty-four hours. 'Hell, no,' retorted Bing, 'it's around midnight in California now. I'll get some sleep at the hotel and see you at 4.00 pm this afternoon your time and we can run through some of the numbers.'

They got together with arranger Pete Moore at Chappell's studios in New Bond Street and Bing sang to Pete's piano playing for two hours—until he suddenly said, 'I think I'm going to get tired in about fifteen minutes, so let's pack it in and carry on later tomorrow.'

A little more than a year after major surgery and with only one complete lung, Crosby arrived at the Chappell studio at ten on 19 February for the first of his fiftieth anniversary sessions.

Awaiting him was a forty-two-piece orchestra, already warming-up for the opening song—the title track of the first album, 'That's what life is all about' (originally written by Peter Dacre of the *Sunday Express* and Les Reed of Tom Jones fame). Bing and Ken Barnes rewrote most of the lyrics to the number which is a philosophical piece much in the vein of Sinatra's 'My Way'.

Bing also reworked the lyrics of the Johnny Mercer number 'Bon Vivant', because he considered some of them too risqué. One line referred to him 'rolling her in the hay'. Mercer didn't mind and in fact two of the numbers on the first album feature him in duets with Bing. It was the first time the pair had sung together since 1940.

Ken Barnes' first problem was how to record Bing. Modern recording techniques decree that a singer should sing in a sound-proof booth, hearing the band through special stereo head-phones. Bing flatly refused to work like this. 'No, I'm a band singer. I've travelled all this way to sing with the band and sing with them I will,' he said firmly.

Ken, greatly concerned about the diminished strength of the crooner's lungs, tried to explain that 'when the brass section gets louder, we won't hear you'. Bing wasn't to be swayed. 'Then I'll get louder,' he said. And he did.

As Crosby ran through the first of the three takes it took to make the master of 'That's what life is all about', the orchestra and production staff listened in amazement. He was not only singing better than he had for more than twenty years, but had also managed to extend his already considerable range to encompass high notes he had not hit for a long time.

At the end of that first date, a few minutes before one o'clock, the entire band burst into rapturous applause; a most unusual demonstration for seasoned session musicians. Afterwards, most of them went to the huge Chappell record shop, bought out the entire Bing Crosby rack of discs and asked that the crooner put his personal mark on them—which he did willingly.

The six-day recording session ran without a hitch and most of the numbers were completed in a maximum of only three takes. Some, like 'Hello, Dolly' Bing knocked off first time round with the laconic remark afterwards, 'next number please.'

His week-long stay at Claridges was supposed to be a secret, but the news leaked out and he was bombarded with calls and callers. The hotel protected him well and so did a massive bodyguard supplied by United Artists.

According to Bing, Claridges barred him in 1961 after he was found playing golf in a corridor. 'One morning,' he recalls, 'it was raining buckets. I had planned to play golf but since I couldn't go I went to an upper hallway—they really are long hallways—with a bag of balls and an eight iron.'

There a press photographer discovered him calmly chipping golf balls into a 'giant cuspidor', Bing says, as he hummed softly to himself. 'The hotel staff was understandably upset. They scarcely need this kind of publicity.'

He left as scheduled the next day, but a month or so later phoned to book a room only to be told 'we don't have a thing'. The story got into print and a rather embarrassed management declared: 'The incident didn't upset the hotel very much. If there's a room next time, he'll get it . . .'

On 22 February, Bing checked out of the hotel that had kept its word and headed for London Airport happy in the knowledge that his two albums were safely in the can. He was, he said, 'looking forward to going home'. His one regret about the trip, was that he had been unable to get in any golf and only managed a couple of race meetings—and one of those was only on TV.

He was able to get to a meeting at Doncaster with a parish priest friend—who was fascinated by a rank outsider with the name The Crosby Dawn and decided that it must be a good bet. Bing was sceptical and would not back it. The priest placed a substantial bet and was well rewarded when the horse was first past the post.

But it was better luck next time. Ken Barnes had been approached about Bing appearing on BBC Television's Grandstand, where he would be interviewed by Frank Bough. When Barnes explained that it was a sports programme, Bing said yes and even agreed to the small fee of £25. Barnes thought the BBC ought to be a little more generous and the offer was revised to £40, to which Barnes promptly replied that £200 would be nearer the mark. 'There was some consternation at the other end of the line,' said Ken, 'but eventually they came back and agreed.' When he told Bing that he was to get £200 instead of £25, the crooner gave a wry smile and said: 'That's not bad walking-around money, is it?'

On the show Bing found that in one of the races being covered by Grandstand there was a horse with the likely tag of Uncle Bing. Remembering his folly at Doncaster, the crooner managed to get a £5 bet on. And, yes, the horse won! Not bad walking-around money . . .

Chapter Twenty-one

There is always the one burning question: how much is the Old Groaner really worth after a lifetime in the big-time and his involvement with so many other business interests?

For years the word has been that he and Bob Hope are two of the richest men in show business and that Bing himself has wealth estimated to be in the region of one hundred and fifty million dollars. Crosby has always denied it and steadfastly refused to place a figure on his fortune. 'Ask the tax man, he knows' has usually been his answer.

Even his late brother Larry, as close as he was and as bound up as he was in the Crosby empire, claimed that he did not know how much Bing was worth. He agreed that there had been some very good investments along the way—'but I don't think he's got the money that Bob Hope has, because Bob worked harder,' he said. And Bing agrees.

'Hope? Oh! God, he's got more money on him than I have,' says the crooner. 'He started way back when he first came to Hollywood. He began buying real estate out where Universal Studios are and out in the San Fernando Valley and you know how that's gone ahead and grown and grown. He still has a lot of it and he sold off some at a tremendous profit. He's very affluent. He's loaded!'

What about the Crosby one-hundred-and-fifty-million-dollar total published in the papers?

'That's completely preposterous,' he says.

'You can't believe any of those figures,' he insists. 'If you have assets, like real estate and some stock, and want to cash them in on a false sale you don't know what you'd get for them. If you do sell them the taxes would be horrendous. Actually and as closely as I can tell, I have a paper-value of 3½ million dollars,' Bing revealed exclusively in 1975.

'I suppose if I really had some good sales; if I decided to liquidate and could sell things at a good figure, and pay the taxes—then if I wound-up with a million and a half dollars, that'd be pretty good. I would be delighted, that's a lot of money.'

So Bing says he's worth a million and a half dollars but at least he admits that his paper value is far greater than that. His comparison between actual wealth and estimated wealth is also a fair argument; the value of land and property can rise and fall like stocks and shares.

But even if one accepts his written-down estimate and bears in mind that trust funds set up for his first four sons years ago have made them 'comfortable'—he's done the same for his second family—it means that a lot of his money must have been spent along the way, even allowing for the fact that Bing has always said he has paid his taxes.

Lawyer John O'Melveny claims to have got Bing's investment programme off to a good start: 'The first investments that I made,' he said, 'were all in tax-free Californian Municipal Bonds and I had a whole box of them.'

O'Melveny refused to speculate on how much Bing is worth, but agreed that at one time the estimates about his and Hope's wealth were true. 'I would say Bob Hope was still very rich, but I don't think Bing Crosby is any more,' said the lawyer.

Bing agrees that a lot of his wealth was wasted along the way. Could it be that he wasn't interested in what happened to his money? 'Well, I was interested in accumulating it,' he says, 'but I never knew where it all went and I brought lots of ventures into the Enterprises that failed and lost money.

'I don't think I ever brought in anything that was profitable. They tried to discourage me, but when you're in the public eye and its known that you're making money, you're approached and accosted by every fly-by-night promoter with every kind of wildcat idea; oil, real estate, restaurants, nightclubs and a thousand-and-one things.

'Once in a while, I'd get sold on something by some guy and I'd tell Everett, or later O'Melveny, to go ahead with it and they'd try to discourage me. Sometimes they were successful, sometimes they weren't. I wish they'd have been successful a lot more, because I wouldn't have lost a lot of those things,' adds the crooner.

But not all of the Groaner's ideas were failures. John O'Melveny told how Crosby and Hope once made quite a killing. 'There was a man Bing knew in Texas,' he said, 'who played golf with both of them and he got them into an oil deal.

'It was purely a wildcat deal, but they both did very well from it. I had one of my partners down there for a whole summer working the deal out and Bob and Bing ended up by having a relatively small lease with just a few oil-wells on it. But some of the big oil companies got interested after it was proven and wanted to buy them out. Hope sold his interest for a lot of money and put it all into real estate, but I was afraid to let Bing do that. I just told him to go along with the oil business, which he did, and that's his principal source of income right now, I believe.'

Says Bing: 'I did hold out for the oil—even though I lost almost a million dollars in unsuccessful exploration before we hit. I was able to keep it going until we were lucky enough to strike an oil field. This has been one of my main assets and still is.'

Bing awards Hope the laurels in the money-making stakes. 'He's a pretty good businessman, I'm not. He's sharp. He's really astute and I'm a sucker for everything. It's a good thing I had this legal staff, because I wouldn't have anything now.'

But Hope always gagged that Crosby 'doesn't even pay tax any more—he just asks the Government how much they need!'

The Groaner found a sure way of raising money for other people. All the profits from his now famous annual Bing Crosby Pro-Am golf tournament go to charity. Almost five million dollars has been raised in thirty-four years.

Crosby felt that some new or different cause should be helped rather than the usual well-known charities. First he started by aiding youth centres—about a dozen of them—and when they became practically self-supporting there were Bing-mobiles— lunch-wagons-on-wheels for the needy.

The next idea was the Bing Crosby Student Loan Scheme—

started in the mid-sixties—which became an instant success. Bing finds it the most gratifying of the many charitable things he does and said to the author in January 1973: 'This morning we made a loan to our seventy-second small university in the United States. Universities of all creeds and sects benefit, it really doesn't matter. We loan the money to the university— say five or ten thousand dollars—and they in turn pick out the students who have a good future, but are not going to be able to continue unless they have some financial assistance. They loan the students the money in three or four hundred dollar bits and when they graduate and start to earn they pay it back and the money goes again into the fund.'

The thing that pleases Bing most about the Student Loan Fund is that—with only a few exceptions—the money is being paid back and in some cases is even being added to by grateful students.

Money for the fund comes from the sale of tickets for the tournament under a volunteer committee of six hundred. To repay them and all the marshalls who make his tournament possible, Bing holds a special stag-night—known as Bing's Clambake—when they get a steak and beer dinner followed by a stage show. There's usually a comedian, a jazz band augmented by Phil Harris and a female singer. Bing himself acts as master of ceremonies and croons some of his hits when he can remember the words.

The first tournament was held in 1937 and grew to become one of the top events in the American golfing calendar. It was the first of its kind and Phil Harris is one of the few to have played in it since its inception. 'The tournament started at Rancho Santa Fé, down near San Diego,' he said, 'and it was just Bing and his friends and that's the way he's kept it. If you're not a friend of Mr Crosby's you are not invited.'

The idea began when America's professional golfers were playing a tough three-tournament schedule out on the West Coast. 'I thought to give them a break from this,' says Bing, 'that it would be wonderful to put on a little tournament. Some of my friends would have an opportunity to meet professionals, get to know them, learn something about the game and perhaps have a little festive affair.

'So we staged this two-day tournament at the Rancho Santa Fé with a pro-amateur set-up and had a great deal of fun, a small purse, and finished with a barbecue and some entertainment. It went on until the war, when we discontinued it. Then when the war ended we came up to Pebble Beach on the Monterey Peninsula and now it's grown into an event of very great national stature.'

The 'little two-day tournament' with pro prize money of about two thousand dollars has now developed into a three-day competition on three separate golf courses with most of the world's top professional golfers competing for prize money in excess of two-hundred-and-fifty thousand dollars.

It is covered nationally by television, with Bing commentating, and each day tens of thousands of people pour in from all over America and brave the inclement January weather to see the stars and the pros play golf. Bing used to take part himself but nowadays confines his activities to playing host and attending as many as possible of the numerous cocktail parties held each night.

The 'Crosby' is highly thought of by the professionals—not only as one of the best organised and most fun tournaments—but as a real test of golfing skill. As double-Crosby-winner Billy Casper (1958 and 1963) explains, it's no longer a gentle romp around a golf course: 'We encounter rain, sunshine and wind, and on one occasion we had two or three inches of snow. So when an individual accomplishes a win in this tournament, he is not only master of the golf course, he's master of the elements too.'

Jack Nicklaus, one of the greatest golfers of all time, won the Crosby in 1972 and 1973, and rates it as unique: 'It's a different thing to what we usually play,' drawls the Golden Bear, 'matter of fact, it's the only one of its kind. Bing's contributed an awful lot to the game through the years and he's not the typical kind of sponsor of a tournament. He stays in the background and doesn't make it a show for Bing Crosby. He makes it a show for the golfers, his friends and the amateurs. It's got a lot of class from that standpoint.'

Chapter Twenty-two

Bing Crosby is probably the most-loved character in the world apart from the creations of Walt Disney. For a half a century he has dispensed much joy and much entertainment for the benefit of millions who were never ever to meet him but felt that they knew him and in him had a friend. A colossal, enveloping warmth of affection has justly come his way through the years. Even if the image of the casual, lazy pipe-smoking crooner was not completely true it would not matter. He was Bing, Mr Family Man, Mr Clean. In his wild younger days of merry-making and occasional drinking sprees columnists scarcely bothered to say so in print. 'No one would believe that of Crosby,' explained one top American writer.

The Groaner has always been open and honest about his drinking and other exploits. He has never lied about them or tried to cover them up and most journalists respected this.

The clean image has been a great asset to him in his career, but he had to be extremely careful to maintain great dignity in public, particularly after he became so closely associated with the Father O'Malley character of *Going My Way*.

A surprising side to Bing Crosby arises from conversations with some of his show business contemporaries. They say Bing is a loner. Far from being an outward-going extrovert, they will tell you, the crooner is very much a man who likes to keep himself to himself.

Bob Crosby believes that it is his way of dealing with the

unprecedented mass-adoration he has had to face over the years. 'Bing is really a very humble person,' said Bob, 'and a very shy person. I've used an expression—I've been criticised for using it—yet I say it very lovingly: once Bing hit success, he placed himself in a little Cellophane bag and he zipped it up and he just will not allow anyone to get inside that bag. He doesn't want to be told that he's good. I've got mine too; I've been in it a long time and I never allow anything to bother me.'

The Crosby butler, Alan Fisher, agrees: 'He's the sort of person that doesn't need anyone else in the whole world. The American expression is a loner and he's happy in his own company. When his wife and children are away, he potters around the house; or goes to play golf; does his work at his desk; comes down for his meals and watches a little television. He doesn't need anybody and I'm sure all the millions of friends that he's got would probably say that this was untrue, but living with him—every day and all day—I feel it's a very accurate description.'

Even in the early days people used to say that Bing had 'a moat around him' and it is evident—if you spend more than a passing moment with him—that there is a point beyond which you cannot go. He will talk freely and candidly about his life and career, but strongly resists any attempt to form a jovial, back-slapping friendship.

There is always the moment with Bing when an 'ice curtain' seems to descend and that is as far as you will get with him. Indeed, his old crooning rival Rudy Vallee has gone on record as saying that all the Crosbys had 'ice water running through their veins'. Bing finds this surprising, saying 'I've never spent more than ten minutes with Vallee in my whole life. Nor has any other Crosby'.

Phil Harris, who is a close companion of Bing's, believes there are other reasons for his apparent aloofness: 'He must spend a lot of time by himself to get various things done. He likes to hunt, he likes to fish and we like to do these things together, and we seem to get along. But he might go away all day long—maybe even two days—and I never see him, but I understand it. Bing doesn't want any pressure.'

Ironically, Bing considers Phil to be a loner: 'He likes the same things I do, I guess,' says the Groaner, 'and he's a great guy to hunt and fish with, because he's very amusing. He's a loner, though. I always go to a fishing-tackle place and find out what the locals are using in the way of lines or gear. He has to use his own gear and wants to fish alone.

'He goes off and fishes his head off and comes back with a very meagre catch, and when he finds me with quite a full creel he's very indignant. He says "you lousy, filthy rat! Fish come to you, fish just come to you" and I say "no, I just listen to the law of the area and follow it. That's the secret." He won't do it; he likes to go out by himself. The same with shooting. If we are shooting up-land game, or duck, he has to pick his own spot. I just follow the people that are having the success.'

Everyone who has ever been close to Bing accepts his need for detachment. Even Kathryn Crosby is well aware of it: 'I understand Bing's great need for privacy,' she confides. 'He's been hurt a great deal and he's a very sensitive man and very shy man. So when he's doing his lonely things, I'm very happy because I'm doing my own things.'

He refused to attend more than a handful of film premières and hated receptions or official dinners.

During a dinner given by top executives of NBC, his radio network, Bing vanished during a break to allow guests to go to the toilets. He went home and missed the speeches. 'How big can you get?' commented an NBC top-dog.

Phil Harris says that, if Bing happens to be with a 'group that's not in his groove—or that he's not especially enjoying—then he won't make any bones about getting up and saying goodnight'.

Even in the closely confined spaces of the recording studio, Crosby could be a difficult man to get to know really well. The Andrews Sisters, who sang with him many, many times, and probably had more fun with him than any other group, found that there were days when it was simply a professional partnership: 'I would honestly say that I don't know Bing,' said Patty Andrews. 'When he'd walk in the studio you'd get to know what mood he was in. I would look at him and if I thought he was unapproachable that day I wouldn't say anything to him and we all felt that way.'

Rosemary Clooney used the term 'ice curtain' to describe his lack of warmth in depth: 'If Bing Crosby is walking down a street in Vancouver—which can happen easily, because he goes there to fish—anybody on the street will say "Bing, how are you?" The immediacy is there and the ice curtain comes somewhere back of that, because he will say "hey, fine—how are you? How's business? How are things?" He always says something that works, so he goes through life in a very informal way on the surface. Others have their ice curtain in front—so that people are kept at their distance when they start to approach. Bing doesn't have that. You can always say hello and be assured of some reaction.'

Gary Crosby analysed Bing the loner this way: 'To me "loner" has two connotations. There's the guy who is a loner because he's afraid of contact with other people and is suspicious of them. Then there's the guy who likes people and if they're doing something that interests him, then he'd love to join them. If they're doing something that doesn't interest him, he expects them to understand that and he goes and does what he wants to do. And I think that's more the way my father is. He's a free soul and he expects the same kind of thing from other people.'

Director Blake Edwards felt there was always a curtain between him and the real Crosby: 'I think that part of that curtain that I couldn't penetrate has behind it a lot of very interesting things and contributed to his ability as an actor. He has really surprised me when I've seen him on the screen reach down and come up with some of the things he came up with in *Country Girl*. I wondered where they came from.

'I think that if you examine Bing's past and consider the era in which he rose to fame, his life with the bands, and some of his tragedies in domestic life—I'm sure that an awful lot of this has gone into making up that reserve.'

Film-maker Mel Frank also found Crosby an extremely complicated human being to work with: 'I would pay for the right to sit in on a psychoanalysis of Bing,' he said, 'to see what really exists between those outer layers that he has—the kind of shell of protection that he has around him. I've found personally, that in a one-to-one relationship with him, there's a bit of discomfort; he seems a bit cold. When another person enters the scene, he warms up a little bit more and with three or four even more so. There is deep inside of Bing a sentimental warmth. But, I suspect, he's a bit shy about it—almost embarrassed about it. So he takes on, without his knowledge, this protective layer.'

Actor José Ferrer feels that the Groaner's reserve is due to the fight that most show business people have put to put up in order to survive: 'There are dogs and jackals snapping at your heels,' he said, 'in the shape of columnists, envious other people, lesser talents and whether you survive smilingly, or you survive with a snarl, you have to survive. Bing has his very, very cold professional side. He's a man who looks very clearly and very unsmilingly at a problem and attacks it and solves it in his own way.

'He is also a charming man and a learned man, but just to think of Bing as "Mr Smiling Happy Singer" and that he gets up and goes around loving everybody he meets all day long is a misunderstanding. Nobody does and nobody should be expected to, and he doesn't. He's survived on sheer talent and you can't expect a man like that to be the "Mr Sweetie-Pie Smiles" that you hear on records or see in the movies. He is what he should be—a great man and from time-to-time, when he feels its necessary, a very tough guy.'

Dorothy Lamour found him a complete enigma. 'There were times,' she said, 'when for short intervals I would feel very close to Bing. Then there were other times when I felt that he looked upon me as a complete stranger. I'm not trying to say he's a snob at all—but it just depended how he felt that day, I suppose.'

Bing confesses himself baffled and astounded by many of these assessments. 'It's fantastic that I should be considered a loner,' he says. 'I really feel that I know more people of contrasting backgrounds to my background than anybody in show business. I know literally thousands of people all the way from caddies, jockeys, touts, trainers, horse breeders, horse fanciers, doctors, lawyers, financiers, royalty, professors, writers, painters —I think I know somebody in every walk of life and some of them quite well. And I am pleased to consider them as friends and I think they feel the same about me.

'My conception of a loner is a fellow who is a recluse; a hermit who doesn't associate with people. I associate with everybody. Always have.

'Of course I like to be alone once in a while—everybody does. You think better when you're alone; you can't think when you're talking. I like to read a lot. I like to watch telly a lot. I like to go out to a movie alone. I can go any place alone;

entertain myself. I don't have to have people, but I enjoy company with people when there's something to do, something to say. I don't like small talk. I'm not very good at it.

'If Patty Andrews thought that some days in the recording studio I wasn't very communicative the chances are that I didn't know the song and I was trying to learn it and in order to do that I had to devote my entire attention to it. I probably hadn't rehearsed it before coming to work.

'I do have a failing—I'm quite aware of it. I don't seem to be able to do anything about it. If someone's talking to me and after a while it becomes not interesting and dull, I sometimes get a glazed expression on my face and my thoughts turn elsewhere. I am probably trying to think how I can improve my golf swing or whether I'll go to the races that day or something of that nature. And when something interesting develops again later in the conversation I may come out of the fog and get back in the action.

'True, also, I'm not very effusive. I'm not very demonstrative. I just never have been. My mother was that way—my father was just the opposite. I don't know why, it's just something I've inherited. I may think a lot of a person, but I seldom tell them so. I'll tell them about their ability; whether I think they're good performers; whether I like the song they sang or the act they have done. Every time I go to a play in New York I write to the leading performer and tell him I like the show.

'I've never told a friend that "I love you" or "I like you" and if any friend told me that I'd be very embarrassed and wouldn't know what to do. It's taken for granted that you like the person or you wouldn't have them for a friend.

'What it all boils down to is that I'm very undemonstrative and that problem has given rise to the belief that I'm a loner and I live behind an "ice curtain".'

This then has been the story and an assessment of the life and times of Bing Crosby; the story of a shy, small-town boy, who started with nothing and asked for nothing, yet achieved everything.

In his entire career there are only two things he has not done: appeared in a Broadway Show—because 'I would have hated to have rehearsed for twelve weeks and then close after a week' —and sung real opera.

But give it time . . .

Postscript

Sammy Davis Jnr.—Entertainer

'I think he'll be remembered for the hat, the pipe and the loud shirts. The kids call it gear today, but he was wearing gear in those days. He always had the hat on and made no bones about the fact that he wore a piece. He wasn't ashamed of it; he was honest with it and I think that was part of the reason why he was accepted by the everyday man. Bing never lost that touch—even with all the fame and the money. And that to me is what I'd like to have him remembered for, because he's a great human being.'

Douglas Fairbanks Jnr.—Actor

'I have known him long enough to know that he is indefatigable; he knows what every instrument in the orchestra should be doing at a particular time; he knows precisely what the rhythm should be; he knows precisely what the interpretation and phrasing of a song should be and he doesn't let anything go that isn't right. He has always liked the open air; to take things easy—to smoke a pipe, to put his feet up—but I think he would have been very unhappy if he had not had something to do as well. He had this artistic drive, which expressed itself in his being a singer and an entertainer, far above the majority of his contemporaries.'

Phil Harris—Friend

'He's an individualist. I think that's why Bing has been so successful and there isn't anybody like him. A lot of people

241

don't understand him; because he goes his own way, minds his own business, picks his own friends and lives his own life.'

Stefanie Powers—Actress

'There was once a famous thing that he did while on a television show; he was asked by the interviewer why it was he had this calm about him and a sort of unruffled air? He reached into his pocket and pulled out an enormous wad of dollar bills, and he said "that helps!" '

Army Archerd—American Journalist

'Bing at least has been honest. He was a loner and would just go off by himself, and people would consider him very selfish. I'm sure lots of people consider him such, but I found him to be one of the most improved human beings I've had the chance to meet in this business.'

Johnny Mercer—Lyricist

'The interesting part of Bing to me is that he likes to be with jockeys, with millionaires, with beach boys and with caddies. He likes colourful people; he likes people who are amusing and who aren't phonies. He's an unphoney man. He's so distant, but he's a very genuine man.'

Sammy Cahn—Songwriter

'Crosby has a special quality of language; Crosby is a great letter writer; he has a flair for language and this comes out in his personality. He would never use a four syllable word if he could think of a five syllable word. His casualness belies his intense determination to be a thorough professional. I don't think there is anything about show business that Bing Crosby doesn't know.'

Jack Mass—Music Publisher

'Bing, if he hadn't have been a singer or an actor, could have been a great writer. Bing has always had a great command of the English language. It was uncanny, the things that he would say and write. He could have been a comedy writer; he could have been a writer of serious things. He's a man that knows many things about many things.'

José Ferrer—Actor

'Al Jolson was like Mr Great Singer of all time. Maurice Chevalier was like Mr Entertainer of all time. Frank Sinatra is like Mr Ballader of all time. But Bing Crosby is like Mr Everything of all time.'

Frank Capra—Film Director

'I rate him in the top ten of all actors. He'd do anything and do it well. He has a complete faculty of being able to work with props; you give many actors props and they can't do it, but he can juggle balls and have Bob Hope cracking ad-libs on the side and still say his stuff. He has complete co-ordination and that is one of the things that is beautiful about him.'

Nelson Riddle—Composer and Conductor

'I know the public have a very warm feeling for Bing Crosby. The fact that personally he was a bit stand-offish and a bit non-committal seemed to have nothing to do with this great feeling the public felt, do feel and will always feel for Bing Crosby.'

Richard Arlen—Film Actor

'One time we were fishing and had hired a boat out of San Diego—this was at the height of his popularity—and California was Crosby territory. He thought that if we came ashore by small boat, nobody would recognise him and we had a car waiting for us. We'd no more hit the beach and they just swarmed on us! He kept saying "I'm not Bing Crosby. I may look like him, but I'm not Bing Crosby!" but there was nothing we could do. He was very courteous about it and signed everything they wanted. We didn't get back to our hotel for almost two-and-a-half hours.'

Bob Crosby—Bandleader

'I think Bing wants security. I don't think his success was pre-destined or anything. I think he got a shot at a picture and felt he should take it; I don't think he had any idea that he was going to become an Oscar winner. It was Mother Necessity that directed a great deal of Bing's career. He does what he wants to do when he wants to do it and he enjoys life. He's certainly not been a spectator in the game of life—he's been a participant.'

Mary Rose Crosby—Younger Sister

'He has a marvellous memory; he has a photographic memory. This is a great help in his business. Many actors and actresses, and singers, don't have that—so he's the boss with that. He puts a lot more into his work than he gives the impression that he does.'

Alan Fisher—Butler

'I've worked for the late Duke of Windsor in Paris and I found that he and Mr Crosby could have been twin brothers, in the way that they reacted to things. They are always amazed at the way people react to them and are kind of surprised when they are recognised and adored by the millions.'

Bob Hope—Comedian

'Nobody has ever reached his proportions and I hope he never reads this because I don't want him to think that I care for him.'

Denis Goodwin—Scriptwriter

'I don't think Bing or Bob Hope could be divorced from one another. I don't think the laws of show business would allow that; they've been a legend for far too long. If Crosby retired a part of Hope would disappear from the scene.'

Bing Crosby—Crooner

'I'm ham enough to like to work in show business and there's a lot of fun in it—especially when you've been in it a long time and you have friends. Now when I go back to see the guys I've worked with for so long—musicians, assistant directors, directors, other actors, other singers—that part of it is amusing and enjoyable. But I don't know, I get bored if the work is slow; if there are too many takes, or it's overtime, and getting late and nothing's been accomplished. I guess I just hate work!'

Index